Computers, Minds and Conduct

This book provides a sustained and penetrating critique of a wide range of views in modern cognitive science and the philosophy of mind, from Turing's famous test for intelligence in machines to recent work in computational linguistic theory.

While discussing many of the key arguments and topics, the authors also develop a distinctive analytic approach. Drawing on the methods of conceptual analysis first elaborated by Wittgenstein and Ryle, the authors seek to show that these methods still have a great deal to offer in the field of the cognitive theory and the philosophy of mind, providing a powerful alternative to many of the positions put forward in the contemporary literature.

Among the many issues discussed in the book are the following: the Cartesian roots of modern conceptions of mind; the nature of Turing's test; Putnam's functionalist philosophy of mind; Searle's 'Chinese Room' thought experiment; Fodor's 'language of thought' hypothesis; the place of 'folk psychology' within cognitivist thought; and the question of whether any machine might be said to 'think' or 'understand' in the ordinary senses of these words.

Wide-ranging, up-to-date and forcefully argued, this book represents a major intervention in contemporary debates about the status of cognitive science and the nature of mind. It will be of particular interest to students and scholars in philosophy, psychology, linguistics and the computing sciences.

Computers, Minds and Conduct

Graham Button
Jeff Coulter
John R. E. Lee
Wes Sharrock

Polity Press

First published in 1995 by Polity Press
in association with Blackwell Publishers Ltd.

Editorial office:
Polity Press
65 Bridge Street
Cambridge CB2 1UR, UK

Marketing and production:
Blackwell Publishers Ltd
108 Cowley Road
Oxford OX4 1JF, UK

Basil Blackwell Inc.
238 Main Street
Cambridge, MA 02142, USA

ISBN 0 7456 1287 3
ISBN 0 7456 1571 6 (pbk)

A CIP catalogue record for this book is available from the British Library
and the Library of Congress.

Typeset in Palatino on 10/12 pt
by Best-set Typesetter Ltd, Hong Kong
Printed in Great Britain by TJ Press Ltd, Padstow, Cornwall

This book is printed on acid-free paper.

Contents

Contents

Preface

This book plunges into controversies which exist chiefly in the philosophy of mind, taking up for often critical treatment a range of topics that have been debated in various ways for a long time (some even for centuries). Our discussions must take some familiarity with these matters for granted in order to make headway in putting our own case, one which goes against currently prevailing views. We cannot, however, present in great detail and at length the background to any particular topic, nor elaborate the full intricate implications of each issue. For the reader who is less familiar with these matters, we hope that this schematic preface will suffice as an outline of the main positions and problems to be discussed in the text.

The problem of the mind/body relationship, which is at the heart of all the matters we shall examine, was decisively formulated in the work of René Descartes at the very beginning of the period commonly characterised as that of 'modern philosophy'. Descartes was a scientist and philosopher, and it was the impressive achievements of the new natural sciences which animated his concerns, concerns in large measure motivated by the problem of how to reconcile these scientific achievements with his Catholicism. The natural sciences (chiefly physics) seemed to tell a very general story about the movement of matter according to definite laws, as though the universe were a vast mechanical operation. Newton himself, a central figure in the science Descartes so admired, had characterised the universe as a giant clockwork.

Attractive though this picture was, it troubled Descartes because it made no mention of, and seemed to leave no room for, human beings and some of their apparent characteristics. The mind (or soul) seemed to fall outside the laws of physics. The idea, for example, of human beings freely choosing their courses of action appeared in direct contradiction to the idea of *everything* in the universe being mechanically compelled by physical causes. Is the existence of the human mind in contravention of the laws of physics? Is a human being a composite of two distinct 'parts', a physical body which *is* subject to the laws of physics and a mental part, the mind, which *is not*? These questions are ones which Descartes bequeathed to philosophy, and they provide the core considerations of the 'philosophy of mind', being influential as a result of that upon many aspects of Western culture, including many of the human sciences. Descartes laid down *the terms* on which many subsequently have confronted the problem.

In relatively recent years, the 'philosophy of mind' has returned to the forefront of philosophical interest and has exercised a powerful influence on the discipline of psychology, especially upon the formation of 'cognitive science' (the name of a certain kind of psychology with which we shall be primarily concerned). Indeed, the Cartesian problematic is in many ways the foundational presupposition of 'cognitive science'.

The dominant question with which the 'philosophy of mind' is engaged is whether an account of 'mind' can be given within the framework of the natural sciences, and especially physics. Popular though (to us, at least) bizarre books like Roger Penrose's *The Emperor's New Mind* try to show how 'mind' must be accounted for in terms of quantum physics. Much more seriously, Noam Chomsky, well known as a linguistic theorist but often much more active as a philosopher, has argued not only for the retention of Descartes' problematic but for the reinstatement of Descartes' fundamental conceptions, though with the (appropriately contemporary) proviso that these are to provide the constituents of a properly scientific theory. Chomsky, rebelling against the limitations he saw in the restriction of psychology to the scientific study of *behaviour* (largely by insisting that language mastery was a proper phenomenon for psychology to explain), held that psychology should once again become 'the science of mind'. Behaviourists (such as B. F. Skinner in psychology and W. V. O. Quine in philosophy) who had recently held sway either denied that there were such things as 'minds' or that, if there were, they had *no* part to play in the scientific explanation of behaviour (including linguistic behaviour). Chomsky countered that Descartes had been right to insist that people do have minds, and that their (mental) states and operations are causes of behaviour. The issue was how best to articulate such a 'mentalist' position in terms consistent with a thoroughly *materialist* philosophical commitment. Jerry A. Fodor took up Chomsky's cause with great vigour and it is often his arguments which we shall encounter below as expressions of the 'neo-mentalist' point of view, one that tries to reconcile various Cartesian mentalistic theses with modern materialist ones.

The development of digital, electronic computing devices in the post-War period has done much to revitalise the debate, and Fodor (among many others) has appealed to their properties in an effort to effect the sought-after reconciliation of mentalist with materialist philosophical conceptions. The computer is unequivocally a machine, but it is one to which human intellectual functions of various kinds can be transferred, and this has inspired the idea that Descartes' problem can be resolved. The operations of the computer can be understood entirely, so to speak, mechanically, but the operations which the computer performs are those which were previously only available to beings with 'minds'. Calculations are prominent operations which computers perform, but, prior to the development of the computer, they were considered to be ones requiring considerable intelligence on the part of human beings. If we can understand how a computer can reproduce human intellectual capacities and functions, then there is no logical barrier to understanding how the human body – in particular, the 'mechanical' functioning of its brain – can give rise to the phenomena of 'mental operations'. Thus, the mind will be understood entirely in terms of (aspects of) 'the body', and the problem of reconciling its properties with the laws of physics will finally be disposed of.

Much discussion in recent 'philosophy of mind', then, is engaged with the question of whether 'the mind' is effectively the same as, or indistinguishable from, 'the brain'. There are many who think that it must be, as do, for example, Paul and Patricia Churchland, who speak of the 'mind-brain' as a unified phenomenon. They, among others, take the view that the laws discovered by the natural sciences (most notably physics) define what really exists, and so if we are to acknowledge the existence of 'the mind' at all then it must be as a *physical* phenomenon, and the only candidate for something which could be physical and carry out the operations of the mind is *the brain*. However, even those who espouse this view about the central role of physics in dictating what really exists do *not* necessarily agree with the above argument. Some, called 'eliminativists' (such as Richard Rorty and, occasionally, the Churchlands themselves), hold that the demonstration that 'the mind' is really equivalent to the operations of the brain (and central nervous system) carries the conclusion that there is no such thing as 'the mind' at all. There is *only* the brain. It is then argued that the notion of 'mind' and the cognate notions which contribute to the concept of mind – such as 'thought', 'belief', 'consciousness', etc. – are basically products of a primitive kind of scientific theorising which sought to explain human behaviour by postulating a series of internal mental states and processes which caused observable conduct. From there, the argument continues, it may be claimed that these notions were postulated *in ignorance* of the nature and role of the brain, and that the impending development in our understanding of the brain and the central nervous system will actually achieve what those 'primitive' ideas sought to accomplish. We shall be able to explain people's behaviour directly in the language of neurophysiology, which has a vocabulary *that does not include* such terms as 'mind', 'belief', etc. Thus, this 'folk psychology', as the supposedly primitive theory is termed, is 'eliminable', obviated by the advancement of a genuine scientific theory. This claim is, however, doubted by, for example, Daniel Dennett who holds that, although there is indeed no such thing as 'mind', nonetheless this 'folk vocabulary' has an indispensable role.

If it is argued that the computer is a good basis for understanding the *nature* of minds, a view most prominently pursued by Hilary Putnam (in an earlier phase of his career), consistently by Jerry Fodor, and, to a lesser extent, by Stephen Stich, it can be suggested that the way the computer *works* is a good basis for understanding how the mind works, so much so that it can even be proposed that the mind *is* a computer – or, in other words, that it operates computationally – and that its workings are to be analysed and described in the ways in which one would analyse and describe the running of a computer program. This idea has been immensely influential on psychology, and has provided the foundation for that major branch of psychology known as 'cognitive science'.

The above ideas are very powerful ones in contemporary thought, and they are the foci of the discussions in this work. However, while these ideas are influential, perhaps dominant, they have by no means gone unchallenged. A crucial move which encouraged the idea that computers could be the equivalent of minds was the creation of the 'Turing test', named after a mathematician, Alan Turing, who played a major role in making the computer possible. The idea behind the Turing test is that computers will develop to a point at which they can match the performance of human beings – it being held that there is no *principled* objection formulable against such a possibility – to the extent that one would be unable to tell the difference between the performance of human beings and machines.

The attack on this underlying idea has been a main platform of the opposition to the tendencies we have outlined above. Thus, it has been argued that the *actual* performance of computers is immensely disappointing relative to the claims which are made about their possible achievements. Hubert Dreyfus has most extensively stated and restated this case, holding that the attempt to transfer human intellectual capacities to machines in the field known as 'artificial intelligence' is often inept and enables the machines to 'match' human performance only in a superficial manner. It is further argued that there is a *principled* objection to the 'Turing' idea, namely, that it is based upon a misunderstanding of the nature of *human skills*, and because of this misunderstanding there are gross overestimates of the extent to which the components of such skills can be transferred to computers.

The analogy between 'the mind' and 'the computer' has also been challenged on the grounds that it misunderstands the workings of computers and the nature of the programs that run (on) them. The extent to which computers can be used to simulate human activities gives a misleading impression of the degree to which the computer is actually 'matching' the simulated performance. Computers may be able to generate strings of words, mathematical symbols and so forth, which correctly correspond to the requirements of human language, systems of calculation and so on, but – to put it very crudely for the moment – the crucial difference between the machine's simulation and the human's performance is that the latter involves understanding of what the strings of words and formulae mean, while the former does not. John Searle has used the ingenious invention of the example of 'the Chinese Room', which we will encounter in some detail below, to demonstrate this point.

In this book, we try to bring a somewhat unfashionable perspective to bear upon this debate in the hope that it will cast some fresh light upon the issues involved. This perspective has been called 'ordinary language philosophy' and has been elaborated from the writings of Ludwig Wittgenstein and Gilbert Ryle. Drawing upon this analytical approach, we suggest (again, to put it crudely) that many of the central intellectual problems which belong to the philosophy of mind and to cognitive science are created in the way in which they are set up. Rather than providing genuine problems which require solution, they generate illusory – and often seemingly insuperable – difficulties. If the initial suppositions behind the formulation of the problem can be explicated sufficiently clearly, it may then become apparent that their premises are spurious. This is essentially what we shall be trying to do with regard to certain selected issues in this area. In particular, we have organised this book around four main themes which we critically examine throughout its course.

The first of these is Descartes' own key assumption, mentioned earlier, that the physical sciences depict a universe which *apparently* precludes the possibility of the human. Descartes and his successors are therefore troubled as to whether a way can (or cannot) be found to accommodate the human mind and its characteristics within the picture drawn by science. They do not, however, question whether the picture which they attribute to science is one which may legitimately be ascribed to it – if they have misinterpreted what the results of physics (or, more currently, neurophysiology) tell us, then their supposed problem simply goes away. The possibility we canvass here is that the ways in which we talk about 'the mind' and in which we explain people's behaviour is not such that they can be considered *either* in contravention of physics' account *or* could be incorporated within physics' story. Our point is *not* that physics itself must give way to *meta*physics here, of one form or another, but is rather that these matters are logically *irrelevant* to physics. This is, essentially, a *conceptual* claim, and will be defended at some length in the ensuing pages.

The second critical issue we examine is the computer simulation of human conduct. The idea that a machine could reproduce the performance of human 'minds' would imply the rejection of any supposition – to which Descartes sought to cling – that there was something exceptional about, and unique to, human beings, that they possess something – the mind – which does not belong within the ordinary course of nature. It would do so because the computer is itself unequivocally *only* a machine, and, as such, to be understood as entirely subject to the general laws determined in the (relevant) natural sciences. The Turing test makes a pivotal contribution to this line of thought by supposedly providing criteria which will enable a determination to be made as to whether a machine *can* actually reproduce human mental life. The idea that the performance of computer and person might be indiscriminable is the key to the appeal of the Turing test, but, as we seek to show, the idea of computer simulation is deployed in such ways that the things it seeks to prove are already built into its terms. If one does not accept – and *we* do *not accept* – the terms on which the concept of 'the Turing test' is set up, then the actual staging of such tests proves nothing.

The third issue is the explanation of people's behaviour, which involves, most centrally, the contention that a scientific psychology must be created which explains people's conduct as the product of the mind, where the mind is considered to operate in the way (or ways) that a computer does. One version of this view – known as the 'functionalist' conception espoused by Hilary Putnam – argues that the relationship between 'mind' and 'brain' is akin to that between software and hardware in the computer, and that, therefore, providing a scientific account of the mind is the same as writing a program for the brain. This conception is contested in various ways, most prominently by John Searle, who insists that mind is the causal product of the brain and cannot therefore be abstracted from it in the way software can be abstracted from the hardware it runs on.

The proposal that 'the mind' is a kind of computer program gives rise to arguments about how the program is to be formulated, and Fodor has created *the representational theory of the mind* to suggest the form this might take. The representational theory has been a main focus of attention for more than twenty years, and has found many supporters and numerous critics. The view that the mind is a program, in fact, involves the resurrection – explicitly embraced by Fodor – of other Cartesian assumptions, particularly about the extent to which 'the mind' is something which is an 'inner cause' (or to which its various operations comprise a set of causes) of external behaviour.

Conceiving the mind as a computer program provides the prospect of a scientific explanation of behaviour, but this raises the question of the relation between this new theory and the kinds of explanations that we already, ordinarily, give for each other's conduct, the kinds of explanations which *allegedly* make up 'folk psychology'. One of the main foci of controversy in recent years has been over whether the vocabulary of 'folk psychology' will be retained in the language of the new psychological science, or whether it will be deleted from the language altogether, to be replaced by a new, scientifically validated terminology, the latter case being put (albeit in different ways) by the Churchlands and by Stich.

The fourth principal theme may seem somewhat arcane in connection with those already mentioned, but it is, in fact, directly and consequentially related to them. The current debate takes the form of a controversy about 'content' and involves asking whether *meaning* is, or is not, *in the head*, an issue which currently divides Fodor from Putnam. If it is argued that people's behaviour is to be explained in terms of the operations of their minds, then it is presumably the case that any such explanation will make reference only to characteristics of individual minds, or to 'inner states' of the brain, on one conception of things. The question is: can this programme of explanation succeed, or must actual explanations of conduct make reference to something external to the individual's mind? Language use is taken to be a prime example of a mental operation, and the question then is: does the meaning of a

language-user's expression depend entirely upon facts about the individual user – about 'what is in the head' of the user – or does it depend
upon facts about the individual's environment? Hence the question: is
meaning in the head? This particular theme is of considerable importance for our overall argument, for it raises the issue of the way in
which, particularly, *language* is understood. This is the very pivot of all
the matters discussed here: the disagreement over whether language is
primarily a psychological phenomenon or a social institution. We will
try to show that many of the positions criticised here underestimate, or
even entirely disregard, the significance of the fact that language *is* a
social institution, something whose properties and operations do not
result from, and cannot be reduced to descriptions of, psychological
conditions or brain states. We hold, in the first chapter, that the recognition of the social nature of language makes an important difference to
the whole *methodology* with which the problems are investigated, and in
the conclusion we seek to give full force to the importance of this point.

In discussing these four main themes and their varied manifes-
tations, we shall not be trying to give other and better answers to these
questions, but will be trying to show that the considerable difficulties in
which those who *do* attempt to give answers find themselves are *not* a
result of the depth, complexity or intractability of the core problems.
They are the result of the way in which these problems have been
formulated in the first place, and of the unacceptable alternatives which
those who argue these cases have *forced themselves into postulating*.
We will try only to show that there is no real need to set things up as
they do, and that, in the absence of certain crucial and problematic
suppositions, their problems just *do not arise*.

Introduction

The recent publication of John Searle's book, *The Rediscovery of the Mind* (Searle, 1992), emphasises the fact that there has been a great resurgence of interest in the philosophy of mind in recent years. Searle is, however, highly critical of many of the tendencies that have developed in the field, and we share his concerns, especially with respect to the re-emergence of 'scientism'. By this complaint, we do not mean to be taken as challenging, denying or belittling *any* development in the sciences as such, whether it be neurophysiology or computer science. Our complaint, like Searle's, is addressed to what we see as a misplaced role assigned to *scientific methods* of inquiry (as well as the appeal to specific scientific findings) in efforts to resolve *philosophical and logical* problems. Indeed, we would go further: many of the claims being advanced in the philosophy of mind involve misunderstandings of what the sciences have indeed accomplished, as well as misconstruals of their scope and relevance to the fundamental questions being posed.

We believe that Searle's strategy for addressing 'scientism' is mistaken. His *constructive* arguments do not unseat 'scientism' because they are as 'scientistic' as those he opposes. Searle, in common with his adversaries, is concerned to advance a (different, better) *theory* of mind. He is also in agreement with them that the contributions of Wittgenstein and Ryle to the debate are outmoded, and, at best, components of a rival, 'behaviouristic' theory. Thus, while we welcome many of his counter-arguments, especially those adumbrated in his 'critique of cognitive reason' (Searle, 1992, ch. 9), we nonetheless

dissent from his strategy. The strategy which we will adopt is to 'rehabilitate' Wittgenstein and Ryle in full measure, and show their continuing relevance – even their centrality – for the contemporary disputes in
the philosophy of mind. We maintain that the difficulties which Searle
identifies in the resurgence of interest in the philosophy of mind are
best tackled by using resources that were furnished by Wittgenstein
and Ryle. The time is ripe not only for grappling with 'scientism' as this
is being played out against a backdrop of recent developments in
artificial intelligence, computational linguistics and neurophysiology,
but for reasserting *the methods of analysis and critique* most powerfully
deployed by these two thinkers.

The modern history of the 'philosophy of mind' has been dominated,
along with Anglo-American philosophy more generally, by materialist
views of one sort or another. The problematic around which the debate
has continued was originally established by Descartes (whose (baleful)
influence we discuss in chapter 2). For Descartes, the place of 'mind'
within a natural, law-governed, causally driven universe was problematic. There are those, namely the 'behaviourists' and the 'eliminativists',
who hold (albeit for different reasons) that there is, in fact, no place at
all for the mind within that universe. They maintain that the very
notion of 'the mind', and all of those expressions in our language
associated with it, is dispensable, especially from that portion of natural science which will eventually extend to cover human conduct.
There has been strong resistance to this position, and there are those
such as Jerry Fodor and Daniel Dennett (whose views we shall discuss
at length in chapter 3) who have sought to reconcile the existence of the
mind with their materialist convictions. Their aim has been to provide
a thoroughly consistent materialist account of the nature of mind and
the mental. Although Searle is severely critical of their arguments,
he has nonetheless shared their principal objective. Searle seeks to
treat 'the mind' as an emergent property of 'the brain', and thus as no
less natural a phenomenon than the liquidity of water, which is an
emergent property of the gases hydrogen and oxygen.

By far the most important idea in the many efforts to reconcile the
mental with the material has been the appeal to the computer. On the
basis of the 'functional theory' of the mind (articulated most cogently
by Hilary Putnam), and fuelled by developments in the field of 'artificial intelligence', many contributors to the philosophy of mind
thought that they had, at last, achieved the long-sought theoretical
reconciliation of the existence of 'mind' with their materialist convictions. In this device, they contended, the 'mental' and the 'material'
came together without any trace of a disembodied or immaterial

substance, a 'soul', 'spirit' or 'ghost in the machine'. Here is something seemingly possessed of mental powers at least equal to, and possibly greater than, those of human beings, but which is unquestionably entirely material: the machine's 'intellectual' performances are attributable wholly to physical causes which are knowable, and its technical elaboration promises an extension of these performances to encompass more and more of the kinds of things which, when human beings do them, we call 'intelligent', 'rational' or 'displaying mentality'. The computer appeared to show that 'mental states and processes' could be 'physical states and processes', that mental states could cause other mental states and could cause bodily behaviour, because, unequivocally, one physical state can cause another.

Searle is thoroughly dubious about the propaganda for artificial intelligence because its theorists (and functionalist claims about 'the mind' more generally) seek to abstract the functioning of the mind from its 'physical realisation', from its connection with *the human brain*. On Searle's argument, the mind, as we know it, is an emergent property of a biological phenomenon, and the materials out of which computer scientists seek to engender mental phenomena do not have the causal powers to produce emergent phenomena which genuinely satisfy the criteria we have for authentic mentality (such as 'intensionality', on which more later). Searle does not hold that *only* the human brain is possessed of the appropriate causal powers, but he does insist that, for a certainty, silicon chips are not.

Our purpose in this book is not, however, solely to challenge (yet again) the fetishism of the computer. Indeed, this is not our *main* objective at all. It is, rather, *to combat the conception of philosophy which gives rise to the fetishism of the computer and of the role of the purportedly scientific rationality which has given us this truly impressive machine.* We also have a number of subordinate aims. Our objections to much contemporary philosophy of mind are apt to be cast as instances of a kind of dogmatism, of a reactionary adherence to notions of 'human uniqueness', and of 'irrational' resistance to the progress of science and of the enlightenment which is supposed to accompany this progress. It is, alas, however, often the case that these criticisms consist of little more than *allegations* of dogmatism, ones which are – as we shall try to document – quite unfounded. We are likely to be grouped together with sundry other proponents of what critics sometimes call 'human exceptionalists', sometimes castigated as 'species chauvinists' (a favourite phrase of Ned Block's), or depicted as in the grip of a purely romantic separatism whereby human beings are thought to be exempt from the workings of the rest of nature, superior to, standing apart

from and above all other forms of existence. Those who make such
charges can thus present themselves as the modest champions of a new
enlightenment vision, one in which all fundamental illusions about our
superiority can be stripped away. They can also portray themselves as
the vanguard of material and intellectual progress, ones who are contributing to a profound, momentous and far-reaching re-evaluation of
our status as, ultimately, sentient *automata*. That such views, and the
criticisms which spring from them, might themselves be the expression
of iron-hard dogmatism is not a consideration widely entertained these
days, perhaps because the correctness of their position seems so obviously true to those who embrace it. We shall do what we can in these
pages to make as reasonable a case as possible for a thoroughgoing
reappraisal of this stance.

The second subordinate aim of this book is linked to the first. It is to
argue that the claims for contemporary materialist philosophies of
mind are based upon *negligible* scientific results, and, more importantly, upon wholly tendentious conceptions of what these can actually
yield. The actual impetus for such claims, we maintain, is not the most
up-to-date science but rather old philosophy. In this respect, Hubert
Dreyfus has patiently gone before us, most recently in *What Computers
Still Can't Do* (Dreyfus, 1993), pointing out the many discrepancies
between the immense claims of 'artificial intelligence' protagonists and
the actual achievements of that field. If our fundamental conceptions of
human nature were indeed at stake, then those who wish to impress
upon us that it is a respect for *science* which requires us to undertake the
'shattering rethinking' they lay upon us, do so on the basis of the most
negligible of scientific achievements.

Noam Chomsky has been a most notable example of parlaying a
modest, indeed deeply problematical, set of scientific (i.e., linguistic)
achievements into a whole array of philosophical claims. Chomsky
would like us to think that it is the (contentious) scientific results of
generative grammar which give credence to his philosophical arguments, but this is not, in fact, the case. It is, rather, Chomsky's invocation of 'rationalist' arguments which provides him with a particular
interpretation of the results of his grammatical analyses, *not* his
'science'.

Thus, we aim to *disentangle* the actual scientific substance from the
philosophical glosses throughout these discussions, showing that the
two are only *fortuitously* interlinked, and that the scientific inquiries
could continue on their course quite independently of the ways in
which they are 'talked up'. We thus do not question the *scientific*
achievements, though the pretensions of some to be 'scientific' *are*
sharply questioned. What we question is the undue philosophical *sig-*

nificance that is attributed to the scientific achievements. For example, we believe that the computer is, unquestionably, an astonishing achievement, and its introduction has made a great difference to human life (indeed, it has *revolutionised* our lives as academicians, to name but one, relatively minor, case). Yet we are witnessing the introduction and proliferation of a new technology, *not a new species of being*.

Not only are those we criticise prejudiced in favour of (a certain conception of) science, they are commonly strongly prejudiced against the likes of us! Though we agree with Searle in many of his criticisms of the main traditions in the philosophy of mind, we do so for very different reasons, and Searle himself shares the same dismissive attitude towards the approach we favour as do those he criticises. This approach is one which directs attention towards, for want of a better summary expression, our 'ordinary language'. Outside of a relatively small circle of persistent practitioners, it is regarded as out-of-date, and it is commonplace in contemporary philosophy to comment disparagingly on the once widely fashionable policy of attending to the nuances of 'ordinary language'.

A ubiquitous basis for this dismissal, and a ubiquitous basis in support of 'scientism' in philosophy, is that the questions being posed do not pertain to just what we say but rather pertain to what is *really* the case. In this respect, the questions *must* be ones for science to settle. The idea that ordinary language – and the pre-scientific understandings which it allegedly expresses – could and should *dictate* to science what it can say is condemned as an absurdity. Indeed, it would be an absurdity *if* 'ordinary language' philosophy, properly done, supposed that 'ordinary language' expressed any such understandings. Therefore, a central charge against 'ordinary language' philosophy will be shown to be largely irrelevant because it fails *to engage what 'ordinary language' philosophy actually does*. The core issue is the nature of *'language'* and it is, of course, the case that the characterisation of the supposed 'pre-scientific' understandings embodied in our ordinary talk is prejudicial, based not upon the consideration of that talk, of how it works and of what it actually says, but, rather, upon preconceptions of what it *must* mean. In chapter 1, we shall be especially concerned with this issue in relation to two major themes in the philosophy of mind: Turing's test for 'intelligence' in machines, and Searle's 'Chinese Room' thought-experiment.

It is not, however, just the approach that we adopt that is concerned with 'language' in the 'philosophy of mind'. Indeed, the 'scientism' with which we contend has made language a central issue in more than one respect. A powerful motivation for many of the recent developments in the philosophy of mind has been Chomsky's neo-Cartesian gloss on his linguistic theorising. The first assumption has been that the understanding of language among human beings must be a *psychological* task, that language is a property of the individual human mind. The idea that language is a matter for psychology means, on materialist assumptions, that it must (ultimately) be a matter of biology, and not just of biology, but of *physiology* – a conviction which Searle has in common with those whom he otherwise criticises.

We certainly do not seek to contest the point that language *is* a matter of biology, for such an assertion can be based on well-established (and even trite) facts (we have vocal chords, Broca's region, etc. and must, when speaking, deploy the articulatory apparatus which is our biological endowment). Chomsky, however, has been particularly adept at providing partisan interpretations of such trite facts. One of these is that it is quite clearly the case that language is something *natural* to the human species and that its development is part of the maturation of the organism.[1] This uncontentious claim about the human capacity for language acquisition is, however, then pressed into the service of a much more contentious claim about the presence of specific 'wirings' in the nervous system. This transition, however, requires (a) some verbal sleight of hand such that the presence of a neurophysiological configuration is to be described as instantiating 'knowledge of language'[2] and (b) a variety of tendentious arguments which *purport* to demonstrate – on the basis of the vastly tendentious assumption that learning a language is a form of inductive theorising – that language learning requires innate rules.

The view which we take, following Wittgenstein and Ryle, is that language is indeed a matter of human biology, but not therefore of *physiology*. The language that we speak is not one which is innate – not even Chomsky argues that it is – and it is not something which has developed as a product of individual *psychology*. That we speak *shared* languages which we did not contrive for ourselves is another very trite

1 We are aware that there are issues to be considered concerning language-like behaviour in other species, such as, for example, apes, but would point out that, even if it were the case that some apes had shown an aptitude for language – which remains, itself, a questionable claim – this would not show that such language was *natural* for them in the way it is for human beings. The immense effort required to instil even a modest aptitude (if that is what it is) in the Bonobo ape, for example, is very far from the ease with which children are brought into the world of language.
2 It is, of course, an even grosser sleight of words by which Chomsky seeks to evade the difficulties in the way of talk of 'knowledge' by the proposed substitution of 'cognising'. For a more detailed critical review of this and related tricks of the Chomskian trade, see Baker and Hacker, 1984b, p. 247 *et seq.*

fact, but one no less consequential than the fact that we take to speaking them as the proverbial duck takes to water. It is *within the collective lives* of human beings that language has been developed, and it is as a phenomenon *of life and activity rather than of neurophysiology* that Wittgenstein and Ryle invite us to consider language.

It is not only the case that the languages we speak are shared but, also, that they have developed over time. The things we say, and our ways of talking, have grown up out of the contingencies of human life, and the language that we speak has been, as the historical evidence plainly shows, elaborated over the course of history, just as the capacity of the individual to speak is elaborated over the course of his or her life. Thus, what Wittgenstein and Ryle contest is the idea that language is a 'mental' phenomenon, that it is something at all separable from human activities and the patterns of those which are developed. The idea that we could have, innately, words for, say, 'bank account', 'water charges' and 'tax bills' is preposterous, as is the idea that we might have such expressions in a language even though we lived in a community which had no knowledge of money, no water supply system, no banking system and no internal revenue system. That monetary systems, water supply systems, banking arrangements and states in need of finance are *themselves* innate or individual 'mental' phenomena is surely not worthy of serious consideration.

The relevance of 'ordinary language' to philosophy is, according to both Wittgenstein and Ryle, due to the fact that the main disputes in philosophy are about topics nominated by words from our ordinary language, as is clearly the case throughout the philosophy of mind. The problematic terms are those such as 'thought', 'intention', 'understand-ing', 'memory', 'belief' and even (as we shall see) the word 'because'. (To which brief list we might add the word 'mind' itself.) Those whom we criticise typically want to offer a *theory* of such things: they seek to answer the question 'What *is* a belief?', or 'What *is* an intention?' or 'What *is* a thought?' Wittgenstein and Ryle complain that such theories seldom result from the wide surveying of the ways in which such words actually appear in the things that people say and figure in the things that people do. As Wittgenstein proposed, a first objective should be to encourage philosophers to weigh (and to weight) the plain facts of the use of words *without prejudice*. The prospect was, or so they claimed, that such surveys (or, better, surviews) of the *assorted* facts about a particular word would show that there was no need for a *theory*. Such suggestions are commonly denounced by, amongst others, Searle, but the fact remains that philosophical theorising, as this is manifest in the philosophy of mind (although not only there),

continues to generate disputes and controversies which remain unre-
solved, and there are no alternative principles or methods commonly
agreed upon to facilitate even envisageable solutions. The parties to the
major debates may all agree, for example, that they are materialists, but
they cannot seem to agree upon what 'materialism' requires them to
say about the nature of mind. From the Wittgenstein/Ryle angle, however, such responses seem only to manifest a determination to continue
looking at those ordinary words *with prejudice*.

We shall provide some practical demonstrations that the advice of
Wittgenstein and Ryle is by no means irrelevant to the problems of
minds and computers which are in contention. In a vernacular para-
phrase, that advice might be summarised as: when you find yourself in
a mess, don't press on, but consider, rather, how you got yourself into
it in the first place. This is the spirit in which we will examine the
various issues that we take up. Instead of seeking to propose how the
problem may be solved, we will seek to show how that problem was set
up to begin with, and to indicate that there is certainly no compelling
reason to set it up that way. More strongly, we will be suggesting that
the problem is *the creation* of the particular philosophical standpoint
from whose vantage-point it takes on the perplexing appearance which
it has. If this is so, then it cannot be to *that* standpoint that we should
(continue to) appeal in order to undertake its resolution. We will (especially in chapter 2) argue that the whole current debate is a result of
the attempt to construe the findings of the physical sciences as an
ontological world-picture, one which (ostensibly) precludes the facts of
'mental life'. We shall contest the scientism which is associated with
this world-picture, and, therefore, we shall repudiate the related conception which is held of our 'ordinary language' as a proto-scientific
vocabulary. We will reiterate the claim that the essentials of the current
positions we contest originate not in the progress of science but rather
in the arguments of Descartes as put forward at the dawn of modern
science. The subject-matter – computers, neurophysiology – may be
novel, but the dilemmas under discussion are not, as Chomsky
(proudly) indicated in his *Cartesian Linguistics*.

In subsequent chapters, we examine the arguments that have been
presented by Jerry Fodor. He has invested much energy in developing
Chomsky's insights, and has made himself a central figure in contemporary debates. Fodor's arguments are, as he often tells us himself,
implausible, but in truly 'scientistic' spirit he insists on 'biting the
bullet' and having to accept an otherwise unpersuasive theory if there
is no other theory, or only a worse one, on offer. Fodor's claim that
there is no alternative is itself unconvincing, resting as it does upon
often superficial and unsympathetic statements of points of view differ-

ent from his own. In the first section of the chapter we devote to Fodor, we cast a critical eye over his account of the opposition before being equally critical of his own theorising, seeking to show that it is *only on the assumptions* of either Fodor or his primary antagonists that there *is* a problem, and one susceptible to theoretical resolution.

Fodor's own theory of mind has been that it is a process of computation. However, various aspects of his theory have fallen foul of developments in computing. Fodor insisted that the operations of the mind must be 'linguistic' in character, embodying, as they must, the transformation of a set of 'representations'. The mind is a process of transforming symbols, and since the programmed digital computer effected such computations in a sequential fashion, then the mind must be presumed to do so as well. However, with the advent of *parallel-distributed processing* systems in computing, and 'network' theorising in the neurosciences, Fodor's model came under attack from a theoretical movement joining these new developments into a perspective called 'connectionism'. The mind and the computer are *still* analogised, but now understood in terms of connectionist principles. The mind and the computer are analogised because the *brain* and the computer are. The brain is not a centralised, linear structure but operates, rather, through networks of concurrent, parallel and interacting neural connections, and this inspires the idea that computing itself can be organised in a parallel way. The point about the connectionist conception with respect to Fodor's position is that it appears to eliminate the need for a *symbolic* level of operation. The connectionists share with Fodor the materialist, philosophical idea that understanding the mind is the same thing as understanding the brain, but we argue that what the connectionist claims accomplish here is, if anything, a *confirmation* of the views of Wittgenstein and Ryle that understanding the brain is *not* the same task as 'understanding the mind'. It is not, however, as though 'understanding the mind' is another, alternative and comparable task to that of understanding the brain, for it is *not a unified task* at all.

The debates engendered by the idea that the mind operates in the same manner as a computer are paralleled by those which propose that the computer is or can be endowed with a mind. The business of simulating assorted human 'mental' activities on computers is often promulgated as the creation of an artificial intelligence, and our attention consequently shifts to a consideration of this issue. Here, we shall revisit a theme first introduced in chapter 1, that of the Turing test, but in terms of a more systematic treatment of the old question 'Can a machine think?'

As remarked in the preface, Dreyfus has highlighted the painfully slow progress which efforts at simulation have made, relative to the hopes and propaganda with which they were initiated. In subsequent chapters, we recognise that simulating linguistic behaviour has a prominent, but highly problematic, role in this story. We shall also examine in some detail various developments in computational linguistics with respect to 'natural language understanding'. Developing technology that can process inputs expressed in a natural language requires the *formalisation* of that language. In computing terms, formalisation is a tool with which computer scientists can build models and representations of language in order to run computers which can accomplish such processing. We do not take issue with the theoretical formulations of linguistic phenomena adduced for these purposes: our objection is to the transposition of such formalisms to the attempt to explain the nature of human language use and comprehension. One theme here will be that such computational theories of *human* linguistic capacities compound misconceptions about language that Wittgenstein had already exposed. Two confusions predominate here: one concerns the role of 'rules' in language, and the other concerns the relationship between 'mental' operations and language use and comprehension.

Disjunctures between claims and actual systems are most telling when considering language generation systems which we consider subsequently. A prominent objective of language processing work is to develop a dialogical or conversing system. However, in order to accomplish this technical task, dialogue and conversation are formalised into linguistic structures and bound by specific sorts of rules. We shall show that these formalisms cannot capture the fundamental properties of conversational phenomena revealed by studies of naturally occurring talk in the interaction of human beings. The issues considered here revolve around a core tendency encountered earlier in our analysis and critique of the current state of the philosophy of mind: the continued insistence upon divorcing language from social conduct and circumstance.

It is fitting, then, to conclude our arguments by re-emphasising the indissoluble link between language and social life and its relevance to contemporary debates in the philosophy of mind. Our critical survey of the field will, if it achieves anything, hopefully reorient students of philosophy and the human sciences to a clearer appreciation, not only of the achievements of Wittgenstein and Ryle, but of the many ways in which a rush to general theorising and a concomitant neglect of the ordinary, everyday details of language and of life can confuse and bewitch our intellect.

1
Philosophy, Language and Mind

This book is a collective enterprise. We are, as will be apparent in what follows, seriously at odds with a variety of theses, trends and tendencies in the contemporary intellectual climate in philosophy and the human sciences which have been cultivated by a widespread adherence to (what we here argue is) a *defective* philosophical vision for these sciences. This vision is, in large measure, we shall argue, the product of an *uncritical* attitude to certain philosophical interpretations of the role of the natural sciences and, especially, of the computing sciences, in the task of describing and explaining human mentality and cognitive capacities.

We are well aware that our attempt to put our case involves something of an uphill struggle, and that we shall need to anticipate many by now standard – though typically rather thoughtless – objections to the line we shall be taking. That line is one which could be stereotyped as an 'ordinary language' approach, one which is widely regarded as *démodé*. We are not, however, too troubled by the fact that the positions we favour were developed in the middle of the twentieth century, since the positions we shall be opposing were, we shall show, essentially the products of arguments and presuppositions which were advanced in the *seventeenth* century. Thus, objections to our views which are based upon their date of initial development do not worry us. Indeed, we share John Cook's view to the effect that so-called 'ordinary language philosophy' comprises a methodology which has not been tried and found wanting, but which has scarcely even been tried at all (Cook, 1980).

At a time when many in the 'philosophy of mind' are busy citing the latest scientific researches to one another, our intervention courts the risk and disdain which rightly falls upon those who seek to settle essentially scientific questions without reference to or possession of the latest scientific results from, for example, studies of the human brain. We risk being treated as being amongst those who think they can arbitrate amongst contending positions in the sciences on the strength of claims about the meanings of ordinary words.

We *do* risk these misunderstandings. However, notwithstanding this risk, we do not believe that we should concede *anything at all* to the philosophical blustering which is often associated with the name of Science, nor to the notion that a recitation of its current results is perforce relevant to (or effective in) confronting the problems we address here. As we shall make plain, it is a *misconception* that arguments such as ours seek to pre-empt the findings of science or to legislate what the empirical sciences can discover. It goes against everything we suppose to imagine that we could settle an intelligible empirical question by conceptual manouevrings, but this is, of course, also why we must look upon philosophers' introduction of empirical materials from the sciences with scepticism: for, just as we refuse to suppose that conceptual elucidations can determine empirical facts, so, correspondingly, do we reject the idea that empirical information can settle conceptual questions.

As to the widespread disparagement of attempts to resolve philosophical problems by way of appeals to 'what we would (ordinarily) say', we would proffer the following comment. It often appears that those who engage in such disparaging nonetheless themselves often do what they programmatically disparage, for it seems to us at least arguable that many of the central philosophical questions are in fact, and despite protestations to the contrary, being argued about in terms of appeals (albeit often inept) to 'what we would (ordinarily) say . . .'. That the main issues of the contemporary philosophy of mind are *essentially* about language (in the sense that they arise from and struggle with confusions over the meanings of ordinary words) is a position which, we insist, can still reasonably be proposed and defended. We shall claim here that most, if not all, of the conundrums, controversies and challenges of the philosophy of mind in the late twentieth century consist in a collectively assertive, although bewildered, attitude towards such ordinary linguistic terms as 'mind' itself, 'consciousness', 'thought', 'belief', 'intention' and so on, and that the problems which are posed are ones which characteristically are of the form which ask *what we should say if* confronted with certain facts, as described.

For example, at a central point in this discussion, we will take up the debate over whether a machine can think or understand, the essential feature of this debate being that we are asked to envisage the output of immensely sophisticated robotic devices, which output can fool us into saying of it that it has been produced by a human being. The test of whether people can discriminate between samples produced by people and those produced by sophisticated computing systems is meant to serve as a test – a 'Turing test' (Turing, 1950)[1] – of whether a machine can possess the same mental capacities as human beings: whether it can think, understand, be conscious and so forth. We shall discuss the Turing test in detail further on, but its intrinsic merits and demerits are less relevant at this point than is its role in *giving the impression* that it has replaced a 'conceptual question' with an empirical one. If we seek to say, on the basis of 'ordinary language', that a machine cannot think, then we will seem to be attempting to counter what we have said is a basic presumption, namely, that these considerations cannot answer an empirical question. After all, was not the Turing test proposed precisely as a means of turning the problem of 'machine thought/intelligence' into an empirical one? Turing sought to provide a precise, quantifiably answerable, question, one of a specifically empirical kind. His test was designed to determine with what frequency people are unable to discriminate between sample output from human beings and sample output from computing machines. If the test results show that the frequency with which the test's subjects can discriminate between the human output and the machine output is statistically insignificant, then the fact that they *cannot* discriminate between these outputs would (it is asserted) mean that *it is right to say that* there is no (essential) difference between a 'thinking' human being and such a sophisticated piece of robotics, and also, therefore, that *it is right to say that* the latter is as much capable of 'thinking' as the former (insofar as the outputs are of the sort which, when produced by human beings, would *be said* to involve 'thinking').

The essential point here, we insist, is not about whether we might obtain the kind of results Turing aspired to obtain from his test, but, rather, about *what we should say if* confronted with results which showed that test subjects could not discriminate between the outputs of humans and machines. We do not, actually, need to be in possession of any such results to determine *what we should say* of them should they be achieved. (Note that we are now recurrently and necessarily emphasising the role of *an appeal to linguistic usage* in this discussion.) The Turing

---

1 For some discussion of this, see Hodges, 1983, p. 266 and pp. 415–17.

test is a smokescreen which makes it look as though what is at issue is essentially an *empirical* matter: could we actually construct a machine which could pass the test? However, the actual question has nothing to do with whether or not the practicalities of building any such machinery are insurmountable. Rather, the fundamental issue (with which the discussion began) remains: *given* that a machine can be built which could pass the Turing test, *should we (then) say that* it can think, understand, be conscious, etc.? The question of whether or not a machine which simulates the behaviour of human beings – to the extent that its output is indiscriminable from the behaviour of human beings – *can be said to think* is not, *per se*, an *engineer's* or a *computer scientist's* question. Nor is it an empirical question to be settled by any empirical, scientific inquiry. It is a *conceptual* question. Whether one can in fact build such a machine that can pass the test is indeed a question about which such scientists might have some authority, but the question of what they would have achieved in building a machine which could pass the test, of *what they have tested for with the test*, is *not* one on which these or any other scientists have any particular authority. We emphasise at this point that the Turing test itself invokes *the judgment of users of ordinary language*, for it is *they* who are invited to say whether or not there is a difference between the output of human and machine. Hence, the question of whether the Turing test has any relevance for determining that one should or should not say that a machine can think has absolutely nothing whatsoever to do with the progress of engineering (robotics) or with any other empirical, natural-scientific endeavour. Thus, disputing the claim that such a test could show that a machine can think in no way impedes or limits the progress of science or engineering. The question of whether or not we should naturally (ordinarily) say that a machine which passes the Turing test can think, understand, etc., *is one which can be answered by those of us who speak the ordinary language from which the words 'think' and 'understand' are taken*. Should we, that is, *in any ordinary sense of these words*, say that what is involved in enabling a machine to pass the Turing test is to be called thinking or understanding (at least on its part)?

Providing an answer to this question does not require that we provide a 'theory of mind' which explains how both human beings and machines could be said to have minds, a theory which would thus supposedly establish how it is possible for machines to have the 'mental' capacities of humans or to enter into states which are called 'mental states'. This was, of course, the role of the 'functional theory of the mind' as initially propounded by Hilary Putnam (Putnam, 1960 and Putnam, 1965), and recently recanted by him (Putnam, 1981). By the time Putnam withdrew his assent from this theory, it had become the orthodoxy in the philosophy of mind. The functional theory held that the workings of the mind were definable in terms of their formal, functional interrelations and their mediating role between environmental inputs and actual behaviours, and it posited a distinction between such relationships and the material forms in which they could be realised along the same lines as the distinction within computer science between 'software' and 'hardware'. Hence, there was no apparent requirement to suppose that 'minds' would only be found in association with biological structures, let alone those biological structures characteristic of the human organism, and, therefore, it was envisageable that these functional interrelationships could be realised in electromechanical constructions, i.e., insofar as the operations of machines (computers) formally parallel the operations of the human mind then that fact endows the machine with mental characteristics. From our point of view, by contrast, what is needed is not any such 'theory of mind' but a perspicuous description of the relevant facts, those making up the envisaged situation of the Turing test.

The much discussed case of the 'Chinese Room' can provide us with a useful occasion for clarification. The 'Chinese Room' is an imaginary example, contrived by John Searle to counter the claim of what he calls 'the strong program of artificial intelligence' (Searle, 1980). The argument, as formulated by Searle, is that though a computer may be able to manipulate symbols according to syntactical procedures (i.e., that its operations can possess a formal similarity to those of the human mind as depicted in the functionalist theory), its operations nonetheless cannot match those of the human mind, for the latter does not merely proceed syntactically because it also possesses semantics. This capacity to operate *semantically* is, for Searle, *necessarily* connected to a human biological apparatus, *contra* functionalism's claims. His 'Chinese Room' is precisely an implementation (by *gedankenexperiment*) of the Turing test. It envisages an arrangement which, *ex hypothesi*, passes the Turing test. It is an arrangement which analogises that of the computer, though it actually involves human beings.

The 'Chinese Room' is equipped with an assortment of dump bins containing cards on which are inscribed characters from the Chinese language. The room also contains manuals which instruct an individual operator inside how to respond when pieces of paper bearing expressions in Chinese are passed to him from outside the room. These instructions tell the individual how to assess the string of characters passed to him, and how to respond to them, by indicating which dump bins to proceed to and how to assemble the symbol-bearing cards into a sequence which is then returned through the door to the outside. Obviously, this is a fantasy, for the operation would be massively too complex for practical use, but its point is, of course, that if the speaking of Chinese could be codified to the extent that it could be expressed in the manuals, then the individual in the room could simulate Chinese exchanges with those outside it sufficiently well to deceive them into believing that the person inside knows Chinese. Now, it is true that the machine operations which are being analogised are themselves enormously fast, but the operating speed of the machine is not something which is fundamentally relevant to its putative 'intelligence' or 'comprehension'. However, this is an imaginary example, and we are thus entitled to imagine that the individual in the room can operate very fast as well! The essential point remains how, by what procedures, the Chinese Room operates, not how fast it operates.

In a way, we think, the scenario of the Chinese Room is utterly superfluous, since it illustrates an argument which is actually much more simple, and which exposes the elementary fallacies involved in so much reasoning in this area. The argument is this: A person who knows no Chinese is given a system of instructions (in his native language of, say, English) which enables him to *simulate* the syntactic, semantic and sequential properties of Chinese conversation without actually acquiring any understanding of Chinese. The fact that the 'output' of the individual – his linguistic behaviour – indiscriminably simulates that of someone who does speak Chinese does not itself demonstrate that the simulator understands Chinese. The simulator's apparent competence results entirely *from his understanding of English*, for it is the instructions provided in *that* language which facilitate the simulation. In short, what we have here is a system for simulating Chinese *without understanding it*. Hence, we should say, *in any ordinary sense of the word 'understand'*, that from the fact that impeccable simulations of Chinese conversation can be given it does not follow that these must manifest an understanding of Chinese. It might be that, *ignorant* of the fact that an arrangement had been produced to permit the successful simulation of Chinese without actual comprehension of it, we might suppose that the behaviour of a Chinese speaker could *not* be simulated, that speaking Chinese could *only* be done by someone who understood Chinese, but in such a case we would *wrongly* conclude that the behaviour must manifest comprehension. However, and by definition, what we have here is a case of someone being able to simulate competent Chinese conversation *without understanding Chinese*.

Turing's own mathematical achievements which led to the development of modern computers and which led him to his own (disastrous) confusions about computing machinery and intelligence involved something comparable to what we have just described. Turing contrived a method for breaking down calculations into such remarkably simplified steps that they could be carried out according to a series of instructions *whose following did not involve any understanding of the mathematical operations thereby being carried out*. They could be instantiated in a very primitive machine. Expressions like 'add two' could be replaced by instructions like 'write that in', 'move to the left', 'rub that out' and so forth. Someone could simulate the carrying out of correct computations by following such instructions, they could do the operations which are the functional equivalent of adding two, and they could do this if they could understand expressions such as 'rub that out' and 'write that in' even if they could not understand the expression 'add two'. Turing, then, had contrived a way of enabling computations to be carried out *without the requirement of comprehension of those computations*, but he seems, on reflecting upon his achievements, to have failed to understand that this was their character, assuming instead that, since, when people compute, their carrying out of computations involves understanding, then if computing can be done on (or, as he would no doubt have preferred, by) machines, then those machines must be capable of understanding!

Of course – but, *of course* – if the Chinese Room or mechanical computation of any kind is to work, then understanding must be involved. Attempts to argue that it is 'the room' or 'the system' which understands Chinese are excluded *ex hypothesi*. The situation is one which is precisely designed to involve no understanding of Chinese at that level, for the operator has only an English competence and the manuals with which he is to operate are written entirely in English. Only the cards in the dump bins feature Chinese characters, but these are, for the operator, only so many squiggles and squoggles – the operator does not even need to know that they are words in Chinese to operate the system, let alone what words they are or what those words mean. The room, the system, operates exclusively on the basis of English; there is no understanding whatever of Chinese. There is, of course, understanding of Chinese involved, but it is, of course, in setting up the room and in writing the manual. One could not write the instructions (in English) for the successful simulation of Chinese linguistic behaviour without an enormously detailed understanding of Chinese. So there *is* understanding involved, but it is that understanding which is expressed in the design of the manual, for example. That such understanding is so expressed does not mean that the manual has an understanding of Chinese! Books may be said to contain knowledge of physics, but they cannot then be said to know or understand what they contain. A physics textbook itself knows nothing of the structure of matter (nor is it ignorant in this regard, either!). Understanding is contained in the manual in the Chinese Room, but the understanding there contained is that of those who have constructed the manual (just as the knowledge in the physics textbook is that of its authors and their discipline) and not that of the manual itself.

There is one further aspect of the Chinese Room situation that deserves to be explored. The idea underlying the Turing test and its Chinese Room equivalent is that for 'the system' to be able to do the same sorts of things a human being can do it must be endowed with those capacities which enable human beings to do what they can do, such as, and especially, thought, comprehension, intelligence and so on. 'The same as' now plays a vital part in the argument. The sense in which the Chinese Room system can be said to do *the same as* the Chinese conversationalist is, then, only a matter of formal similarities between their respective 'output'. Though the output from the room may parallel the output of someone who speaks, who *understands*, Chinese, the output of the system cannot *mean* what the Chinese speaker meant when he said whatever he said. The operator of the Chinese Room, *ex hypothesi*, does not understand Chinese, hence he is outputting stuff without any idea of its meanings; thus, he does not know what the output might be used to say and hence he cannot mean any such thing by it. We do not, of course, wish to deny that the output of the automatic teller machine which displays the current bank balance of a customer does not mean that he is, say, overdrawn, but this is not to say that an automatic teller has the power to mean what it says, any more than we should say that the fact that a 'No Smoking' sign tells us not to smoke means that cardboard signs have the power to issue injunctions.

Our argument here might be criticised because once again, focusing entirely upon the human operator of the room seems to overlook the possibility that it is *the system as a whole* which understands Chinese. However, this particular strand of the discussion in fact provides a rebuttal of the 'system as a whole' argument. It does so by making quite clear that the onus is upon those who press this latter case to explain how 'understanding Chinese' is present in the room, i.e., in the system. The understanding of Chinese is indeed involved in setting up the room in such a way that simulation of Chinese linguistic behaviour can be achieved entirely on the basis of an understanding of English. The question is, therefore, if the room (i.e., the system) is to be said to 'understand Chinese', just how is the understanding of Chinese introduced into it? To someone who *does not know* how the system was set up, the simulation of Chinese linguistic behaviour (based entirely upon a command of English) produced by it may *appear to manifest genuine comprehension* of Chinese. Appearing to understand, however, is not the same as genuinely understanding. Someone who was repeating lines whispered into his ear by someone else may succeed in giving the impression that he understands Chinese, but it would not therefore establish that he did. Producing appropriate expressions in a language does not, then, *invariably* manifest comprehension of that language.

If we are not guilty of the charge of attempting to restrict the progress of science, can we not be convicted on the charge of attempting to dictate the meanings of words? And isn't this another aspect of an effort to obstruct science? The expression 'ordinary' in the phrase 'ordinary meanings' or in the phrase 'ordinary uses of language' may mislead, and has often done so. It is taken to contrast with 'technical meanings' or with 'technical language', the vernacular with the vocabulary of science. It is indeed the case that attention is paid to expressions which can be called 'ordinary' in this sense, ones like those mentioned above, such as 'thought', 'belief', 'intention', 'meaning', 'understanding', etc. These are ordinary words in the sense of being plain English ones, and they would contrast, certainly, with technical expressions from the sciences, such as 'proton', 'boson', 'neutron', etc., and also with technical expressions from the professions such as law and medicine, with 'mandamus', *'mens rea'*, 'hypothyroidism' and the like. The emphasis here upon *ordinary* words such as belief, consciousness, understanding, etc. is, however, quite *incidental* to the 'ordinary language' argument – incredible though this suggestion may at first seem. The prominent emphasis upon such ordinary words is a contingent consequence of the fact that many of the important philosophical problems (i.e., confusions, misconceptions, fallacies) centre upon words which *are* ordinary in this sense. However, this does not mean that there cannot be philosophical puzzles and confusions over *technical* words as well, for indeed there are such cases, and they do, as such, provide occasions for treatment in 'ordinary language' terms. The essential contrast, then, is not between 'ordinary' and 'technical' terms, but between 'ordinary uses' and 'philosophical abuses' and *that* contrast could apply to technical (including scientific) terms just as readily as to plain English ones. We digress into this issue here because, of course, the case we argue does not seek to inhibit the capacity of scientists, engineers or other professionals to create a technical vocabulary to suit their needs. However, can we not therefore allow engineers/computer scientists to call machines which pass the Turing test 'thinking machines' or to say that they possess 'understanding'? Are we not trying to dictate to computer scientists and engineers whether they can say that machines think and understand? This is not merely a falsification, it is the very reverse of the truth.

If engineers wish to term computers 'thinking machines' we have absolutely no objection to their doing so. We can, likewise, have no objection (save perhaps for their sexist overtones) to the fact that the owners of cars and ships often refer to their possessions as 'she'. Nor do we mind that the owners of *Electrolux* vacuum cleaners talk about using their machines to 'hoover' the floor. We do not suppose that someone who talks of his car as 'she' supposes that the vehicle possesses the sexual characteristics of a female (any more than we suppose that the putting together of 'male' and 'female' plugs provides a sexual – rather than an electronic – connection). The users of vacuum cleaners have come to use the expression 'hoover' as a generic expression for such cleaners despite its origin as a proprietary name, and those who speak of their *Electrolux* as a 'hoover' are not making any mistake about the brand of vacuum cleaner that it is. Words do indeed acquire new meanings, and the expression 'thinking machines' might come to be universally used of computers; the question is not whether this might happen (and certainly not whether it would be acceptable if it did). It is, rather, what it would mean for this practice to become so widespread.

We have absolutely nothing against the coining of new, technical uses, as we have said. Rather, the issue is that many of those who insist upon speaking of machines' 'thinking' and 'understanding' do not intend in the least to be coining new, restrictedly technical, uses for these terms. It is not, for example, that they have decided to call a new kind of machine an 'understanding machine' where the word 'understanding' now means something different from what we ordinarily mean by that word. On the contrary, the philosophical cachet derives entirely from their insisting that they are using the words 'thinking' and 'understanding' in the same senses in which *we ordinarily use them*. The aim is quite characteristically to provoke, challenge and confront the rest of us. Their objective is to contradict something which the rest of us believe. What the 'rest of us' believe is simply this: thinking and understanding is something distinctive to human beings or perhaps as well to other higher forms of life, and that these capacities set us apart from the merely mechanical. Many of us are supposedly attached to the notion that a machine cannot think because it secures our sense of superiority, and this kind of arrogance would be badly damaged if it could be shown that a machine can in fact think, understand, be conscious, etc. The argument that a machine can think or understand, therefore, is of interest *precisely because* it features a use of the words 'think' and 'understand' which is intendedly the same as the ordinary use. Otherwise, the sense of challenge and, consequently, of interest, would evaporate. The impact of theories based upon work in artificial intelligence computation is due to their insistence upon the view that machines *can* in fact do what we would ordinarily claim they could not do. If engineers were to make 'understand' and 'think' into technical terms, ones with special, technical meanings *different and distinct from* those we ordinarily take them to have, then, of course, their claims to have built machines which think or understand would have no bearing whatsoever upon our inclination ordinarily to say that, in the ordinary sense, machines do not think or understand. Hence, if anyone seeks to dictate to others what they must say, it is the proponents of the 'strong program of artificial intelligence' (Searle, 1980).

At the outset of this discussion, we endorsed John Cook's (Cook, 1969) contention that 'ordinary language philosophy' has seldom been tried, let alone tried and found wanting. The fundamental attitude of this kind of philosophy is that the problems of philosophy can be dissolved rather than solved, and that there is nothing for the theories of philosophers to explain. This attempt to 'dissolve' philosophical problems and to do so by reference to the 'ordinary' use of words is certainly condemned in many circles these days; it is alleged to divest philosophy of its dignity and grandeur, to abandon the important problems, to invite participation in a tedious and uninteresting exercise, the inspection of the fine nuances of word meaning. Such responses are abusive and dismissive, but they are hardly relevant. They simply beg the question which Wittgenstein and Ryle raised, and they merely assume that what they take to be philosophy's problems can withstand the persistent and thorough application of the method they oppose. However, the approaches of Wittgenstein and Ryle are not ones to be argued with *in abstracto*, but are ones to be *tried out*, and to be tried out systematically and not in a brief, perfunctory and half-hearted manner. Above all, nothing in Wittgenstein and Ryle should be treated as the espousal of alternative theories, competing *solutions* to the problems of philosophy (as when Ryle, and sometimes Wittgenstein, is treated as embracing a form of behaviourist solution to the Cartesian mysteries). Attention is to be directed *exclusively* to exposing the *source(s)* of philosophical confusion and to *dissolving* the problem.

For the whole of the arguments covered in this book, it is clear that much depends upon what we are understood to be doing when we make use of words such as 'intention', 'belief' , 'purpose' and so on.

Whether such expressions are used in the way that 'theoretical terms' are used in a scientific vocabulary, and whether they are used in ways which make them the putative equivalent of terms in such a scientific vocabulary, must be decisive in connection with the case for 'eliminativism' for example, but the problem of how such words function in our language is not itself a matter for thoughtful examination by most of the participants in these debates. Rather, *a priori* conceptions of how these words work are depended upon, often rather dogmatically so. In this chapter, we argue that the provision of some *method* for establishing how these words work ought to be unavoidable in even approaching these issues.

Many of the issues which we have to confront pertain, then, to the misrepresentation of philosophical approaches, rather than to substantive issues. We have sought to establish in our exemplary discussion of the Chinese Room that:

1 Philosophers who may make the most vigorous protestations that they have no interest in (mere) questions about the meanings of words are not necessarily to be taken at their word, for claims about the prospect that a machine might think (etc.) have been shown to be about the employment of the words 'think' and 'understand' rather than having anything to do with the complexities of the science of robotics, with the actualities of the latter being entirely immaterial to the issues.
2 Despite allegations to the effect that work of the kind that Wittgenstein and Ryle initiated involves claims to *a priori* knowledge, attempts to say in advance of empirical inquiry what will happen, what is possible, in, for example, the world of robotics have been shown to be canards, for the arguments have been shown not to hinge in any way upon the technical realities and possibilities of engineering science. The argument, as we have put it, against the possibility that a machine can understand a language, does not involve the slightest suggestion of a restriction on the practical ambitions of engineers, for that argument concedes that engineers have developed robotics that are as advanced as anyone could imagine, and asks: what *then* should we say about the case?

In addition to the above objections to 'ordinary language philosophy' with respect, mainly, to its putative 'trivialising' of the nature of philosophy itself, there is another, and significant, objection which is made, one which relates to some central and profound differences. The complaint is that 'ordinary language philosophy' is *anti-scientific*, the alleged (although, as we have shown, actually non-existent) opposition to robotics being supposedly the product of a reactionary, conservative resistance to 'progress' in the form of the progress of a branch of science. There is a distinctly *historicist* cast to the formulation of issues in terms of assigning people to 'the side of science' or in opposition to it, and such efforts are, in our judgment, just more of the bluster of which we complained above, aimed at intimidating others into acceptance of suppositions or conclusions, without examination of their true merit, solely on the grounds that they are claimed to be in harmony with the spirit/findings of science.

There is no reason why anyone should take philosophers who avow their attachment to science at their word, and especially no reason why any such claims should be taken to confer any sort of authoritative status to their arguments. Those who insist that what they do is in harmony with science do not seem to us particularly scientific in the spirit with which they approach things. For example, in the work of the Churchlands (Churchland, 1979; 1984; 1986), we find a touching, but troubling and strange, certainty about the *future* prospects of the neurosciences, about what they *must* show, which seems at odds with the idea that these are empirical and *open-ended* inquiries. We certainly could not agree that a refusal to accept that the Churchlands represent any kind of 'voice of science' or that their arguments in any way express a 'scientific point of view' involves any form of *opposition to science*. Rejection of *pseudo-science* (or, to put it more kindly, of speculations about the future of science) does not put one in the position of 'opposition to science', and neither Wittgenstein nor Ryle, any more than ourselves, are to be placed in that camp. Our argument is precisely that being on the side of 'nonsense' is certainly not being 'on the side of science' and that, therefore, the successful prosecution of our case simply *cannot* limit the prospects of science's development.

In an epoch in which some of the natural sciences have enjoyed great prestige, it can be profitable for people to align themselves with the sciences, and it certainly seems that to dub an argument or a conclusion 'scientific' is to aid the cause of its wider acceptance. The doubt about whether all of those who *call* themselves 'scientists' or who *say* that their approach is 'scientific' are entitled to the same acceptance as that already conceded to the natural sciences has nothing whatsoever to do with any kind of reservation about the achievements thus far of those sciences. The doubt is over whether one is being offered in the name of science something which has nothing authentically scientific in its character, something which may, rather, be a product of the ideological status which *the idea* of science has now assumed. Wittgenstein and Ryle were both resistant to the *ideological* promotion of science.

In contemporary Britain, we have the misfortune to be subject to endless perorations about the importance of useful, productive activities in our life relative to the useless and the unproductive (amongst which the pursuit of sociology and philosophy are frequently listed). Manufacturing industry is the embodiment of all that is virtuous. These perorations originate, very often, with those who make their livings as career politicians and who were, in previous careers, pamphleteers, journalists, lawyers and even academics themselves. In comparable fashion, as we must distinguish between those who practise scientific inquiry and those who campaign on its behalf, so we must distinguish between those who practise scientific inquiry and those who appoint themselves to express 'the scientific point of view'. Just as scepticism that those who speak on behalf of industry necessarily know what is best for it, and resistance to the philistinism of those who hold forth about the value of manufacture, involves no necessary opposition to industry itself, so even the most resolute disregard for so-called, self-styled 'scientific' strains within philosophy does not of necessity involve any 'opposition' to science.

There is no earthly reason why philosophers should be allowed to 'freeload' on the achievements of science. The arguments which would elevate science to a very prominent place in our lives, one more prominent than that which it now occupies in fact, are not ones which themselves *originate* from within the sciences. They are not arguments which follow from or contribute to any specific scientific findings, nor are they arguments which favour the cause of science's advance by *adding to* the assembled body of its results. They seek to advance the cause of science by *improving its institutional position*, by transplanting the so-called 'scientific point of view' from the practice of scientific inquiry into the organisation of *other* spheres of our lives, into the conduct of our day-to-day affairs, making it the basis on which to reform the very ways we speak. Indeed, the demands that we accord with the requirements of science are such that they call upon us to anticipate what these will be. Thus, 'eliminativists' (among them, Richard Rorty, Paul Churchland, Stephen Stich and the 'eliminative connectionists') advise us of the need to be rid of 'intensional[2] expressions' from our ordinary language

---

2 In this work we shall use 'intensional' to mean that property of an expression which marks its non-detachability from an object-complement. We do so to avoid confusion with the ordinary meaning of 'intentional' (with a 't').

(e.g., 'I intend to ...', 'he believes that ...', 'he hopes to ...', 'she expects that ...', 'they wish that ...' and the like), and they urge this transformation upon us in the light of 'results' from the neurosciences. They do not, however, show us that the neurosciences *have* developed a vocabulary which can and should displace that which is made up of intensional expressions. Rather, we are hectored about the necessity to give up these expressions on the grounds that a successfully developed neuroscience *will* show us that they can be displaced. We should be even further misled if we were to imagine that these fateful implications for our 'ordinary' vocabulary arose from the *actual* state of development of the neurosciences, for this would ascribe to those sciences much greater progress (and 'progress' of a very specific kind) than they genuinely exhibit. The 'eliminativist' argument can be, and is, pursued in the absence of genuinely relevant 'findings' of neuroscience because, of course, it does not depend *in any way* upon the specific character of any such findings. This is because, for making an eliminativist case, *it does not matter in the slightest* what the neurosciences have found or even will find, since if it did, then the eliminativist case could not be put *prior* to the determination of these findings! The truth is that talk about the neurosciences (even especially elaborate, summarising and speculative discourse about their contents) is a *red herring*, a distraction which makes it look as though the argument is somehow based upon or *hinged* upon the results of empirical, scientific research, when it is actually based upon the prior acceptance of a *philosophical* position, one in terms of which the results and prospects of science are to be interpreted. We say this even though it may also be the case that some practising neuroscientists themselves look with favour upon some such arguments of these philosophical interpreters. That such interpretations form no *necessary* part of the actual conduct of neuroscientific research itself is clear from the fact that it is no precondition for doing successful work in that field that practitioners subscribe to *any* philosophical gloss upon its achievements or objectives, and from the fact that many neuroscientists disdain *all* such (metaphysical) speculations. It is also clear from the fact that various and *different* philosophical interpretations can be made consistent with the same range of (undisputed) research findings. What is noteworthy in this regard, however, is the observation that most such philosophical glosses actually postulate *conjectured* outcomes from current research enterprises.

The philosophical position whose prior acceptance is indispensable to the promotion of the 'eliminativist' view is one which has to do with *language*, and is one which embodies *preconceptions* about the respective roles of scientific and 'ordinary' vocabularies. It is, after all, only possible to argue that the vocabulary of neuroscience can replace that of our ordinary 'intensional' vocabulary if the former adequately fulfils the purposes for which the latter is intended. Ironically, these assumptions about the purposes of the respective vocabularies is typically *a priori*.

What we are usually offered *in the name of science* is almost anything but what science itself has to offer. We are offered a particular kind of philosophy, one which is commonly called 'naturalism' and which operates from the assumption not that science has escaped from or has displaced metaphysics, but that it has provided the answer to one of the central questions of metaphysics itself, namely, 'What exists in the world?' Metaphysics asks about what, *ultimately*, there is, and the assumption that science should be elevated into a special place in our lives is because it provides an answer to that question, tells us what *ultimately* there is. Certainly, W. V. Quine, one of the most influential of modern naturalists, affirms that the purpose of philosophy (as he understands it) is to illuminate the true and ultimate structure of 'reality' (Quine, 1960; 1961; 1981), and he places science (especially *physics*) at the centre of his philosophy on the grounds that it provides (or facilitates the production of) the best account available of the true and ultimate structure of reality. Since the sciences, on this account, tell us what *ultimately* there is, it must seem that their results should matter in all walks of life, because in each of these we will proceed on the basis of assumptions about what kinds of things there are and insofar as the sciences will show us to what extent such assumptions are valid (or otherwise), so, to that extent, they will lead us to revise the terms on which our other activities are conducted.

The 'eliminativist' programme (which is one about which, of course, naturalists themselves disagree) is one which arises not from the results of the neurosciences themselves but from the assumption that one major role of science is to adjudicate the question of what, ultimately, there is. 'Science' is a partially misleading locution in this respect because it is actually the position of naturalist philosophers that it is the *physical* sciences which can adjudicate what, ultimately, there is. The role of neuroscience in this connection depends upon the assumption that its identification of authentic phenomena may (eventually) be rendered in terms of *physics*. With respect to the explanation of human behaviour, then, it is first of all assumed that its explanation must be causal, and, secondly, that the causal determinants will be such as to be formulable (ultimately) in the terms of physics. The phenomena of neuroscience *unquestionably* are ones which can be formulated in terms of physics (let us agree) and in that respect, or so the logic of the argument proceeds, they cannot fit into the 'intensional' terms we use to explain each other's conduct in ordinary, everyday life. At the very least, the question as to whether such things as intentions, motives, desires, thoughts and the rest really, in the sense of *ultimately*, exist, becomes the controversial one.

The main opponents of the 'eliminativists' within contemporary naturalist philosophy of mind are those who deny that intensional expressions can be eliminated from our vocabulary, but who dispute this, obviously enough, on commonly shared, *naturalist* grounds. They argue that the progress of the neurosciences will show that the phenomena identified in an intensional vocabulary are *real* phenomena, in just the sense shared by eliminativists, that is, in the sense that they *can* (eventually) be described in the vocabulary of physics. In other words, 'naturalist' anti-eliminativists maintain that they will be shown to be states of the nervous system, including the brain. Hence, the eliminativists can proceed to press their case by arguing that progress in neuroscience could show otherwise, that there are *no* states of the central nervous system or brain which correspond to, or are identical with, for example, having an intention, believing something, desiring something, expecting something and the like. This possibility cannot be ruled out, and thus eliminativists have a counter to the view that intensional states *must* have a physical basis. (Recall that Putnam's 'functionalism', for example, argued against *any* direct or 'smooth' reduction of intensional to biological – thence physical – phenomena.)

The assumptions are, note, beginning to accumulate. Note also that they are not themselves assumptions which originate in science in general or in neuroscience in particular. They are, instead, assumptions which belong to arguments about the role of the sciences in providing answers to the *metaphysical* question of 'what there (really, ultimately) is' and about the special role of physics within those sciences in answering that question, as well as connecting to assumptions about the canonical role of the kind of causal explanation found in that science in *defining* what 'explanation' could be. In this sense, then, it would seem to follow that, if physics furnishes solutions to the question of what ultimately there is in the world, and physics explains by giving causes, then, since there are only physical phenomena, the only things that can be cited as causes must be physical phenomena. Therefore, the science of psychology, which is in the business of 'explaining human behaviour', must itself proceed according to this paradigm, must give causal explanations, and ones which explain by citing *only* physical causes (i.e., physical states/processes of the behaving organism).

Talk about *a priori* determinations of what must, empirically, be the case! Talk about attempting to predetermine what shape a science must take, and what science can discover! The fact is, with respect to the putative science of psychology, that kind of naturalism provides a *stipulation* of the character of that science. Thus, one finds in the arguments of Quine, Fodor, Dennett, Stich, Block, the Churchlands and many others, despite their internal differences, the view that 'scientific' psychology is to be *defined* in the terms which permit the accommodation of these contestable naturalist preconceptions. In Fodor's case, the subject-matter of such a psychology is to be narrowed down to that which can be implemented only through a 'methodological solipsism' (Fodor, 1980) in order that it may be confined within the *a priori* parameters that he has, on naturalist suppositions, set for it.

Reluctance to accept that science provides the fulfilment of the objectives of metaphysics, and that the vocabulary of physics provides, therefore, definitive statements of 'what there *ultimately* is', reflects neither favourably nor unfavourably upon the sciences themselves, and thus a criticism of such an account of science is not any kind of criticism of science itself. Just as criticism of those who wrap themselves in the flag is a criticism of those who do this and not a criticism of the flag they wrap themselves in, so opposition to those who *appoint themselves* as the authoritative bearers of the scientific point of view does not necessitate reservations which diminish the achievements of the sciences whose prestige they seek to borrow. The naturalistic viewpoint is a *philosophical* one, and the fact that it proclaims itself the possessor of a high regard for science (even of the highest) does nothing to ensure that it is possessed of a correct understanding of that which it holds in such esteem, that its terms are *thereby* the ones which are appropriate to characterising that which is ostensibly venerated. The idea that science requires and depends upon justification in terms of philosophical doctrines, and that it requires guidance from and interpretation in terms of a set of metaphysical presuppositions, does not strike us as providing such an unmitigatedly *complimentary* view of science.

Within the terms of naturalism, it is made to seem as though the *essential* problem is that of the relationship between different orders of phenomena; that the root problem is to identify those phenomena which 'ultimately' exist, that is, which are authentically physical phenomena, and to describe the ways in which they causally interact with one another. The sleight of hand of naturalism is, then, to make it seem that this problem *arises from* the successes of physics. However, if we stand apart from the terms of naturalism for a while, it becomes apparent that the problem does not actually arise from the results of science but, instead, is one which originates in the articulation of two vocabularies, that of physics and that of the 'ordinary' language we use, and the corollary problems are generated entirely by the assumption that the vocabulary of physics has the *primary* role. It is not common for naturalists to be particularly reflective upon their assumptions. Perhaps this is because they take their assumptions to be self-evident. One will not find the naturalists wondering whether their assumptions are compelling, whether there might be alternatives to them, and what might be said for those alternatives, or whether the *only* course open is to adopt these assumptions. Do we really *need* to locate the vocabulary of physics in *prime* position, to treat it as though it were an all-purpose one? Or can we, as Ryle remarked, and as we shall discuss in more detail further on, treat it rather as a *specialised* vocabulary which has been developed to serve certain distinct purposes, to characterise things in certain ways and *in (principled) disregard* of many of their characteristics?

The physicist speaks of a 'falling body' and specifies that its rate of acceleration in a vacuum will be such-and-such. The physicist's specification does not mention the nature of the body that is falling, nor the manner in which it began its descent, for those matters are, from the point of view of describing acceleration, irrelevant. It does not matter, from the point of view of physics, which is here concerned *purely* with motion, whether the falling is that of a human being or not, nor whether, if the body is that of a human being, it is falling because it has tripped, jumped or been pushed/thrown. It is not that from the point of view of physics there is no difference between accident, suicide or homicide but, rather, that whether or not there is such a difference is irrelevant to the determination of the rate of descent. The difference between accident, suicide and homicide is not to be made within the vocabulary of physics but is, instead, one which is made in the vocabulary of legal discourse. The various specialised vocabularies characterise things in different respects, and they do not rival each other or compete for priority, for they serve different interests and operate, in important respects, *in disregard of* each other. Just as a statement of a book's length or of the composition of its paper and type is a statement about something quite different from a statement about what it says, what knowledge it conveys and the like, so also a statement about a falling body within and for the purposes of physical science is *indifferent to* (although does not by that token *deny*) distinctions between accident, suicide and homicide. By extension, then, there is no need to assume that because physics (and physiology) make no mention of 'intensional expressions', they are therefore in the business of denying the existence of intensionally expressible states of affairs. That a difference does not matter to physics does not mean that there is no difference, and that a distinction is irrelevant to physics does not mean that it cannot legitimately be drawn for *other* purposes.

The treatment of physics as a specialised rather than a prime vocabulary does not entail *any* restriction on the *generality* it has, or entail any limitations on its (widespread) *utility*. Insisting, however, upon its primacy, the naturalist treatment of the discourse of physics can register only one conclusion: if physics does not mark it, there is no distinction between 'physically' and 'intensionally expressible' phenomena, and from here one or the other of two (seemingly exhaustively) available but opposing conclusions is drawn. The first is that there are only physical phenomena (because physics talks only of these but does not mention and thus must deny the existence of intensionally definable phenomena), and the second is that there is no difference between physical and intensionally definable phenomena and thus intensionally definable phenomena *must really be physical phenomena*. There seems to be no acknowledgement of the alternative possibility: that intensional phenomena are *irrelevant* to physics, and that though there may be a difference between an event or state of affairs which is intensional and one which is not, it is not a difference that physics needs to mark or to register in any way and, further, it is not a distinction which is to be made *in physical terms*.

The collection of naturalistic suppositions also engenders the problem of a 'folk psychology' which involves a view of the nature of intensional predicates such as intention, belief, thought, etc. The problem arises in the attempt to set out the character that a truly scientific psychology must have. If a scientific psychology is to be created then it must, it seems, have its own scientific vocabulary. The question then arises as to whether *any* of the words used in our 'ordinary' vocabulary can be taken over for the purposes of constructing that vocabulary. The primary objective of such a vocabulary is to provide terms which can be used in the scientific explanation of people's behaviour. It is clear to the naturalists that such terms as 'intention' and 'belief' are ones which we ordinarily use to explain people's behaviour, and that these are amongst the terms that should be considered as candidates for inclusion within any scientific theory of such behaviour. The issue then arises: are they acceptable for inclusion within a properly scientific theory? Can such terms be used within scientific explanations? And these issues are now said to depend exclusively upon whether or not such expressions, predicates, terms, etc. can satisfy the basic requirement set down by the naturalist philosophical conception, that is, whether they identify physical states, processes or events of (or in) the behaving human organism. It is over this question that naturalists disagree. Fodor, for example, in his early work, insists that 'folk psychology' (that is, the pattern of explanation of people's behaviour employing ordinary intensional predicates) will be vindicated by scientific psychology. He argues that by using notions such as 'intention', we can and do successfully predict the behaviour of others – people usually do what they say they intend to do – and no doubt this is so because the concept of 'intention' picks out *real* states of the mind (or, rather, brain). Stich (1983), by contrast, insists that there is no reason to include such notions within any scientific psychology, for there are *no* physical states, etc. which correspond to 'folk-psychological' concepts or predicates. Since the vocabulary of physical science serves, for naturalists, to define 'what there really is', then if the vocabulary of a scientific psychology proves to have no use for expressions such as 'intend' or 'believe' ('intention' or 'belief'), principally because the naturalists cannot identify any physical states or processes which correspond to these expressions, then this is the same as saying that *there are no such things as beliefs and intentions*.

Such claims have the advantage of sounding startling indeed, and thus of drawing attention to, and ensuring much discussion of, the work in which they are advanced. The spirit of *épater les bourgeois* is widespread in contemporary culture, and it perhaps helps to fuel the energies of such contemporary naturalist philosophers who embrace eliminativist positions. They appear to stand our existing preconceptions on their heads: after all, what could be a more stark and straightforward assault upon our 'ordinary' preconceptions than that we actually do not have intentions and beliefs? What could be more radical than to tell us that we have never had an intention, do not hold beliefs, possess no desires and the like? Much like the claims that computers might understand, the claims that it is up to scientific psychology to decide whether there *really are* any beliefs and intentions are set forward as though they bear directly upon our 'ordinary' or 'pre-scientific' beliefs (or they would if there were any beliefs for us to have!). However, perhaps these challenges are not quite what they are sometimes cracked up to be. Like many sceptical contentions, they do not *directly* challenge our ordinary ways of thinking.

The naturalist argument is about whether or not there are such things as 'intentions' and 'beliefs' in the sense of there being physical states or processes which correspond to these notions. *If* what we mean by the attribution of an intention or a belief is that the person to whom such attributions are made is in a certain physical state, *only then* would our claim that the person had the intention or held the belief be falsified or vindicated by the demonstrations of this envisaged scientific psychology. From the point of view of the naturalist, and only from this point of view, the expressions which together make up folk psychology (as he describes it) are ones which essentially involve hypotheses about the brain. They *must* be, because for naturalism there is nothing else to discuss in this respect except, so to speak, states of matter or material processes. If a word like 'belief' is to be used to speak about anything at all, then it must, on naturalist premises, be used to speak about states or processes of the organism *or else it must be used to talk about nothing 'real' at all*. Once again, we can only note the stringently *a prioristic* character of such an insistence as this one, deriving as it does neither from close inspection of the actual ways in which we speak nor from the explanations which we actually give to one another when we use these words. The actual 'confrontation' with our ordinary ways of talking is, however, a little more complicated than it appears, and perhaps is not a genuine confrontation at all. The conflict is not of the form: 'You say that there are beliefs, but we deny that there are any.' The actual confrontation is, rather, this: if you take beliefs to be brain states, then we deny that there are any. On those terms, there is no confrontation between our position and that of the naturalist, for we can fully agree with this claim. We do not hold that beliefs, intentions and thoughts are brain states (events, processes, etc.), although it is crucial to note that we do not say this as a statement of a philosophical position of our own. We say this as ordinary speakers of the language. When we speak of someone's intention to catch the 4.15 train or of his belief that he is late for an appointment, we are not thereby hypothesising about any *brain states* he may have.

The insistence upon the view that we hypothesise about neural phenomena whenever we attribute, say, an intention is not one which the naturalist can sustain on the basis of an examination of what we are up to when we *do* attribute an intention. The insistence is, we argue, the result of the constraint imposed by what is possible within the terms of the naturalist's own preconceptions: whatever we might *seem* to be doing, whatever we might *think* or *believe* that we are doing when we ascribe an intention or belief, we *must*, for the naturalist, be hypothesising about states of matter, for there is nothing else that could possibly suffice to give meaning to such terms and we must, therefore, be hypothesising either correctly or incorrectly about these. The confrontation with what we ordinarily think or believe does not, in fact, take place at all. Such a confrontation is not with anything that we, as competent users of words like 'intend' or 'believe', would accept as our purposes in using these terms. They are instead artificially foisted onto us by virtue of an adherence to a philosophy to which we, in our capacity as ordinary speakers, have no need to give assent. What do we actually do when we ascribe an intention or belief? We shall return in chapter 3 to the topic of 'belief': at this juncture, let us focus upon some examples of intention attribution.

We, the speakers of an ordinary language, make a distinction between the correct and the incorrect ascription of an intention. When we see the orange left indicator begin to flash on the car in front of us, and the red brake lights light up, we say that the driver in front intends to turn left. What are we talking about when we say this? We are talking about what the driver is *going to do*. When the car reaches the left turn, the driver will turn his car into it. We are not putting forward *any* philosophical theory here, and certainly not a behaviourist one, but are, rather, pondering the ordinary use – the meaning – of the word 'intention'. Why do we say that the driver of the car in front is intending to take a left turn? Because of what the driver is now doing, which is signalling such an intention, something that we can state equally well without reference to the term 'intention' at all, for the driver is signalling *what he is about to do*. Thus, we ascribe an intention to the driver *on the basis of what he is now doing*. We are *not guessing about the driver's being in some kind of brain state*: such a guess would be entirely empty. We have no idea, *qua* routine ascribers of intention, what brain states people are in, for, *qua* ordinary ascribers, we know no neuroscience. *Philosophers* sometimes make arguments about what kind of brain states people must be in to have an intention: for example, do they, perhaps, have an imperative sentence inscribed in their brain?[3] But could this be a necessary hypothesis of someone who is simply noting that the driver in front is intending to turn? Such a person is *not* attempting to make an inference from what the driver is now doing to what is going on in his brain! Rather, the person is inferring from *what the driver is now doing* to *what he will do next*. This is a *direct* inference, *not* one which goes through an inference from what the driver is now doing to something that is taking place in the driver's brain to what he will do next. *It is a direct inference from what the driver is now doing to what he will do next*. The inference is, of course, from the driver's *telling us what* he is going to do next to what (actually) he *is* going to do next. The driver's telling us what he is going to do next is, in this case, a part of his *getting ready* to do something next. In taking a left turn, part of the activity of doing this is to *prepare* for it, to give others warning that you

3 See 'Brain Writing and Mind Reading' in Dennett, 1987, pp. 39–50.

will be making this move, and slowing down your vehicle so that the turn can be safely controlled, and it is the driver's activities of preparing to turn by signalling and slowing down which tell us what he is prepared (intends) to do. It is by virtue of these being the earliest stages of a particular sequence that we can see that the driver has undertaken to go through this sequence and that leads us to expect its later stages. *What we are talking about*, then, when we talk about this driver's intention is about what he is doing, about the relation between what he is now doing and what he will shortly be doing, and where these are linked as steps in a sequence of activities. If the driver is signalling, slowing and then turns into a side street, *then that confirms that he did intend to take the turn*. What we said was *correct*: the driver *did* have the intention to take the turn. Our claim that the driver had the intention was not *any kind of* claim about his being in a particular brain state, for we certainly did not look, either in making the determination of the intention, or in satisfying ourselves that we had been correct in our determination, for evidence about his brain's having certain features, for we did not want, *in identifying his intention*, to make findings about the state of his brain, but, instead, to anticipate his conduct on the road.

In saying that our attribution of an intention to turn left was correct, we are saying only that the left turn was not adventitiously related to what went before, that the turn was the outcome of a prepared sequence, not an abrupt and unprepared turn or one which resulted from the car's swinging out of control. That the driver took the final step in the sequence of which the signalling and the braking were the earlier steps establishes that he did have the intention to make the turn. When we say that someone has an intention, then, we are often saying something like 'they are getting ready to do X', just as in the instance of the driver described above. Saying 'he intends to turn left' in this case is the equivalent of saying 'he is now getting ready to turn left', and the capacity to say that does not *depend upon* the existence of neurological states but, rather, upon the relationships between various kinds of activities in the circumstances in which they are produced. Some activities are conventionally prior to others, and the notion of intention has a great deal to do with the relationship between an outcome and the actions which led up to it; whether these were preparatory, for example. The *test* of whether a person has an intention is not whether they do the things they may avow as their intention(s); if someone says that he intends to take the afternoon flight, then there are various things which *he must do* if we are to say that he does (indeed) have that particular intention and these are, naturally, things which he must do *if* he is to catch the afternoon flight. Someone who is to take (who genuinely intends to take) the afternoon flight *must do* such things as obtain a flight ticket, reach the airport, hire a cab as a means of doing so, ensure that he has a (valid) passport with him, gather his luggage together and so forth. The test of whether he intends to take the afternoon flight is whether he makes any effort to do so, whether he gets a passport, buys foreign currency, arranges a taxi or other means of transportation to the airport, sets out for the airport, etc., etc. If such a person does *not* do such things, then, he does *not* intend to catch the afternoon plane: to say, in such a case, that he does not have the intention is tantamount to saying that *he is not even trying*! We should point out that someone who does all the things preparatory to boarding the plane and who eventually does board the plane does not merely provide us with *evidence from which the existence of his intention can be inferred*: rather, doing all these things *qualifies* the person as possessing the intention. To undertake all these activities and to carry them through to their conclusions *is* what 'intending to take the plane' is. J. L. Austin's remark about seeing signs of bread when one sees some crumbs is apposite here, for one does not see signs of bread when one sees the loaf.

The paradigm of the 'inner' and the 'outer' is a paradigm which is deep in philosophical psychology, and it is one to which the naturalist tradition adheres, even in its 'behaviourist' form. Behaviourists (from Watson to Skinner) suppose that the identification of intentions and other 'mental' states (etc.) must be a matter of *inference from* 'observable behaviour' (whether 'thinly' or 'thickly' described) to *unobservable, inner* phenomena. The behaviourists simply ruled out the legitimacy of any such 'inferences'. However, one is not *inferring* from the buying of the plane ticket, the hiring of the cab and so on to an 'inner state' which is the having of the intention. Where inference *is* involved, it is often from *part of* the pattern of activity to the *outcome* of that activity. That someone sets out to obtain some foreign currency allows the inference that he or she is going to take a trip abroad and that, therefore, he or she is going to take a plane, so one may infer that he or she is going to take a plane from his or her buying the foreign currency, that is, one may infer what his/her intention is, what he/she is *going to do*. This, however, consists solely in inferring about the role of this activity within part of a pattern, *not from an outer behaviour to an inner state.*

It is because of the inner/outer paradigm that naturalists (often despite themselves) adhere to a Cartesian dualism, for they seek to persuade us that when we attribute intentions we must be attempting to make hypotheses about 'inner' states on the basis of outer ones. Their naturalism comes into play because they suppose (and here, again, we do *not disagree* with them) that there is only matter (i.e., brain matter) 'within' and that, therefore, *if* we are inferring from what we can see to what is 'within' then the inference would have to be about states of the brain. Yet this picture is a product of the inappropriate retention of the 'inner/outer' dualism as omnirelevant in the first instance. It is because of the retention of this picture that the naturalist is driven to the conclusion that talk of intentions (etc.) *must* involve the postulation of 'inner' states, and that these must be, on naturalist terms, brain states. Declining, as we do, to set up an 'inner/outer' dichotomy in an *a priori* way exempts us from the necessities that the naturalist sees and leaves us free to ask the following. What *evidence* is there to show that users of 'ordinary words' such as 'intention' and 'belief' actually operate in terms of this inner/outer dichotomy *when they speak*? How would someone who believed that an intention *was* a physical state of the brain differ detectably from someone who did *not* believe this when they engaged in such things as ascribing an intention to take the afternoon plane to someone else, or when they announced their own intention to take the plane?

The reason why a person who does not acquire foreign currency, ensure that his passport is valid, arrange a taxi to the airport, etc. cannot be said to intend to take the plane is simply because without doing some such things they *cannot in fact* take the plane. The doing of such things is a precondition of being able to board the plane, and the necessity of doing them has nothing to do with *psychology*. The connection between the acquisition of passports, air tickets, etc. and the taking of the afternoon plane is *not* made through any psychological regularity, or through any generalisation made about the conjunction of these, but is, rather, made through the fact that the possession of a passport, air tickets, etc. comprises *requirements* for boarding the plane: the former are (simply) means to the latter. There is, of course, the fact that intentions are sometimes avowed rather than attributed. If someone tells us that he intends to take the afternoon plane, he does not do this on the basis of *evidence* (of *any* kind, and certainly not on the basis of a scrutiny of his brain states). We do not, for example, find ourselves buying an airline ticket, acquiring foreign currency, booking a taxi to the airport, and then *concluding* that we must, therefore, have the intention to go to the airport, to take the afternoon flight, etc. We certainly do not seek evidence that our brain is in a certain specific state: we have no means of introspecting the character of our brains, and so we do not, in declaring an intention, report to others that we have found that our brain is in a certain condition. When we state an intention, we tell other people about what we will be doing, we report not on our brains but on our plans. We are not advancing a *predictive hypothesis*, such that, having issued it, we will now wait to see if it turns out to be true. When we inform someone of our intention(s) we are not providing them with an empirical prediction about our future behaviour such that they, too, can wait to see whether our prediction was correct. When we tell someone of our intention, we tell them what we will be doing, but our telling them this is more of an assurance than a prediction. If we fail to fulfil our expressed intention, then others can *blame* us for having let them down, for having *misled* them, and not merely that we have unfortunately given them (as it turned out) erroneous information. We have not thereby misled people about the state of our central nervous system but about, for example, where we will be that afternoon, or what we will be doing later that week, etc.

It should now be apparent why we have serious difficulties with the eliminativist idea that we could give up our intensional expressions ('intending to' do X being one of the most common of these). The formulation of an intention does not portray a state of the brain but, characteristically, a course of action or its outcome. We require, for a multitude of practical purposes, to be able to mark distinctions between intended actions, accidental outcomes, adventitious occurrences, unintended consequences, inadvertent conduct, involuntary behaviour, unforeseen results, anticipated and expected effects, obligatory conduct, purposive activity and the rest, and we need these distinctions *quite irrespective of* the kind of distinctions which may be needed to advance *scientific* research. It is *only* if we suppose that an intention is a particular state of the brain that the announcement that there are no such things tells us anything. And, since we have shown that this identification leads to absurdities, we are, indeed, not being told anything. . . .

In the next chapter, we shall try to track down some of the historical roots of this obsession with the 'mental' construed as an *interior* forum, comprising 'inner phenomena', ripe for some (future, hypothesised) reduction to the physiological. Much of what we have here characterised as 'naturalism' has its roots in seventeenth-century philosophising, but it is a peculiarity of our contemporary intellectual culture that we have not yet emancipated ourselves fully from the fall-out of that philosophy. It is to the task of arguing for such an emancipation, in the face of so many trends to the contrary, that the remainder of this book is devoted. Consequently, having in this chapter outlined the thrust of our general approach to the problems with which we contend, we turn in the following chapter to a more detailed examination of the first theme we are addressing in this book: mind/body dualism.

2

The Cartesian Nexus

Descartes was impressed by the portrayal of the world by the natural sciences, and contributed extensively to the mechanistic world-picture bequeathed by the Galilean enterprise. A central feature of this world-picture was the austere ontology of existence which it advocated. In his *The Assayer* (1623), Galileo had expounded an essentially *philosophical* conception of the world, according to which Nature possesses only those properties recognised by the physical sciences: the remaining properties are bestowed upon her by the human senses. He wrote: 'I think therefore that these tastes, odours, colours, etc., so far as their objective existence is concerned, are nothing but mere names for something which resides exclusively in our sensitive body, so that if the perceiving creature were removed, all of those qualities would be annihilated and abolished from existence.'[1] In his *Optics*, Descartes argued similarly that one need not suppose that 'there is something in the objects [of perception] which resembles the ideas or sensations [of light and colour] that we have of them.'[2] The fundamental conundrum with which we associate Descartes, namely, the problematics of the *mind/body relationship*, originates within a broader, philosophical depiction of the nature of the universe. Human beings are thought to exist within a mechanically operating material reality, a reality available exclusively

1 Galileo's *The Assayer*, cited in Hacker, 1987, p. 3.
2 Descartes, *Optics*, as reproduced in Descartes, 1985 translation, p. 153, cited in Hacker, 1987, p. 10.

through scientific research and interpretation. The world-according-to-science, then, was claimed to be quite *unlike* the world-as-available-to-the-senses. Whatever experiential properties it appeared to have to the plain man, but which were not recognised as properties within the natural-scientific world-picture, such as colours, odours, sounds and tastes, were construed as bestowed 'subjectively' upon material reality by the operations of the human sensorium and the human mind. This conception, necessarily, endowed both mind and sensorium with *meta-physical* qualities. The world is essentially physical in a specifically restricted sense of that term, but the human mind is transcendental. The human body is a feature of the physical world, is a *res extensa*, but the human mind is cut from non-physical cloth, and is a *res cogitans*, lacking mass and having no spatio-temporal co-ordinates. One of the most important operations of the *res cogitans* is to endow the otherwise colourless, tasteless, odourless and silent world with its actually ex-perienced colours, tastes, odours, sounds and so on. It accomplishes this astounding feat by integrating the input from the sensorium and presenting us with a rich *internal* representation utterly unlike the 'real' material world whose causal forces acting upon us help to generate this *illusion* of itself, an illusion which, apparently, only a scientifically grounded philosophy can show us to be such.

The doctrines of primary and secondary existential qualities, the doctrine of the 'mind' as a *res cogitans*, and the doctrine of the world as given only in internal representations, all have contemporary counter-parts within cognitivism. All are rooted in a world-picture inherited from the seventeenth century, and all hinge upon the effort to derive holistic conceptions of the essential nature of phenomena from the findings and results of particular scientific theories. Although Descartes is often remembered primarily as the progenitor of a tran-scendentalist account of the human being, this aspect of his thinking was a product of coming to terms with a foundationally mechanistic view of inanimate as well as animate beings: creatures (other than humans) were construed as 'thoughtless brutes' whose bodily func-tions and behaviour could be assimilated to a *mechanistic* account. As such, animals are depicted as sentient automata, and Descartes' great challenger, Julien Offray de la Mettrie, was actually only extending this basic vision in his effort to *encompass* human beings when he denied the existence of a Cartesian metaphysical entity, the 'mind', and became one of the first of a wave of 'scientific materialists' in Europe.[3] Materi-alist doctrines about the human mind and conduct were given a boost

3 For some discussion, see Coulter, 1993b.

by the success of evolutionary biological theory after Darwin,[4] as well as by the steady process of secularisation which characterised much of European culture in the nineteenth century. However, it must be clearly understood that 'materialism', even 'scientific materialism', is not a *scientific theory* which has been borne out, but a *philosophical* doctrine which depends for its cogency on a certain (mis)conception of how best to interpret the significance of the findings and theoretical claims advanced by the physical sciences.

The objective of recasting philosophical thought and speculation along 'scientific' lines has been, arguably, a dominant trend within philosophy in the twentieth century, and it is one against which both Wittgenstein and Ryle, amongst others in their tradition, argued extensively. Their arguments, however, have routinely been miscast as arguments directed against the relevance of science for human understanding, or as comprising an uncritical glorification of what critics think of as 'pre-scientific' reasoning, typically engaged in by scientifically illiterate or semi-literate 'plain' folk. A hierarchy of sorts was postulated, according to which *all* describing and explaining, *all* inferring and deducing, *all* reflective thought and reason, was to be understood as connected together in a pyramidal structure, with Science at its apex and 'commonsense' at its base. Education was taken to involve a steady ascension toward the apex of scientific description and explanation, and all other forms were treated as lesser versions, essentially corrigible formulations – in other words, as *'pre*-scientific' *approximations* – some of which may serve practical goals in the everyday world of pragmatic and short-term interests and judgments, but each of which could be shown, given training, intelligence and patience, to be misinformed, or predicated upon defective lay theorising and an absence of rigorous methodicity, when set against the standards and achievements of the sciences. After all, hasn't science demonstrated that, contrary to the plain man's pre-scientific judgment, the earth is ovoid and rotates around the sun? Hasn't science penetrated to the core of the atom and shown that matter is not as 'solid' as its outward appearances might lead us to believe? This story is endlessly recycled, both in textbook treatments, classroom pedagogy and materialist philosophies of all kinds. It is, however, an essentially *philosophical* account,

4 This is a favourite theme in much current materialist philosophy of mind. See, for example, Churchland, 1979; Churchland, 1984. An earlier attempt to 'naturalise' the human mind so as to facilitate a philosophical defence of the comprehensiveness of evolutionary theory is to be found in C. D. Broad's 1923 work (see Broad, 1951).

and, as such, stands in need of logical evaluation and, ultimately, logical dissolution.

Wittgenstein and Ryle were *never* in the business of trying to *deny* the achievements of any genuine natural science, nor the efficacy of logico-experimental methodologies upon which so many of the sciences' achievements indeed depended. Nor did they ever deny that scientific discoveries had overturned many cherished beliefs about the ways in which so many phenomena worked, or about their composition, or their origins. Their target was, by contrast, a philosophical *scientism* which insisted upon (what they argued was) an *overgeneralised deployment* of criteria of conceptualisation, description and explanation of mundane events or states of affairs, drawing upon the hierarchical model of human reason established by the intellectual inheritors of the Galilean-Cartesian world-picture.

A major problem they faced, then, was how to delimit the *bounds* of a specifically *scientific* rationality, how to illuminate *the ways in which scientific relevances are truly circumscribed*, without falling prey to the charge of intellectual conservatism, theoretical inertia or a kind of *a priori* stipulation of where science shall inquire and of what it can aspire to find. Put metaphorically for the moment, their task was partly one of discerning clearly when a game of poker was being incongruously judged according to the rules of chess, when apples were being compared to oranges and illicitly found wanting for not being proper oranges, and when our practical commonsense was being anomalously addressed as if it was all of a piece in comprising a *proto-scientific theory* of the world.

Like Husserl before them, Ryle and Wittgenstein saw clearly that each science is always, and necessarily, a part of a broader world of everyday life and workaday reason upon which it depends in a plethora of ways, and from within which it differentiates itself for its own investigatory purposes. No science can cultivate a thoroughgoing *amnesia* for commonsense judgment and ordinary language, even if it aims, selectively, to combat a widely held empirical belief or to overturn a common prejudice about the properties of the phenomena to which it directs its theoretical interest. However, materialist philosophy articulated a vision of scientific achievement according to which it is *thoroughly and comprehensively subversive*: our 'ordinary' conceptions of ourselves and of our everyday world are doomed to *total* replacement by an alternative characterisation (or set of interrelated characterisations) which will be the fruit of science, in particular, of physics and biology. The lineaments of this total alternative vision are already within sight, it is claimed, and it is to the specification of this alternative which philosophy must dedicate itself, albeit with an appropriately modest openness to whatever new developments are bequeathed to us from the sciences themselves. In a striking passage about this contemporary conceit, Ryle wrote:

> Botanists, entomologists, meteorologists, and geologists do not seem to threaten the walls, floors and ceilings of our common dwelling-place . . . No, there are, I think, two branches of science which, especially in collusion with one another, produce what I may describe as the 'poison-pen effect', the effect of half-persuading us that our best friends are really our worst enemies. One is the physical theory of the ultimate elements of matter; the other is that one wing of human physiology which investigates the mechanism and functioning of our organs of perception . . . So, the so-called world of science which, we gather, has the title to replace our everyday world is, I suggest, the world *not of science in general* [our italics] but of atomic and sub-atomic physics in particular, enhanced by some slightly incongruous appendages borrowed from one branch of neuro-physiology. (Ryle, 1987, pp. 71–3)

Ryle here depicts as the source of philosophical confusions the same two sciences which had earlier, albeit in a less developed phase, figured so prominently in the construction of the philosophical world-picture enunciated by Galileo and Descartes. In fact, it is clear that the influential twentieth-century philosophical writings of Bertrand Russell and W. V. Quine are overwhelmingly beholden to physics and physiology for their respective specifications of 'what there really is'. Ryle, very powerfully, exposes the root confusion involved in elevating the findings of these special sciences to a more general, ontological status:

> There is nothing that any natural scientist studies of which the truths of physics are not true; and from this it is tempting to infer that the physicist is therefore talking about everything, and so that he is, after all, talking about the cosmos. So, after all, the cosmos must be described only in his terms, and can only be mis-described in the terms of any of these other more special sciences . . . or, most glaringly of all, in the terms of every-day conversation. (Ryle, 1987, p. 74)

As Ryle goes on to remark, the sheer fact that correct physical theories 'cover' every physical phenomena at some level of detail does not mean that what they do not *mention* in so covering these phenomena – such as, for example, the colour, odour or texture of a chemical substance – is supplied or tacked on by human physiological processes. Philosophical popularisers of natural science may encourage us to believe that what the joiner says to us about the table is somehow 'unscientific', whereas, in fact, physical theorists do not describe tables *at all* 'any more than the accountant describes the books bought for the library' when doing the college's accounts (Ryle, 1987, p. 79). Nonetheless, what the physicist says about elementary particles, if true, will *cover* this or that particular table. Because the physicist's formulae do not *mention* or describe its colour or texture (or the period of its construction, etc.) this does not mean that colour and texture are not themselves *physical* properties of the table. 'It is not true', says Ryle, 'that what is not and cannot be mentioned in a formula is denied by that formula' (Ryle, 1987, p. 83). *Scientifically* physical descriptions of phenomena are descriptions framed *for the purposes of doing physics*, and these can neither contradict nor undermine our ordinary workaday descriptions of the *same* phenomena as those to which the physicist's explanations apply. Now, it is true that *some* of our everyday characterisations will indeed be incorrect proto-theories or articulations of false empirical beliefs about the properties of what is being characterised. However, this cannot be true of all – or even *most* – of our descriptive expressions for physical phenomena, on pain of denying the physicist any starting-point for his own enterprise. And the relevances of an experimental physicist cannot be conflated with the relevances of the carpenter, accountant or painter, nor can his explanatory and experimental purposes of description be mixed up with those (perhaps more mundane) ones of complaining about the price, praising the style or arguing over the quality of any 'physical object'. The practices, courses of action, worldly purposes and interests – the 'language-games', if you will – involving physical phenomena of all sorts manifest criteria for adequate description which are often wholly disjunctive and which cannot, therefore, be treated as rungs on the same ladder, nor as *rivals*.

The contrast of science with commonsense in *general* terms, then, has inculcated a further set of spurious contrasts according to which there are the *genuinely* physical phenomena (recognised exclusively as that of which a physicist speaks when doing physics, such as kinetic energy levels, photons, neutrons, protons, bosons and the rest), our 'everyday' physical phenomena (such as tables, chairs, apples, rivers, mountains, trees and so on) and the merely *apparently* physical (such as tastes, fragrances, colours and the rest of the putatively 'secondary qualities' of physical phenomena). The everyday phenomena we recognise as 'physical' (e.g., apples) are thought by some to be 'logical constructions' fashioned out of what our senses register of the phenomena-as-described-by-physics (such that the apple is a cognitive construction of

ours, interpretively derived from what are *in essence, only*, impinge-
ments of millimicrons of wavelengths of light on our photoreceptors).
The colour of the apple, and its texture, are claimed to be deeper-level
constructions from the same phenomena-as-described-by-physics, only
now the 'redness' and the 'smoothness' are *addenda* contributed by our
sensorium (perhaps with a modicum of help from our internal supply
of concepts and memories) in a first-order processing operation on the
basis of which the *further* 'recognition' of the phenomenon *as* an apple
is effected.

The confusions within these contrasts, and corollary efforts to relate
them, can be seen to result from a fetishism of a mode of description
appropriate to atomic physics and physiology, from its treatment as a
uniquely adequate and context-free generality about the essence of the
world, and from its juxtaposition with ordinary, non-technical modes
of description in our everyday lives. If atoms, photons, etc., which are
among the primary properties characterising visible natural phenomena, themselves are depicted as intrinsically without 'colour', then it
must, according to this scheme, be we as perceivers who contribute to
Nature what she inherently lacks!

In his great treatise *Physiological Optics* von Helmholtz wrote: 'all
properties ascribed to [physical phenomena] by us only characterise
effects which they exert either upon our senses or upon other objects in
nature. Colour, sound, taste, smell, temperature, smoothness and solid-
ity . . . characterise effects upon our sense organs' (von Helmholtz,
1977, p. 168). This distorts the actual scientific account itself, however,
for the *effects* exerted by physical stimuli are not *themselves* colours,
sounds or smells: the effects are, rather, electrochemical transforma-
tions in receptor cells (Hacker, 1987, p. 46). Nonetheless, the overall
philosophical picture is clear enough: colours are *not* genuine physical
attributes of bodies but 'are introduced by our eye into them'.[5] We say
'philosophical' here, because nothing von Helmholtz had to say about
the locus of colour was a result of experimental investigation (how
could it be?), but resulted from his uncritical pursuit of an ontological
vision that is traceable to Galileo and which was embraced by
Descartes, Newton and a panoply of major scientific and philosophical
thinkers over three centuries. This scheme surely merits more detailed
investigation here, not only because of its august intellectual history,
but because one or another form of such an ontology inhabits modern
cognitive science.

5 von Helmholtz, cited in Hacker, 1987, p. 44.

Having correctly objected to the idea that a colour (e.g., red) inheres in an object, say, a rose, precisely parallel to the way in which its pigment does, speculative scientific realists move directly to what they conceive of as the only alternative: the colour must be a 'subjective' phenomenon, caused to appear *within us*[6] (by the wavelengths of light emitted by the object).[7] However, we quite naturally distinguish between the colour which an object *appears* to have or to be, and the colour which it actually *is*. Further, we do not, when we consider the idea that colours are genuine properties of objects and not of their perceivers, thereby take it that a colour is *in* an object[8] in the way in which an ingredient may be: objects *are* coloured or *have* a colour (or colours), but colours are not the sort of properties of which it is even intelligible (let alone true) to assert that they are *parts of* coloured objects. By contrast, if 'colour' were merely a *subjective* projection onto a physical phenomenon, then any object would have as many colours as there would be different ways it looks under different conditions, to different perceivers, etc. But this is absurd. Red things are not red solely by virtue of how they 'look' or 'appear' to the normal-sighted under normal lighting conditions, since something which only 'looks' red or 'appears to be' red *may not actually be* red. Rather, red things can be seen *to be* red by the normally sighted under normal-lighting conditions, and this is (part of) 'what it *means* to be normal-sighted' (Hacker, 1987, p. 125 *et seq*.) as well as (partially) constituting what could *count as* 'normal lighting conditions'. Thus, it seems that the attempt conceptually to

6 It is still worth repeating an early philosophical *objection* to this form of subjectivism: if the colour of an object seen is alleged to be interior to the perceiver, but the remainder of the object is external to him, by what method of projection are the colour and the object perceptually united? It certainly cannot be by any empirically determinable *physical* method of projection. And what internal analogue to one's eyes can be posited as the *'inner* organ of vision' which enables one to see *interior* colours? And against what *background* are these (now 'disembodied') colours visible? Here, by insisting upon a detailed scrutiny of its entailments, we truly expose the depths of the *incoherence* of the subjectivist thesis.

7 Of course, the varying light frequencies do not cause the 'sensations' of colours *in us*, but rather enable us to see the varying colours which objects actually, themselves, *have*. We shall discuss the abuse of the notion of 'sensation' later.

8 Even though we may (harmlessly) say that someone 'has some colour in his cheeks', by which we mean that his cheeks are not pallid but flushed, somewhat red, etc. We scarcely take it to signify that, in addition to the flesh, cells, etc., which compose his cheeks, we could expect to find an added physical component, namely, their colour!

fit the grammar of colour to *either* side of a simple dichotomy of 'objective'/'subjective' is bound to fail, at least if one construes this contrast class, in purely 'materialist' terms, as omnirelevant to this issue, and as exhaustive of the conceptual possibilities in the traditional ways of philosophical ontology.

Turning now to the perception of an 'apple' as such: in what does *this* achievement consist? At least since Kant, many theorists have agreed that 'perception without conception is blind'. What this esoteric dictum means is, essentially, that one cannot be said to have seen an X (for example, as in 'He saw the Great Bear') without having some *concept* of what an X is. So, if you don't know what, for example, a 'stamen' is, you cannot *see* the stamen, even if it is (silently) laid before you. And, by parity of reasoning, one cannot see *anything* (except *analogically*, for example, as in the case of pre-linguistic infants and non-linguistic animals) if one lacks the conceptual means wherewith to look. Of course, this does *not* entail that photons are not striking photoreceptor cells: it simply means that the ascription conditions of quotidian visual accomplishments are tied, conceptually, to linguistic competence.[9] However, the notion promulgated by inferential theorists of vision since von Helmholtz (including many 'information-processing' theorists) that one must 'recognise' an apple *as* an apple every time one sees an apple, is, of course, to abuse the concept of 'recognition'. As Baker and Hacker indicate: 'I [do not] *recognise* [our italics] . . . what time it is when I look at the face of my watch [n]or recognise my wife when I sit down to dinner with her of an evening' (Baker and Hacker, 1984b, p. 232). To 'recognise' something *as* something is a distinctive achievement, not at all characteristic of ordinary, unremarkable instances of merely seeing something (and knowing what it is that one has seen). Thus, the (philosophical) doctrine that to see an apple is to *recognise* 'sensory input' *as* an apple, or that it is to *construct* ('internally') 'applehood' from such 'input', is, at best, a violation of the logical grammar of 'see' and 'recognise'.

If colours, fragrances, tastes and textures cause (pseudo-)problems for the classical Galilean-Cartesian ontology, 'consciousness', *the putative medium within which these 'secondary qualities' are determined or 'constructed' by perceivers*, poses the deepest (pseudo-)mystery of all. It is to an assessment of this issue which we now turn.

'Consciousness', which, for Descartes, was the primary property of the *res cogitans*, appears to materialist ontology as an enigma. Quine, for example, seems to think of it as a supreme mystery: 'We know what it

9 For a more elaborate defence of this position, see Coulter and Parsons, 1991.

is like to be conscious, but not how to put it into satisfactory *scientific* [our italics] terms' (Quine, 1987, p. 133). Johnson-Laird, speaking from within the cognitivist paradigm, asserts that: 'No one really knows what consciousness is, what it does, or what function it serves' (Johnson-Laird, 1983, p. 448). Such dicta betray an adherence to a specific theoretical version of 'consciousness' which treats it as a peculiar kind of phenomenon with remarkable properties and powers. However, as Ryle, Wittgenstein and those working in their tradition[10] have argued, 'consciousness' is not properly understood as a discrete kind of *phenomenon* at all. Once again, a noun appears to 'stand for' some 'substantive phenomenon', albeit, in this case, one which is neither empirically determinable, measurable or truly physical in kind. Hence the 'enigma'. Yet this 'enigma' is a function of an impoverished grasp of the logic – the logical *grammar*, as Wittgenstein would have it – of the concept of 'consciousness', partly ordained by an *a priori* adherence to an austere materialist ontology which is itself inspired by a deep misunderstanding of the logical scope of the natural sciences' (especially biology's and physics') legitimate application. For, of course, 'consciousness' is not, and cannot be, a physical or biological concept: but it does *not* follow that, therefore, it must be an enigmatic phenomenon or a 'mystery' of any kind. It is, rather, a commonsense concept – an ordinary word with a range of mundane communicative functions – which stands in need of logico-grammatical *clarification*. Once such clarification is achieved, the enigma vanishes, and its roots can be clearly seen (in retrospect) to have lain within a *forced* extension of the relevances of biology and physics. It was Franz Brentano who first contributed to this process of clarification. Brentano argued that 'consciousness' is a *transitive* notion, and that, therefore, it cannot be the name of any discrete object, whether of the 'mind' or of the body. One is conscious *of* something (Brentano, 1924). Thus, 'consciousness' is not a name for any detachable or isolatable phenomenon, but is an *essentially* relational word. Edmund Husserl, the founder of 'phenomenology', repeatedly emphasised this point in various of his writings. He sought to decompose the concept of consciousness into an array of unified 'acts-and-objects' (*noeses* and their *noemata*), claiming that the various ways in which we are 'conscious' of something, e.g., perceiving X, hearing X, recollecting X, imagining X, thinking (of/about) X, reflecting (upon) X, etc., are all 'acts'. However, the idea that these are, in Husserl's terms, *'acts of* consciousness', goes somewhat against the grain of the prior (Brentanoan) thesis of the 'intensionality of

10 See, especially, Malcolm, 1984.

consciousness', the thesis that 'consciousness' *necessarily* takes an (explicit or implicit) object, since there cannot be (logically, grammatically) a construction such as 'an act of consciousness of *X*'. Consciousness cannot itself 'act': it is not an agent, but a term for a *relational* property of an agent, a term which is susceptible to decomposition into its constituents, such as 'seeing', 'hearing', 'noticing', 'recognising', etc., with their correlative, and *non-detachable*, 'objects'. If philosophers remain wedded to the idea that words (especially nouns) must necessarily 'name' things, they will *never* emancipate themselves from such a profound misconception as that 'consciousness' is a word which 'stands for' something ineffably mysterious. This root idea – that nouns are names which 'stand for' things – is at the basis of the resistance to the Rylean/Wittgensteinian recovery of the nature of the 'mental.' However, this *kind* of resistance will not work.

Ryle, who had earlier in his philosophical career been much influenced by Husserl's phenomenological project, argued at length (in a much-neglected discussion of his erstwhile mentor's writings)[11] that Husserl's listing of putative 'acts of consciousness' embraced many verbs which are *not* genuine action verbs. Remembering, perceiving, seeing, and many others listed as 'acts of consciousness' in the Husserlian analysis, are not acts but capacities or *achievements*, and various others, such as 'thinking', are polymorphs whose grammar is in many ways unlike that of regular action verbs. There are also many verbs which are neither achievements nor polymorphs but *dispositional* verbs, and so forth. Their analysis is misrepresented if portrayed in simple dichotomies. Furthermore, the proper locus of predication of *all* of these verbs is the *person*, and not an aspect, dimension or putative component of a person (such as his or her 'mind' or brain). The proper logical analysis of the uses of expressions such as 'I (you/he/she, etc.) am (are/is) conscious (of . . .)' and 'I (you/he/she, etc.) have (has) consciousness' shows that this ordinary word does not function as a name for *any* kind of phenomenon, object, entity or discrete 'referent' putatively investigable by psychology, the neurosciences, or any other empirical science.[12] This is not because it names a transcendental or metaphysical 'mystery', but because it never has been the *name* of *any* kind of object, however theoretically conceived. Only by reifying 'consciousness', and then pondering the ontological implications of such a

11 Ryle, 'Phenomenology', in Ryle, 1971b, pp. 167–78. See also Ryle's essay 'Phenomenology versus "The Concept of Mind"' in the same volume.
12 For a more detailed treatment of the logic of the concept of 'consciousness', see Coulter, 1993a.

reified commitment, could it ever have seemed to constitute a genuine puzzle for philosophy or for the behavioural and life sciences.

One's 'consciousness' is not, then, a locus for, nor the agent of, the sorts of functions theoretically ascribed to it in the Galilean-Cartesian ontology: *inter alia*, the 'filling in' of the colours, textures, odours, etc. of an otherwise colourless, odourless, dull world, a world depicted as such only by falsely universalising – and raising to omnirelevant and ontological status – the descriptions and conceptualisations of (particular) phenomena appropriate solely to the specialised work of physics and biology, and to the exclusion of all other descriptions and characterisations of things. If, then, objects *are* genuinely coloured, phenomena of various sorts *do* have fragrances and textures, and various things *do* emit sounds, then there can be no colour-endowing, fragrance-adding, texture-constructing or sound-appending work for 'mind' or 'consciousness' to do.[13] Of course, we can be conscious of the sound something makes (meaning that we can hear it), conscious of the colour of an object (meaning that we can see it), conscious of the odour of something (meaning that we can smell it), but in *every* case the sound (of the birds), the colour (of the flowers) or the fragrance (of the fruit) is *there* to be heard, seen or smelled: it is not our 'consciousness' (nor our putatively 'unconscious minds', either) which put these qualities *into* the world. And these sounds, colours and fragrances are not 'sensations' in us (e.g., 'in our brains'). It is *only* in metaphysical discourse that one encounters such locutions as 'sensations of colour' construed as on a par with, for example, sensations of pain. The *ordinary* meaning of a 'sensation' in connection with seeing a coloured object would be explained as something like being transfixed by the brilliance of a red sunset or dazzled by the white light of the sunlit snow. These (extraordinary) experiences, precisely because they are exceptional, cannot serve as exemplars of *all* mundane instances of 'seeing something that is red' (or white), and this shows that the concept of 'sensation' is either being abused (if it is thought to be equivalent to 'seeing' or 'hearing', or part of an elucidation of their ordinary meanings) or that it is already prepackaged with the contested elements of the theory or ontology which is itself supposed to be providing an account of quotidian colour perception, acoustic perception and the rest.

So much of the perplexity about the 'mental', which we ultimately derive from the Cartesian world-picture, originates within a philosophical commitment to a restrictive and scientistic conception of the

13 And, by parity of reasoning, nothing of *this* sort for the central nervous system to do, either.

'physical' which is still alive today in many intellectual circles, and which has not fundamentally changed since Descartes' own period (technical details and modifications notwithstanding). There are many ordinary and intelligible uses of 'physical' which have little or nothing to do with the concepts of physics *as a natural science* as such (for example, 'physical beauty', 'physical pain', 'physical needs' and 'physical illness', to name but a few). If 'all that there really is, physically', or 'all that *actually exists*', is thought of as given *exclusively* in the conceptual frameworks of physics, chemistry, biology and related natural sciences, then, obviously, the 'mind' must either remain a metaphysical enigma, be banished from the human conceptual apparatus, or be somehow *reduced to the terms of* one or more of these sciences. Naturally enough, given the imperious ambitions of the sciences, philosophers have frequently succumbed to the latter temptation: namely, to theorise the nature of the mental in terms drawn exclusively from physical and biological science. The result has been rampant, albeit deep and disguised, conceptual confusion, much of which displays itself in the cognitivist theorising which we criticise in this work. Very few philosophers and cognitive theorists would characterise themselves as straightforward 'Cartesian dualists' these days (Eccles and Popper being clear exceptions in this regard). The tide has turned, and, as Ullin Place has remarked: 'Truly a remarkable transformation [has taken place] from the situation that existed thirty years ago, when every philosopher you met was quite convinced that whatever answer to the mind-body problem, if there is one, is true, materialism must be false' (Place, 1988). But such materialisms as abound are as arid as the ontologies they embrace, and are all latter-day variants of the same seventeenth-century world-picture which gave us the mind/body dualism against which they pit themselves.

It has frequently been remarked that 'behaviourism' and 'mentalism' (or 'Cartesian dualism') are twin sides of the same (defective) philosophical coin. Behaviourists such as Skinner construed the 'mental' phenomena of human life (thinking, understanding, imagining, reasoning, etc.) as basically 'private inner events' inaccessible to scientific penetration and therefore to be relegated to a kind of non-scientific or pre-scientific limbo. The attack upon this treatment of the 'mental' by the cognitive scientists and their philosophical protagonists only reestablishes their ontological status as genuine phenomena, but now via the metaphors of computing systems. Yes, the mental phenomena are real, the story goes, and must be admitted into the rarefied scientific canon as such: indeed, they are still to be construed as wholly *internal* phenomena, but their reality is now said to consist in either a purely biological mode of existence (the mind-brain identity postulate) or in an emergent, 'computational' or 'functional' set of properties of neural events and processes. An immense amount of the literature in the modern philosophy of mind is dedicated to efforts to make these theses coherent, to try to reconcile the logic of our mental concepts and predicates to such an ontological account, or to try to banish such concepts altogether as inadequate to a fully developed, speculatively realisable science of the mind. This second objective, sometimes called 'the critique of folk psychology', will be considered in greater detail elsewhere in this work: suffice to remark at this juncture that the dismissal of all of our mental concepts from the purview of a theory or analysis of mind would appear instantly self-negating for the purpose of constructing any such 'theory'. If one denies oneself the ordinary conceptual resources for characterising one's *explanandum* in the first phase of reflection or inquiry, one has cut off one's nose to spite one's face. However, we are told, since the 'mind' and the 'mental' are themselves *theoretical* concepts, we can well do without *pre*-theoretical concepts of them.

This treatment of 'mind' and the 'mental' as if they are now to be regarded as *theoretical entities* (after the manner of hypothetically postulated entities in, say, theoretical subatomic physics, which may or not survive the further scrutiny of the scientific community) – a line (at various times) endorsed by Jerry Fodor, Daniel Dennett, Paul Churchland and Stephen Stich, to name but four prominent contributors to this debate – is itself rarely defended as the contentious claim which it is. Rather it tends to be merely asserted as a precondition for pursuing the cognitivist and/or materialist enterprise. Little effort is made to think through, or to come to terms with, the paradoxical implications such a position actually would entail. For example, would I be merely advancing an *hypothesis* if I claimed to 'have a lot on my mind', to be unable to 'make up my mind', or to have let something 'slip my mind'? And could it be merely a contestable theoretical claim, defeasible by reference to neurophysiological data alone, were someone to insist that he 'believed that so-and-so' was the case, or 'was thinking long and hard about a problem', or had 'recognised his attacker', was 'hoping for a raise', 'expecting a friend to come', or had 'become conscious of his obesity'? The decontextualisation of the concepts of 'mind' and of the 'mental' is a first false step prior to the subsequent false step of assuming that these words have (only hypothetical) internal *referents*. John Cook has written:

psychologists as well as philosophers have long been in the habit of assuming that our ordinary use of 'mentalistic' words involves a dualistic conception of human beings. And Sherrington . . . was clearly assuming that our everyday use of the words 'life', 'living' and 'alive' embodies a commitment to vitalism. Still other philosopher-scientists have attributed to the plain man's words a metaphysical theory of time. Now this repeated tendency to read metaphysics into our workaday words is not merely a series of unrelated misconceptions about these various words. (Cook, 1980, p. 58)

The root problem has been to assume an exclusively referential, object-describing function for (*inter alia*) our so-called 'mentalistic' words: 'Accordingly, when a psychologist asks himself, "What have people intended the word 'thinking' to stand for?" he is bound to suppose that the answer must be a dualistic one . . . for the word "thinking" has been in use since long before modern psychology and neurophysiology' (Cook, 1980, p. 58). Such a supposition gives rise to the misconceived ambition to 'reform' our ordinary language of the 'mental'. And yet, as Cook (and others) have observed, the entire 'problem' apparently posed by such words is a pseudo-problem, an artifact of far too narrow a view of how these words actually work, their grammars of actual use in contexts of communication of many diverse kinds. Indeed, an *amnesia* for how it is that we can and do ordinarily explain our uses of our workaday words seems to be a prerequisite for any such scientistically motivated and generalised onslaught against them to appear even remotely plausible.

If our arguments are right, and the enigma of the 'mind' is an artifact of a misconception of how language works, coupled to an overextension of the domain of applicability of 'description-according-to-physics-and-biology', then the stage is set for a reappraisal of the gamut of problems bequeathed to us by the Galilean-Cartesian philosophical tradition. Amongst the major principles of any such reappraisal is the following: no empirical, scientific inquiry will be relevant to a solution of the problems involved in untangling the putative enigmas of the mind, consciousness and the 'secondary qualities' of phenomena in the world, because these are not in any sense truly scientific problems but are *philosophical* problems, and philosophical problems are only dissolved by a perspicuous survey of the logic of – the principles of intelligibility governing – the relevant concepts. As Hacker reminds us:

It is not the task of philosophy to affirm or deny the existence of things, but rather to clarify what assertions or denials of existence signify, if anything. Ontology is as defunct as metaphysics. It is not philosophers who make discoveries about the furniture of the world, but empirical scientists. The task of philosophy is to check the inventory for double counting, to clarify the list-making principles when confusions arise (in science and philosophy alike) through miscategorization or cross-classification. (Hacker, 1987, p. 238)

It is because we believe that so many of the puzzles and arguments besetting the investigation of human capacities articulated within the cognitive sciences are, at root, philosophical puzzles and *not* genuinely scientific ones, that we have devoted so much attention to logical clarifications and conceptual elucidations in this work. Clearing away the debris of defunct ontologies and metaphysical schemes, which, we are arguing, hinder a clear understanding of the nature of the *explananda* for the human sciences, is an absolute prerequisite for pursuing rigorous and meaningful inquiries into those topics which interest us all.

It was Gilbert Ryle's *The Concept of Mind* (1949) which most explicitly and systematically elaborated a range of criticisms of the 'dogma of the Ghost in the Machine' (Ryle, 1973, p. 17) in large measure by exposing errors of 'miscategorization or cross-classification', in Hacker's terms. Ryle's patient logical dissection and classification of the various conceptual categories pertaining to the mental and experiential domains (identifying distinctions between, *inter alia*, the episodic, occurrent, dispositional, semi-dispositional, achievement, task, heed, mongrel-categorical and the rest) enabled philosophers to work their way through the conceptual confusions, misclassifications and 'category mistakes' which plagued the Cartesian world-picture of the 'inner' and the 'outer'. Although Ryle sometimes misapplied his *own* classifications (for example, wrongly treating 'believe' and 'having a motive' as exclusively 'dispositional' expressions), and sometimes forced some concepts to fit his scheme where a more flexible, example-driven approach would have served better (e.g., the strict subsumption of *all* instances of 'understanding' under the 'achievement-verb' class, ignoring ill-fitting but intelligible constructions such as 'he understands women'), the general methodology of attack was fundamentally sound. However, it was not very long before many philosophers (especially in the United States) began to retreat from the minutiae of conceptual clarification and also to reconceive of Ryle's project of dissolving the Cartesian knot as merely a sophisticated variant of behaviourism. (This revisionist assessment was also to afflict the appraisal of the later Wittgenstein's contributions to the dissolution of the same array of problems.) Ryle himself anticipated this reaction when he wrote towards the end of *The Concept of Mind*:

> The general trend of this book will undoubtedly, and harmlessly, be stigmatized as 'behaviourist' . . . But it has not been a part of the object of this book to advance the methodology of psychology . . . Its object has been to show that the two-worlds story is a philosophers' myth, though not a fable, and, by showing this, to begin to repair the damage that this myth has for some time been doing inside philosophy. (Ryle, 1973, p. 310)

We do not quite agree with Ryle's diagnosis of the 'harmlessness' of the stigmatisation which was, indeed, in store for his work. For it blinded many serious thinkers to the radical character of his assault upon the Cartesian foundations of psychology, and enabled them to pursue theoretical constructions which simply rehabilitated the vanquished pseudo-phenomena of the Cartesian mentalistic mythology in a new form. It is to a detailed and extensive consideration of several efforts at such a rehabilitation (especially that developed by Jerry Fodor, originating within an explicit confrontation with Ryle's work) that we now turn.

3

Minds, Machines and 'Folk Psychology'

Jerry Fodor looms large in this chapter because he has been amongst the most determined in pursuing the 'computer metaphor' for the human mind and, in so doing, has been perhaps the most influential figure in stimulating renewed debate within the philosophy of mind. Fodor essentially elaborates upon the 'mentalistic' initiatives of Noam Chomsky's Cartesian linguistic theorising. Fodor is certainly one of the first to recognise that many of his own arguments are unpersuasive and implausible,[1] but he commends them to us even so, commonly on the grounds that no better ones are currently available. However, an unpersuasive and implausible argument is simply that, and it cannot be accepted even for want of a persuasive and plausible one. Taken at his own estimation, many of Fodor's arguments are patent non-starters, but his occasionally frankly expressed scepticism about central aspects of his own case has not deterred him from continuing to press his case nor others from taking it seriously.

Fodor justifies the project in which he is engaged on the basis of the degenerate state into which theorising about the nature of the mind and human behaviour had fallen. Such theorising had been dominated by behaviorism in psychology and by 'logical behaviorism' in philosophy, and these doctrines, in Fodor's view, are simply inadequate. Fortunately, the situation can be saved, or, at least, significantly trans-

---

1 For example, Fodor writes: 'Some of the things we seem to be committed to strike me, frankly, as a little wild. I should be glad to know if there are ways of saving the psychology while avoiding those commitments' (Fodor, 1975, p. ix).

formed. A main element of the solution to the predicament confronted both by psychology and by the philosophy of mind has been available for centuries as the basis of Cartesian dualism. In contradistinction to the modern doctrines of psychological behaviourism and 'logical behaviorism', Descartes had maintained what Fodor takes to be a patent (and fundamental) truth, that 'mental states' can be, indeed are, *essential* to the explanation of human behaviour. However, Descartes' dualism itself *cannot* be accepted as it stands. Fodor is a thoroughly modern materialist and he cannot, therefore, countenance the supposition that there are two distinct substances, one material and the other not. There is no immaterial substance. If, then, Descartes was correct to treat mental states as *causes* of bodily movements, it must be that the mental states are themselves resolvable into material states, for only a material state can be the cause of a material motion or of another material state. There is only *one* serious candidate for such a causal role, and this must be the central nervous system. At a stroke – literally, *by* a stroke – the mind/body problem is settled: we are dealing with the phenomenon of the 'mind/brain'.

Fodor's project is, or so he tells us, not to develop a 'philosophy of mind' but to vindicate the possibility of a 'scientific psychology', one which becomes – again – a realistic possibility if one accepts that 'mental states' are causes of 'bodily movements', for one thereby opens up the possibility of what to Fodor is a *sine qua non* of a genuine science: causal generalities.[2] It had been the possibility of these which 'logical behaviourists' had prominently denied, thereby casting doubt upon the prospects for an explanatory psychological science (or, at least, of the kind of 'scientific psychology' that Fodor envisages).

The aged Cartesian arguments can be complemented by that most recent of technological developments, the digital computer. While Fodor wants to insist – good materialist that he is – that central nervous system states are the causes of bodily movements, he must, if his case for a 'scientific psychology' is to be carried through, *preclude* the possibility that the work of explaining our behaviour in a scientific sense should fall entirely within the province of neuroscience. The states of the brain must be material states, but they must *also* be mental states – how can this be? According to Fodor, the nature of the inner states of the computer establish that this *can be* the case. The inner states and operations of the computer are the causes of the behaviour of the computer, and they are electrical phenomena, but the states of the

2 The original case for this view is spelled out in Fodor's early book – Fodor, 1968.

computer are also describable at a more abstract level, and in 'functional' terms, as a series of 'symbolic' states. The computer, therefore, operates over 'symbolic' states, and thus it provides an existence-proof of the way in which symbolic states are realisable in material form and, thereby, can play a causal role in the production of physical behaviour.

The computer's functioning may involve computational operations over symbolic states, but is there any basis for thinking that 'the mind' is to be understood, comparably, as involving computational operations over symbolic states (or, as Fodor terms them, 'representations')? At the very least, there is the evidence of natural languages. Following Chomsky, Fodor seeks to argue that, though we speak natural languages, we do not actually learn how to speak *from scratch*. We acquire concepts: but this, in his view, requires a language within which to express them. Such a 'language' must be innate. The acquisition of concepts presupposes language, language presupposes concepts, therefore, according to Fodor, one must already possess language/concepts if one is to learn anything. One must already have one language in order to acquire another! Hence, the so-called 'first language' which a child acquires cannot truly be the first language – the child must *already* have a language to enable the acquisition of this 'first' language. Thus, the child must have a language which it has *not* acquired, one which is built into the brain. There is, therefore, a language – the 'language of thought' – which is innate (Fodor, 1981a, pp. 142–62). We shall return to consider the argument about language learning at a later point, and in some detail.

In Fodor's theory, it is not the case that the computer operates upon the 'representational' states within it by virtue of their 'representational' or 'symbolic' character. The computer does not perform arithmetical operations because it, the computer, is obedient to the rules of mathematical calculation. The computer operates over these 'representational' states by virtue of their *form*, and that alone. It is, in Fodor's view, the form of the representations to which the computational processes are sensitive – in other words, and in the crudest terms, it is to the presence or absence of an electrical pulse that the computer responds. It is, of course, the case that the computer cannot be responding to the representational character of the representation, but only to the *material properties* of the representation – it is, after all, only the material properties of something which can play a causal role in bringing about the behaviour of a material body.

These are the lineaments of the position which initiates Fodor's many years of sustained argument. Some aspects of the way in which he develops this argument will be presented below, but we shall concentrate upon four main issues to which Fodor's work gives rise. These are: the adequacy of Fodor's response to the putative doctrine of 'logical behaviourism'; the relationship between the explanations which the putative 'scientific psychology' and the alleged 'folk psychology' provide, particularly with respect to the issue of 'narrow content'; the question of the 'reality' of beliefs; and the adequacy of the rationale for the 'language of thought'. To begin this discussion, we must first confront:

The behaviourist bogeyman

A substantial part of Fodor's rationale for taking the line that he does is provided by his complaints about the inadequacy of the behaviourism which prevailed prior to Chomsky's and his own interventions. We have no brief for the psychological theorising called 'behaviourism' as espoused, especially, by Skinner. As we mentioned in chapter 1, we see Chomsky's and Fodor's 'mentalism' as sharing basic and vital assumptions with behaviourism, particularly the assumption that the relationship between 'behaviour' and 'mind' must, if there is to be one, be an *inferential* one. The disagreements between behaviourists and mentalists *au fond* is essentially in their philosophy of science. Behaviourists supposed that scientific inquiry should traffic only in 'observables', whilst the mentalists insisted that it is legitimate to postulate 'unobservables'. These ostensible rivals think that the line between the observable and the unobservable is to be drawn in precisely the same place: between observable bodily movements and unobservable – hypothetical – 'mental states and processes', but they disagree over the *scientific* legitimacy of inferences to the mental. The antinomy of 'body' and 'mind' is, of course, a shared inheritance from Cartesian dualism, and the mentalists seem, in their basic conceptions, much closer to behaviourism than they proclaim themselves to be. This is certainly the case *vis-à-vis* the arguments of Wittgenstein and Ryle which, at the very least, (a) point toward the possibility of eliminating the pairing, in this Cartesian way, of 'body' (behaviour) and 'mind'; and (b) eschew the assumption that the relation between behavioural and mental characteristics is one of problematic inference.

Fodor repeatedly combines together the behaviourists and the so-called 'logical behaviourists' (amongst whom both Wittgenstein and Ryle are to be included, with Ryle being a most prominent representative) as the leading players in an intellectual 'dark age' from which he is leading us. We have given some reasons for asserting that Fodor has much more in common with the behaviourists in the human sciences than do his 'logical behaviourists', for he shares with those behaviourists both the framework of fundamental assumptions which provides their central problematic and a preoccupation with developing a 'scientific psychology' within the bounds set by an *a priori* conception of proper scientific explanation.

Fodor writes:

> I am suggesting that the reason why there is no serious psychology of central cognitive processes is the same reason why there is no serious philosophy of scientific confirmation. Both exemplify the significance of global factors in the fixation of belief, and nobody begins to understand how such factors have their effects. In this respect, cognitive science hasn't even *started*; we are literally no further advanced than we were in the darkest days of behaviorism (though we are, no doubt, in some beneficent respects more disillusioned). If someone – a Dreyfus, for example – were to ask us why we should even suppose that the digital computer is a plausible mechanism for the simulation of global cognitive processes, the answering silence would be deafening. (Fodor, 1983, p. 147)

It is significant for the evaluation of his project that, though his work is developed as a counter-behaviourism, it is still, in such central matters with which it is concerned, 'no further advanced'. Nonetheless, there are constant reminders about the supposed deficiencies of behaviourists and 'logical behaviourists' alike. For example:

> modern philosophers – like Wittgenstein and Ryle and Gibson and Auty – *have* no theory of thought to speak of. I do think this is appalling; how can you seriously hope for a good account of belief if you have no account of belief *fixation*? But I don't think it is surprising. Modern philosophers who haven't been overt behaviourists have generally been covert behaviorists. (Fodor, 1987, p. 147)

We have already indicated that Fodor does not, in our view, do very much to reach down to the roots of behaviourism in his own beloved Cartesianism and he does not, therefore, recognise the extent to which *psychological* behaviourists are his close kin. As far as the so-called 'logical behaviourists' are concerned, some are characters of considerably greater philosophical sophistication than the would-be behaviourist psychologists, yet Fodor displays a questionable understanding of their position and rarely manages better than caricature presentations of it. The arguments of a Hempel[3] or a Carnap[4], who wished to advance the thesis that statements about mental phenomena could simply be 'reduced without residue' into statements about behaviour, are conflated with the arguments of a Wittgenstein and a Ryle, who nowhere defended such a simplistic style of 'logical reductionism'. It is not, therefore, surprising that Fodor's rebuttals of 'logical behaviourism' leave so much to be desired. Indeed, as we expound upon Fodor's position and the issues which surround it, we shall show that the situation in which he and his contemporaries find themselves is exactly that which Wittgenstein and Ryle would have prognosticated for them.

So numerous and gross are Fodor's misrepresentations of what he calls the 'logical behaviourism' of Ryle and Wittgenstein that we cannot encompass even the major ones, and can provide only a brief account and relatively perfunctory critique of one or two of the dismal parodies of philosophical debate in which Fodor purportedly rebuts this 'logical behaviourism'. He asserts, *inter alia*, that:

> Denying the etiological involvement of mental states was really what behaviorism was about; it is what 'logical' behaviorists and 'eliminativists' had in common. Thus, for example, to hold as Ryle did, more or less, that mental states are a species of disposition is to refuse to certify as causal such psychological explanations as 'he did it with the intention of pleasing her', or for that matter, 'his headache made him groan', to say nothing of 'the mere thought of giving a lecture makes him ill'. (Fodor, 1987, p. 155, note 3 to chapter 1)

Further, we learn that it is 'no doubt a travesty to say that for a logical behaviorist "Smith is thirsty" means "if there were water around, Smith would drink it." But it is a travesty which comes close enough for our present purposes' (Fodor, 1987, p. 155). It is always easiest for us to agree with Fodor when he disparages his own views, and we can

3 See Hempel, 1949.
4 See Rudolph Carnap's (strange) claim: 'a sentence about other minds refers to *physical processes in the body* [our italics] of the person in question. On any other interpretation, the sentence becomes untestable in principle, and thus meaningless' (Carnap, 1932–33, p. 46). Elsewhere, Carnap refers to 'processes *of* the body'. This 'unified-science' conception of psychological language presaged the later work of Quine in its refusal to countenance any meaningful discourse which could not be strictly paraphrased into the 'language of science' – largely meaning physics. The remark about 'untestability' and its linkage to 'meaninglessness' is a clear reflection of the Vienna Circle's doctrine of verificationism. According to this doctrine, no statement (although its proponents tended to use 'sentence' and 'statement' interchangeably) could mean something unless what it said could be verified by empirical (preferably scientific) means.

certainly agree that he has provided a travesty of, specifically, Ryle's arguments by formulating them in *this* way.

The first significant mistake which Fodor (and numerous others) make in their treatment of Ryle is in interpreting his work as providing a 'theory of mind' and as seeking, therefore, to provide something which would satisfy the requirements of a 'scientific psychology' as Fodor and others would envisage it. Ryle's arguments are, in essentials, not a contribution to 'the philosophy of mind' but are, instead, an exercise in philosophical methodology. Like Wittgenstein, Ryle held that philosophical problems were largely confusions that were best dispelled, and that these problems arose as a result of philosophers' misapprehensions of superficial features of language. These problems were, therefore, to be dispelled by a more perspicuous view of (as Ryle termed it) the logical geography of our ordinary language. Fodor, of course, persistently treats Wittgenstein and Ryle as though they were putting forward a psychological theory such that, as in the quotation given above, he thinks it relevant to bewail their failure to provide a theory of thought. The alleged absence of such a theory in the writings of these prominent 'logical behaviourists' allows Fodor to proclaim his own theory of thought as the sole contender for the title, as 'the only game in town'. However, as we shall see, Fodor's purported theory is quite a feeble construction which does as much to make the case that Wittgenstein and Ryle put up against the need for 'theory' in such connections as anything could. We will take Ryle as the primary example of the so-called 'logical behaviourist' position designated by Fodor.

Ryle himself says of *The Concept of Mind*:

> This book offers what may *with reservations* [our italics] be described as a theory of the mind. But it does not give new information about minds. . . . The philosophical arguments which constitute this book are intended not to increase what we know about minds, but to rectify the logical geography of the knowledge which we already possess. (Ryle, 1963, p. 10)

We, for our part, are inclined to think that Ryle does not emphasise the reservations about describing his book as providing a 'theory of mind' strongly enough. The fact that he registers reservations about so describing the book's contents can easily be overlooked and is unlikely to deter someone like Fodor from seeking to extract from the book a 'theory of mind' of the sort that Fodor himself aspires to, the sort that *will* provide 'new information about minds' and that can be criticised for failing to meet the standards which someone seeking a 'scientific theory' of mind would set for an adequate explanation of people's conduct. The attempt to assess Ryle's *supposed* theory of mind in respect of its adequacy in providing an explanatory theory of behaviour will take us in entirely the wrong direction. Ryle's purpose is not, as he makes plain in the quoted remarks, to put forward any theory on his own behalf but is, instead, to survey and describe the 'logical geography' of the expressions which comprise the so-called vocabulary of 'mental' terms and which are expressions that belong to and are taken from our 'ordinary' language – careful, stupid, logical, unobservant, ingenious, vain, methodical, credulous, witty and self-controlled being ones which Ryle identifies, from amongst 'a thousand others'. The way in which Ryle's arguments would have to be contested is not, then, in respect of their adequacy as putative theoretical terms for the explanation of behaviour, but in terms of their accuracy as a description of the 'logical geography' which they purport to survey, as a *description of the 'ordinary' language of which this 'mental' vocabulary is part.*

We are reluctant to consider *The Concept of Mind* as an exercise in 'philosophy of mind' except in an incidental sense, for it is primarily an exercise in philosophical methodology. Like Wittgenstein, Ryle held that philosophical problems were largely confusions that were best dispelled, and that these problems arose as a result of philosophers being misled by superficial features of language. These problems were, therefore, to be dispelled by a more perspicuous view of the way in which relevant expressions actually function in the language, and it is towards the provision of a *method* for conducting an effective survey of appropriate aspects of the 'ordinary language' that *The Concept of Mind* is primarily devoted. That it is the vocabulary of 'mind' which is being reviewed is incidental to the primary purpose of the work. The vocabulary of 'mind' is the exemplary focus for the formulation of the method because an incidental, but important, feature of modern philosophy is that one of the most crucial and influential of its founding figures was Descartes, whose arguments for dualism have provided a continuing source of provocation. Descartes' dualism is, therefore, a prominent and influential example of the kind of confusion Ryle is claiming philosophy is prone to, and the purpose is, therefore, to show that dualism can be dispensed with and that there is no need to seek any alternative to it. What *The Concept of Mind* actually puts forward then is not any alternative to Descartes' account of 'the nature of mind', but an account of language as having a 'categorical' structure.

Ryle's argument is that the words in our ordinary language are allocated to different 'logical categories', on the basis of the ways in which they function there. Words from different 'logical categories' behave in significantly different ways, but they do not *invariably* do so, with the result that words from different 'logical categories' may sometimes behave in superficially similar ways. This similarity may wrongly be taken by philosophers as indicating that the words work in the same ways throughout, and this leads them to overlook significant differences between the actual functions of these words, thus inducing confusion. Ryle argues that those crucial terms 'body' and 'mind' belong to different 'logical categories' but are, in Descartes' thinking, treated as if they belonged to the same categories. Descartes' philosophy of mind thus originates in what Ryle terms 'a category mistake'. He explains this kind of mistake with the notorious example of the visitor who is shown the various colleges of the university and then asks to be shown the building which is the university. 'College' is a term that identifies a building, but 'university' identifies an organisation made up by a collection of buildings, and in that respect they belong to different 'categories', but the visitor who asks to be shown 'the university' has mistakenly supposed that this term belongs to the same category as 'college'. *Very crudely put*, it is Ryle's argument that Descartes *mistakenly* takes the words 'body' and 'mind' as belonging to the same 'logical categories', as both naming, so to speak, different 'parts' of human beings, for, *as those expressions are used in our 'ordinary' language*, they are no more different parts of a human being than 'the college' and 'the university' are different parts of the university. Thus, Ryle's claims are about the part these crucial words play in the language from which they are taken, whether or not they *do* belong to the same 'logical categories', but these are not the grounds on which Ryle is characteristically challenged by his critics. It is a most common counter to Ryle's position to say that no serious philosopher wants to be concerned with examining *the language* in its fine detail and nuances, when they want to talk about real phenomena. It is not, of course, therefore possible for such critics to respond to Ryle's arguments directly for, of course, Ryle is making arguments about the role that words in the language play, and these arguments can only be directly answered by demonstrating that Ryle's survey of the 'logical geography' has gone awry. That, though, would require the sort of inquiry into *the language* and its detailed workings that the critics eschew. Consequently, many critics – like Fodor – suppose that the way in which to counter Ryle is to attribute to him his own 'theory of mind', one which is to be judged as an alternative to Descartes', and it is common to assign to him, just as Fodor does, a theory called 'logical behaviourism' which *does* offer a 'theory of mind' in a substantive sense, which proposes that 'mind' is (effectively) *a collection of dispositions*. It is because of such responses that we feel that Ryle gave a hostage to fortune when he allowed, *albeit with reservations*, that he was dealing with 'a theory of mind'.

One prominent form Cartesian category mistakes take is that of mistaking many expressions for 'episodic' ones. There are many expressions in our ordinary speech which identify episodes. 'Thirsty' and 'headache' would be two prominent examples. Someone who is thirsty is in a particular state, and one which continues over some period of time, as is someone with a headache. Someone who is thirsty has a number of feelings – discomforts, even – and these will persist and intensify if the person does not have something to drink. Similarly, someone who has a headache feels pain which is located in his head, and he feels this pain continuously for some period of time. Taking 'headache' and 'thirst' to be terms which identify 'mental states' – something which seems, outside of the philosophical tradition of so dubbing them, entirely perverse – does not, however, provide a licence for supposing that all 'mental' terms must identify episodes, though this is what those within the Cartesian tradition are inclined to do. This is, furthermore, a tradition which Fodor seeks to maintain. It should be noted that though 'having a headache' and 'feeling thirsty' may identify episodes, it is misleading to suppose that 'believing X', 'thinking Y' and 'intending to do Z' comparably do so. These terms, although very prominent in the 'mental vocabulary', do *not* identify episodes.

Let us contrast a word like 'irritable' with a word like 'thirsty'. We have said that the latter identifies an episode. It is clearly the case, though, that the word 'irritable' does not. 'Being irritated' is something that *is* episodic. One is irritated by something, and one can remain irritated for some time after the provocation is over. If we say of someone that he is irritable, we are not saying that he is now irritated, that some episode is taking place. That prior episodes of irritation have occurred is something that provides us with a basis for attributing 'irritability' to someone. However, when we say of someone that he is irritable, we do not say that he is someone who has, in the past, been irritated. We make a prediction about his future behaviour. Someone who is 'irritable' is someone who becomes irritated, and who is easily irritated. If this person is irritable then he will become irritated, and it will take relatively little provocation to precipitate a bout of irritation. Thus, the characterisation 'irritable' has a sort of hypothetical, predictive nature. When we say 'X is irritable' we are saying that X is prone to irritation. Expressions such as 'believing', 'thinking' and 'intending' are closer to 'irritable' than they are to 'thirsty'. If we treat them as though they were close kin to 'thirsty' then we would generate confusion, as those in the Cartesian tradition (amongst others, of course) have done. This is Ryle's primary claim. A prominent problem is, crudely, that of conflating expressions which identify 'dispositions' with those that identify 'episodes'.

Ryle's claims are about the ordinary role of expressions within our language. Ryle's arguments are about *what we mean when we say* of someone that he 'believes *X*', 'thinks *Y*' or 'intends to *Z*', for example. His would-be critics, such as Fodor, are apt to overlook this essential aspect of Ryle's work and to treat his arguments as though they were designed to be components of a kind of theoretical psychology. It is precisely because of the ways in which all such projected psychologies have been conceived to appropriate the matters spoken of in that ordinary language that Ryle's work engenders a deep scepticism about such projects. It is hardly likely, therefore, that the notion of 'disposition', for example, was intended to bear the burden that the would-be critics assign to it. Insofar as Ryle is concerned with the notion of 'disposition' as an *explanatory* notion, then, it is not within the context of a putatively 'scientific' or 'theoretical' explanation of our conduct but, rather, as explanatory within the context of the kinds of explanations that we give one another for our respective actions during the course of our everyday conduct. Of no small importance is the fact that Ryle does not seek to answer the same question as that which troubles other philosophers: *their* characteristic form of question is 'What sort of thing is a belief or a thought?' whereas Ryle's is, rather, 'When do we say, and what are we saying of someone when we say, that he believes something or has a thought about something?'

As happens on several occasions, Ryle's (and Wittgenstein's) would-be critics stand in full agreement with him on important points. If those would-be critics assert that 'disposition' does not provide an acceptable theoretical term for a scientific psychology, then they are in full agreement with Ryle; he, of course, concludes that, since many of the alleged 'mental' terms have a dispositional character, then the prospects for a theoretical, scientific psychology cannot be promising. His would-be critics draw a quite different conclusion, however: since dispositional concepts are not propitious for the kind of scientific psychology they envisage (fantasise might be a better term), then some *other* kinds of expressions must be used or, indeed, the allegedly dispositional character of key concepts must eventually be disputed.

'Dispositions', the argument often goes, do not really explain. They are, for example, little more than tautologies. A classic 'dispositional' property would be the brittleness of glass. To say of a glass that it is brittle is to say that it is disposed to break. Actually, it is to say something a little more precise than that, for it is to say that it is disposed to break easily. If we say that something is disposed to break, and it breaks, then to say that it broke because it was brittle is, surely, to provide no information at all? To say that something broke because it was prone to break, because it was breakable, is virtually a tautology. If it wasn't breakable, it wouldn't have broken.

We must be wary, first of all, of supposing that 'dispositional' and 'causal' explanations are mutually exclusive. This is another mistake that Fodor makes, perhaps as a result of the misconceptions embodied in his attempted attack on Ryle over the 'clever clown' argument (Fodor, 1987, pp. 3–9). What, asks Ryle, makes a clown's performance clever? The Cartesian idea is that what makes it clever is its causes, that it is the occurrence of a set of 'inner' mental operations which cause the performance, and it is, of course, the 'inner' and 'mental' operations which are clever. Ryle holds that the question 'What makes a performance clever?' is, so to speak, a 'conceptual' question, not a causal one – what characteristics of a performance do we single out as marking it as a clever one? The cleverness of the performance is itself a characteristic *of the performance* and not of any interior goings-on accompanying the performance. The cleverness of the performance is *on open display* to the clown's audience, says Ryle, and we certainly do not need to appeal to any putatively hidden 'inner' or 'mental' operations to establish that the performance of this clown is much cleverer than the performance of the one who came on before him. Fodor thinks that he has a knock-down answer to Ryle, one which consists essentially of two complaints: (a) that Ryle is seeking to give an *a priori* answer to an empirical question, is trying to do empirical science by purely conceptual means; and (b) that whilst it is true that there is a 'conceptual story' to be told about the cleverness of the performance, Ryle denies what is also true, namely, that there is *also* a *causal* story to be told.

Fodor is wrong on both counts. Ryle is at pains to distinguish conceptual from empirical, causal, *scientific* questions, not least because the Cartesian approach conflates the two. Since 'intelligence' is (held to be) a 'mental' attribute, and bodily movements cannot possess mental attributes, then the bodily movements of the clown cannot, therefore, themselves be intelligent. The bodily movements are caused by the 'mental states or operations'. Any intelligence in a performance must reside in its mental causes (for they, and they alone, can be intelligent). Thus, to explain what makes a performance intelligent involves identifying its mental causes. So goes the Cartesian story, and it is the one to which Fodor wholeheartedly subscribes. Against this, Ryle's argument proposes that it is the *performance* (*not* 'a series of bodily movements') that can be characterised as intelligent or clever, that there are criteria for differentiating a more from a less intelligent performance, and that to explain to someone what was clever about a performance one would not refer to its (hypothesised) inner mental causes, but to aspects of the performance, those which satisfy those criteria. What characteristics of the clown's performance single it out as more intelligent than other performances is *not* a scientific question but is, of course, a conceptual one. 'Cleverness' involves such considerations as, *inter alia*, whether what is done is original, inventive, imaginative, skilled and so forth. Ryle's arguments do not rule out the possibility of a causal story concerning a clever performance at all: there may well be one to be told, but it would not be the kind of causal story that would suit Fodor's needs. Fodor, recall, wants to hold to the Cartesian idea that there is a need to invoke a set of inner, concurrent mental operations to explain behaviour, and the admission that there could be a causal story to be told would be, for him, the admission that it is *that* sort of causal story. But there are quite other kinds of causal stories. The kind that is (conceptually) appropriate to the explanation of how this performance came to be as clever as it is would involve reference, not to a sequence of inner, mental events, but to *a history of prior activity*, to the preparation, planning, rehearsal and so on that has gone into organising and staging the performance.

Suppose, then, that someone throws a ball, it strikes the window and the window breaks. Here is a causal explanation. The ball broke the glass. However, someone may be puzzled by the event. Plainly, it was the ball that was the cause of the glass's breaking, but the ball was a soft one and it was not thrown very hard and, in someone's estimation, it should not have broken the window. Subsequently, it is determined that the glass was of a type known to be brittle. It takes very little to shatter that kind of glass, and, therefore, the way in which the cause brought about the event that it caused is now explained. The (soft) ball did break the window, but only because the glass was brittle, i.e., easily broken. The same kind of argument applies to the case of 'irritability'. The office manager is an irritable character. He becomes irritable, but his irritations have causes (although we will just note that 'cause' here means something akin to 'provocation'). The point is that someone who did not know the office manager well might see that, indeed, some occurrence has precipitated his irritation. That the manager is irritated at what someone has done is plain enough to see, but our visitor to the office might be bewildered and troubled that such a minor matter has brought about such intense annoyance. Has someone unwittingly done something which is much worse than it appears? To have it explained to him that the office manager is an irritable person can reassure our visitor: no-one has done anything especially serious, and with someone else it would scarcely have caused notice, but the manager is prone to disproportionate reactions to minor derelictions and the offence, slight though it was, has been enough in this case to trigger the enraged response. *The identification of a disposition may, then, play a part in identifying a cause.* '

Ryle's invocation of dispositions is taken by some as suggesting that certain mental concepts can 'cash out as' behaviours. To believe a certain thing is to behave in certain ways: if someone believes in God, then he will pray, read the Bible, go to church, etc. Yet this occasions the kind of worry which one finds expressed by Smith and Jones:

> Having a certain belief is often the cause of some consequent behaviour; but according to Ryle, having a belief is a matter of there being lots of 'iffy' facts concerning one's behaviour, and surely packages of 'iffy' facts about behaviour can't themselves be causes of behaviour. (Smith and Jones, 1986, p. 92)

However, as Smith and Jones add, 'to avoid unnecessary complications it is worth shifting ground a little, and talking not of causes but of explanations'. Thus,

> reconstructed, the argument runs as follows: It is surely uncontrovertible that we appeal to people's beliefs in explaining their behaviour patterns. But if having a particular belief just is the matter of there being certain patterns in one's behaviour, then how can citing a belief explain the behaviour? On Ryle's theory, this would seem to collapse into a vacuous attempt to explain something by reference to itself. (Smith and Jones, 1986, p. 92)

Smith and Jones' reconstruction is, in fact, not a reconstruction at all. The unnecessary complications they wish to avoid are about 'mental causation', but their argument simply retains the assumption that genuine explanation just *is* causal explanation. However, this is by no means the case.

Ryle is, again, presented as someone who is putting forward a general policy of explanation, proposing an explanatory theory on his own behalf, but he is actually not doing anything of the kind. He is, rather, seeking to describe the kinds of explanations that we give one another in the course of our everyday affairs, and his claim is therefore about the 'dispositional' character of the *word* 'belief' as it is employed in everyday discourse. Rebutting Ryle would mean demonstrating that the word 'belief' does *not* operate as, for want of a better word, a 'dispositional expression' in that discourse. An answer to Ryle requires not comment on explanatory theoretical strategies, but upon the precise workings of the word in the language. The question which Smith and Jones, and Fodor, and many others, wish to answer is this: 'What is it to have a belief?', even 'What kind of thing is a belief?', which is why Smith and Jones construe Ryle's work as giving an answer to *their* question, which answer they derive as: to have a belief is 'a matter of there being lots of "iffy facts" concerning one's behaviour'. However, the question which Ryle might actually be seen to be dealing with is, rather, 'What is it to believe something?' The answer to that, recall, ought not to be one which he offers on his own behalf but, rather, that which reports how we should 'ordinarily' answer that question. And, of course, the answer to the question 'What is it to believe something?' which is appropriately given on such terms (at least for *some* uses of 'belief') is something like simply: to accept or agree with something. Someone who believes in God accepts the contention that God exists, agrees with the teachings of the Christian church, rejects assertions that God does not exist. Someone who believes that the ice is thin affirms the assertion 'The ice is thin', holds that the ice is thin, assents to someone else's assertion that 'the ice is thin', etc., etc. This *is* to answer the question about what it is to believe something, and it is *otiose* to ask further questions such as 'What is it to have a belief?' Only if we treat that question as meaning the same as 'What is it to believe something?', can we answer it as we have just done: it is to agree to or accept a certain contention, to hold certain things to be the case and so on. However, it is not as if philosophers of mind are *unaware* of the existence of this answer but it is, rather, that they regard it as necessary to make further inquiries, to ask (for example) '*What does one have when one has a belief?*' That is, 'What state is one in when one has a belief?' Rylean arguments, however, indicate that to take this step is to transgress the boundaries of what can intelligibly be asked: to say what one has when one has a belief is to ask a question to which *there is no answer* – the question makes no sense, and there can be no answer to a question which makes no sense.

Let us not now contend over whether the question actually does or does not make sense, for the determination of that would be a time-consuming matter, but let us simply persist in the point that it is only too likely that Ryle's case about belief is likely to suffer if it is construed as an answer to a question which he *denies can be posed* and which, therefore, he certainly cannot be trying to answer.

The first point to make about the relation between 'beliefs' and 'behaviour' is that the connection between them is not, in the first instance, a *causal* one, but more like a criterial one. The connection between believing a certain thing and acting in certain specific ways is of the sort often called 'internal' or 'logical'. With respect to believing certain things, it is the case that whether or not one behaves in certain ways is a *test* of whether one does indeed believe them, is a criterion for the *determination of whether or not one does hold that belief*. The extent to which behaving in specific ways functions as a criterion is, of course, complicated, for the circumstances relevant to settling *whether or not a given individual does have a certain belief* may be numerous, and their interrelations complex, but it is nonetheless the case that we do take a person's behaving in certain ways as evidence that they have a certain belief, and sometimes as *decisive* evidence that they hold the belief. Thus, if *under suitable* circumstances a given individual is not willing to say certain things or to act in certain ways we must refuse to accept that they do hold a given belief. Unless someone is willing to say, for example, that the world is flat when asked whether the world is round or flat, then we shall have no basis to say that they believe the world is flat. If they are prepared to book a 'round the world' holiday with a tour company then we shall have every reason to insist that they believe the world is round, not flat, even if they *say* they believe the world is flat and so on. A certain degree of *consistency* in the ways people behave, in the relation between the various things they do, including the things they say, is a prerequisite for our saying that they believe a certain thing. This is, of course, well testified in Stich's (1983) discussion of the lady who would say that President McKinley had been assassinated but who could not answer other questions about President McKinley such as whether he was dead, and thus exhibits massive inconsistency in her behaviour. In this case, we just do not know what to say she believes, are perhaps inclined to conclude that we can't say that she believes anything. We have not, in such a case, found any *flaw* in the concept of belief but have only highlighted the extent to which possessing a belief requires conducting oneself with a degree of consistency. In the various courses of action which depend upon or involve X's being the case, then a person who believes X is the case must act as though it is the case. 'Assassinate' is a 'success verb': someone is killed. If President McKinley was assassinated, then he is dead, and someone who genuinely believes McKinley was assassinated therefore believes that he is dead.

That the necessity for consistency between the various things a person says and the things he does is a precondition for attributing a particular belief is the basis for our suggestion that to describe a certain person as believing something is a hypothetical statement about them. We are not, however, saying that they *will* do certain things, but, rather, that there are certain things they *must* do, *if we are to be able to say that they believe this*. Ryle's 'dispositional' account of belief is often criticised on the ground that I may hold a certain belief, without ever doing anything about it – if I believe that Alpha Centauri is a planet, then there may be nothing that I will ever do that results from my believing that. Ryle's discussion of 'belief' is not, for one moment, incompatible with the contention that someone who read in a book that Alpha Centauri is a planet believes that 'Alpha Centauri is a planet' even if they never say or do anything remotely connected with this belief. To say of someone that they 'believe Alpha Centauri is a planet' is to say nothing other than that they accepted without question what they read on this matter, that they assented in this claim. However, though we have said that attributing to someone a belief is offering a sort of hypothetical assertion, we did not say that it was a matter of predicting in a flat-out fashion that a person will do certain things, is actively *disposed* to do certain things. If we say that someone believes Alpha Centauri is a planet we do not say that this person is actively *disposed* to go around saying 'Alpha Centauri is a planet', do not predict that they *will* say this and act in certain other specific ways. Of course, someone who believes Alpha Centauri is a planet may *never* say so, may never do anything on the basis of this belief. Very often, when the expression 'disposed to' is used, it is used to suggest that a person is on the edge of, is strongly inclining towards doing a certain thing, what we have called 'actively disposed'. Thus, if someone says he is disposed to give Smith a piece of his mind, he is maybe saying that he is currently getting ready to tell Smith off, is on the edge of performing this action. To employ this particular usage of 'disposed' to summarise Ryle's views will result in their misrepresentation, for it will suggest the very interpretation we are denying – that Ryle is suggesting that for a person to believe something is to be actively disposed, currently inclined, to do a particular thing – in which case, the objection that a person who believes something may have no disposition to do anything whatsoever about it would be cogent.

However, the kind of prediction we do make about someone when we say 'they believe a certain thing' does not necessarily involve the flat-out unconditional prediction that they will do any particular thing. On the contrary, the 'hypothesis' is a thoroughly conditional one. We can only say of someone that they do believe that 'Alpha Centauri is a planet' *if, when asked* 'Do you believe that Alpha Centauri is a planet?' they do such things as: *sincerely* answer 'Yes'; if when completing multiple choice questions like 'Is Alpha Centauri a planet, star, or galaxy?', they tick the 'planet' box; if, trying to find Alpha Centauri in a catalogue, they look under 'planets' not 'stars'; and so on. This is why we said that someone *must* do certain things if they have a certain belief, but, as should now be plain, we did not assert that they must at any point in their lives actually perform these particular actions. The 'must' has the following force: *if* certain conditions arise, then someone who believes *X* must act in way *Y*. We do not contend that those conditions need arise. If, however, they do, then someone who believes *X* must do *Y*. They *must* do *Y* in the sense that if they do not, then it makes no sense for us to say that they believe *X* – someone who, when giving a sincere answer to the question 'Is Alpha Centauri a planet?', responds with 'No' is someone to whom we *cannot* attribute the belief that Alpha Centauri is a planet. It just makes no sense to do so. Thus, for someone to believe *X is* for them to be disposed *under circumstances such as A, B and C* to perform action *Y* – if they are not, then it is nonsense to say that they believe *X*.

Having defended Ryle against the attribution of a 'dispositional' account of belief which cannot, we submit, be one which he would actually give, we can further point out with respect to Smith and Jones' complaint, that there is nothing remotely exceptionable about explaining some item by linking it to the pattern to which it belongs. When we explain our behaviour to each other in the course of our everyday affairs we *do* explain particular doings by relating them to the pattern of which they are a part. Such an explanation, of course, does not postulate a *causal* relationship, but then, as we have said, many explanations do not purport to provide causes. Thus, to explain someone's current irritation in terms of his 'irritability' is not to offer a cause for their irritation, but to explain something about the current irritation, which is that it is part of a pattern, that it is quite the normal and unremarkable thing for this individual and that, therefore, the outburst requires no explanation other than its ostensive local cause. That someone who 'never gets irritated' is currently irritated is not something that is fully explained by the ostensible cause: the fact that the current irritation is atypical of this person advises us that we should seek something in addition to the ostensible cause, such as, for example, stress, troubles at home, etc., which might render him much more prone than usual to irritation.

We must bear in mind as well that the word 'believe' has first-person uses, and that such uses are neither dispositional nor do they involve the reporting of inner states. Someone who says 'I believe the ice is thin' is making an assertion about what the ice is like – that, for instance, it will not support anybody's weight. However, in saying that he believes the ice is thin, the speaker may be providing a *qualified* claim, one which expresses less than full confidence about the state of the ice. 'To the best of my information, the ice is thin' is by no means the same as 'The ice is thin'. The first-person use of 'believe' has more than one role to play in communicating information. It often serves to contrast with 'know', for example, and thus to indicate the degree of certainty with which one's conviction is held or the extent to which speculation might enter into the information one provides. Thus, 'Do you *know* the ice is thin?' may be replied to intelligibly with a remark like: 'No, but I *believe* it is.' This tells your interlocutor that you are less than one hundred per cent certain about the actual state of the ice, that you have not yourself been out and tested it, for example.

Can beliefs be used to give *causal* explanations? The question is not *whether* beliefs can be used to give causal explanations, but *how* they figure in causal explanations when they do. It is commonplace amongst the philosophers with whom we are dealing to take the occurrence of the word 'because' as a straightforward indicator of a causal connection. Stich, for example, cites the case of someone who is asked about Harry's whereabouts, and is told that Harry is in Chicago. It transpires that Harry was not in Chicago, and the person is asked what led him to tell the police that he was. He answers: 'Because I believed he was in Chicago.' This is sufficient for Stich (1983) to assert that appeals to belief provide causal explanations. However, in making such an assertion, the informant is not claiming to have been in an internal state that caused him to utter those words but is, rather, commenting upon the *information* that he had, information which *to the best of his knowledge* was reliable but later proved to be incorrect. In other words, his action was offered as a correct one, but its correctness depended upon the information on which it was based, and it was the *misinformation* which caused his mistake.

A person's complaining that he hears voices through the radiator in his room, that these voices are hostile and critical, and that he does not like to hear them, *does* explain why he engages in the use of earplugs and covers his head with his pillow. It would be a travesty to suggest that this involves vacuous efforts to explain something by reference to itself (i.e., behaviour by behaviour). That someone's earlier behaviour explains his later behaviour is another quite normal and unexceptionable feature of explanation. Earlier in the evening, Larry was drinking many pints of beer. Later in the evening, Larry was staggering around the room and falling over the furniture. Larry's earlier behaviour explains his later behaviour – his drinking has made him drunk, and has (in this case) caused his staggering and falling. Alternatively, on a road journey, Larry, who is driving, engages in talking to his companion Barry, rather than watching the road and monitoring the road signs, and eventually becomes lost – Larry's getting lost is, of course, to be explained in terms of his earlier behaviour, of his carelessness with respect to tracking their route. When Smith and Jones complain about there being a *circularity* to explanations of behaviour by reference to behaviour, they need to consider examples such as these. Nothing mentioned here by way of behavioural explanation has been circular. To identify Larry's current chess move, in his game against Barry, as part of a strategy is, precisely, to locate this move *informatively* as part of a pattern, to see it as building upon prior moves and as opening up the prospect of further moves. To explain 'pawn to Queen's bishop six' as part of a chess strategy is hardly vacuous. It shows the *connection* of this move to prior moves and to likely future moves, a connection which, for those who had not discerned it, can afford quite a deep *explanation* of the current move.

Are we then in a position to defend Ryle (his arguments, his methodology) against the charges of behaviourism? It is not, we submit, really necessary for Ryle to be defended against such charges because Ryle was not a psychological theorist of *any* stripe. Ryle's claims pertain not to the adequacy of 'dispositional' concepts as candidates for inclusion into any theory propounded under the auspices of a scientific psychology. They pertain instead to the meanings of expressions in our ordinary language and to the part which such expressions play in the kinds of explanations (and other discursive activities) we produce in the course of our daily lives. We do not see that Ryle's would-be critics offer any counter-arguments to his actual case. For instance, is there an *argument* which might show that 'belief' – as we ordinarily use it, saying what we ordinarily do say with it – is more like 'thirst' than it is like 'irritable'? Is there an *argument* forthcoming from the critics which shows that the word 'clever' is, contrary to what Ryle says, used to identify things going on inside someone's head? We think not. In fact, many of the would-be critics do, in their deployment of the word 'belief', characteristically employ it in the ways in which Ryle described, as a dispositional word. As mentioned above, Stich encounters the same difficulty with his lady who spoke of the assassination as any one of us would have in saying exactly what beliefs she had about it, and this difficulty arises for him because he is using the word 'belief' in the same way that the rest of us do, a way which Ryle's account (to a substantial extent correctly) describes. While these philosophers polemicise against Ryle they do, in practice, confirm what he says.

It is simply false to say that Ryle advanced the view that *all* 'mental' concepts have a dispositional character for, as mentioned earlier, the whole point of his argument was that there is a great *heterogeneity* amongst the so-called 'mental' vocabulary. He devoted space to considering the way in which 'dispositional' notions relate to 'episodic' ones: 'irritated' is an episodic expression, 'irritable' a quasi-hypothetical, dispositional one. It is, of course, to revert to Fodor's comment about the word 'thirsty', just an elementary mistake to think that 'thirsty' might conceivably be a *dispositional* word!

There is a vast gulf between those who want to expound upon the way 'the mind works' after the fashion of scientific theorists and those who are engaged, instead, with the careful characterisation of some aspects of our ordinary ways of talking. It remains the case that, despite the self-image of the former, much of what they actually do depends deeply upon assumptions – albeit ones adopted in very cavalier fashion – about the ways in which we ordinarily talk. Indeed, despite their overt disparagement of Wittgenstein and Ryle they are, as we shall see, compelled into practical, perhaps unwitting, acceptance of the arguments already advanced by both men. The continuation of our argument raises again the issue of 'explanation' and involves the complaint that:

There's no bear there: the strange case of the disappearing psychology

Fodor's work exhibits many typically Cartesian elements, but their deployment is much influenced by his determination to shape them into the constituents of a 'scientific psychology'. As he frequently reminds us, he is interested in 'science', not philosophy. Considerable trouble arises, however, from this juxtaposition of (fantasised) science with mere philosophising, for, as we have noted, much of his work requires its justification from the rejection of Wittgenstein's and Ryle's arguments. Fodor rightly sees that these thinkers are deeply sceptical of the prospects for a scientific psychology of the kind he envisages – the kind which Ryle characterised as a 'counterpart to Newtonian physics'. That there is no room or need for a mentalistic 'counterpart to Newtonian physics' does not eliminate all prospects of anything that might, legitimately, be called 'scientific psychology'.

We cannot reinforce often enough the point that Wittgenstein's and Ryle's scepticism was not about the prospects for psychology nor, even, about what might properly be termed 'scientific work' within psychology. It was a scepticism towards the 'Newtonian counterpart' conception. A major aspect of Ryle's case against such a programme consisted in pointing out that there did not appear to be any genuinely explanatory work for it to accomplish. If we ask ourselves the question 'What is the explanatory role of Fodor's projected scientific psychology?', we find that it is to explain things which we can already explain. Not for the first time must the notion of 'folk psychology' enter the discussion.

Whatever Fodor says about his concern for 'scientific' questions, his actual problem is a classical philosophical one. He is concerned with the form that our explanations of each other's actions take. Fodor holds that the *explanandum* of those explanations are 'body movements' and the *explanans* are 'mental causes'. This accounts for Fodor's preoccupation with behaviourism (apart from the fact that it was, in his version of the history of the human sciences, the only other significant candidate psychology on the scene prior to Noam Chomsky's and his own interventions). Behaviourists *deny* that 'mental causes' can explain 'body movements', but they share with Fodor the conviction that it is 'body movements' that are to be explained. Fodor's most basic claim, then, is about the kinds of explanations that we give each other for our actions – as when, say, someone asserts that 'he gave her the flowers with the intention of pleasing her'. Such explanations, as he construes them, are of a causal kind, and they invoke 'mental states' such as 'intending to please her' as the causes of such 'bodily movements' as 'giving her the flowers'. Fodor construes the presence of such terms as 'intending' as identifying 'mental causes', and as thereby indicating the presence of a theory of our bodily movements, a theory which explains them in terms of 'psychological' phenomena and which, therefore, makes up a 'folk psychology'. Fodor is convinced that our folk psychology is (broadly) correct. That it is correct is an essential element in his argumentation.

Fodor claims that behaviourists are mistaken insofar as they deny the operation of 'mental causes', and his principal evidence for their actual existence is his construal of the form of the explanations which we ordinarily give each other. 'Intentions', 'beliefs' and 'thoughts' are the things that Fodor identifies as mental causes. Therefore, if these notions do not identify causes of our behaviour, if, in some sense, the 'folk psychology' is fundamentally mistaken, then Fodor's position is eliminated. Thus, his initial assumption is that the explanations which we give for each other's actions are (broadly) correct, and it is, hence, the case that if Fodor's projected scientific psychology were successful, it would give (broadly) the same explanations that we now do give for our conduct. We should explain his 'giving her the flowers' as resulting from his 'intending to please her', having, presumably, always previously understood this statement as specifying a *causal* connection.

The contentious question which arises from Fodor's work is, then, one which pertains to the meanings of things that we ordinarily say. The difference between Fodor and, for example, Ryle, is, as Fodor himself says, over whether 'he gave her the flowers with the intention of pleasing her' qualifies as a causal statement. That it is appears to be a matter of dogmatic assertion on Fodor's part, and this is perhaps to be expected since he nowhere concerns himself with establishing any method for ascertaining that we do indeed understand our words in the way he claims we do. The presence of the word 'because', for him, is enough to signal the existence of a causal claim, but this is merely posited and not demonstrated in his account of the matter. At the very least one would need to inspect a range of constructions involving the use of the word 'because', but Fodor does not supply examples and any analysis of them.

At the very least, then, a cognitive science as envisaged by Fodor seems to be projected to explain what we can (and do) already explain, and, furthermore, to explain those phenomena in much the same way as we already explain them. Fodor, though, is of a scientistic inclination and he is, therefore, inclined to think that only those things which have been established or confirmed by science can be confidently accepted as the case. Thus, from Fodor's Quinean perspective, our 'folk psychology' is very likely to be correct, but we shall only know that this is so when a scientific psychology has been developed which can show that the ingredients of our 'folk psychology' can be incorporated into a properly formulated and empirically tested scientific theory. His inclination to turn to science for such vindication is due to the assumption, common to so many of his contemporaries, that science has inherited the task of metaphysics. This turns out to mean, effectively, that science alone shall determine what kinds of things there are. In the version of this doctrine which is nowadays masterminded by Quine, and which remains so influential, there are only those things which must necessarily be postulated to satisfy the requirements of science (especially physics), and concepts cannot satisfy that requirement unless they proffer identifications for which there is some (physical) 'fact of the matter'. Unless the concepts in question correspond to some distribution of material states, they do not identify something which can play a part in the science described by Quine and so, from the point of view of such a science, the concepts cannot qualify as identifying *anything*. Thus, as far as Quine is concerned, there are no 'meanings' and there are no 'mental states'. It is in relation to this stance that Fodor seeks to achieve the vindication of 'folk psychology'. Fodor is no less a materialist than Quine, and consequently he perceives that the 'challenge' to 'folk psychology' is that it might not be included within a developed science, that notions such as 'belief', 'intention' and so forth might not identify anything that actually exists within the compass of the developed scientific psychology, and that there will be no (material) 'fact of the matter' as to whether a person has an ascribed/avowed belief or intention, and therefore, from the point of view of this science, there would be no such things as beliefs or intentions. Since science is the arbiter of what there really is for those such as Quine and Fodor, for a science to discover that it has no need for notions such as 'belief', 'meaning', 'intention' or 'thought' in its explanations would be for it to establish that there are no such things. Thus, if 'folk psychology' is to be vindicated, it is necessary to establish that the purported 'mental causes' such as 'beliefs', 'intentions' and 'thoughts' actually do exist, that they can truly be the causes that they are (in Fodor's construal, at least) alleged to be. In other words, 'mental states' must be shown to be material states, since for materialists only one material state can be the cause of another.

All of this might seem to make an exercise like Fodor's imperative. Suppose that it were the case that someone like Quine (or like the eliminativists, such as Rorty, Churchland or Stich) were right? Suppose that the progress of science did indeed establish that there are no such things as beliefs, intentions and thoughts. This would presumably make an immense difference, and would have to have extraordinary and far-reaching consequences. It would, it seems, profoundly affect the ways in which we think of ourselves, how we behave towards one another, how we explain ourselves to each other and even how we treat one another. It is, by contrast, part of Wittgenstein's and Ryle's argument about the confusing character of philosophy that it gives the misleading impression of directly controverting our 'ordinary' ways of talking, thinking and understanding and that, therefore, if its arguments are shown to be correct, then this will engender upheavals in our lives. However, on closer inspection, it typically proves that the challenges are by no means so direct as they are made to seem, and are, rather, most usually at cross-purposes with our 'ordinary' ways of thinking, talking, etc., making no substantial contribution to what we do. Having to give up completely the use of expressions like 'belief', 'intention', 'purpose', 'meaning' and so on, because they have been

shown to be scientifically baseless, would surely be a momentous occurrence. But just a moment . . . it is not at all clear that these notions
would have to be given up. The discovery that there are no such *things*
as, for example, beliefs, might seem like an occurrence which would
make an immense difference, but it transpires that it might make no
substantial difference to anything at all.

Fodor's actual attempt to set out a subject-matter for a cognitive
science gradually leads to a significant retrenchment in what that subject-matter could be, since he is compelled by his fundamental conception of the nature of that subject-matter to adopt the restrictive policy of
'methodological solipsism' and to focus upon what he terms 'narrow
content'. (We shall discuss these issues extensively below.) His insistence is that it is the business of psychology to explain the behaviour of
human beings in terms of inner causes, of properties which depend
exclusively upon the physical states of the individual. Thus, in the first
instance, the tactic would be to argue that such 'mental' things as
beliefs, intentions and so forth are, in fact, physical (computational)
states of the organism, because if beliefs are indeed to play an explanatory role relative to physical behaviour, then that must be a *causal* role,
and, of course, only physical phenomena can be causes.[5] Thus, Fodor's
version of the role of 'the language of thought' is that mental (computational) operations are carried out on the formal, physical properties of
representations, rather than their representational character as such.
He endorses Descartes' argument that the states of my mind are independent of the external world, that my thoughts would remain the
same even if the external circumstances changed, and this provides a
further basis for his stipulation that psychology must explain purely on
the basis of properties which are *intrinsic* to the individual. It is the
Cartesian supposition which first comes under pressure, because it is
conceded that when we attribute such 'mental states' as thoughts and
beliefs to people their characterisation depends upon *the context* in
which the people are situated. This is, of course, a rediscovery of a point

---

5 John Searle makes a parallel argument. He claims that: 'The brain is all we
have for the purpose of representing the world to ourselves. . . . Each of our
beliefs must be possible for a being who is a brain in a vat because each of us
is precisely a brain in a vat; the vat is a skull and the "messages" coming in are
coming in by way of impacts on the nervous system' (Searle, 1983, p. 230).
Norman Malcolm gives this peculiar idea a brusque but effective rebuttal:
'Searle says that each of us *is* a brain in a vat, the vat being one's skull. Now if
you *are* your brain then you are inside your own skull. You cannot walk or talk
or see your friends. Searle says that you can receive "messages". But in that
predicament, who wants messages?' (Malcolm, 1986, p. 186).

which was central to Wittgenstein's (and Ryle's) work, though it has been recently reiterated by, amongst others, Putnam (1981), Burge (1979 and 1986) and Stich (1982).

A good example would be one which we have previously used, that of the belief that 'the ice is thin'. As we indicated, someone of whom we might say that he believes that 'the ice is thin' is someone who believes that, for instance, 'the ice is thin relative to the purposes of someone's walking or skating on it'. This person, then, with *this* belief, is someone who could be thinking about the ice on the lake at the bottom of his garden, and about the prospect of a skating party in the afternoon. If, however, we attribute the belief that 'the ice is thin' to a scientist working in an Antarctic research base, then this person would be believing, not that the ice was thin relative to supporting someone's weight whilst skating, but, rather, that the measured thickness of the ice was considerably less this year than, say, a year ago. This clearly shows that what someone can be said to believe, what his or her belief *is*, does not depend upon his or her intrinsic characteristics, but upon features of their context. This case, as put by Putnam, Burge and others, however, is put within the framework of the assumption that the crucial idea is that the 'mental' must 'supervene' upon the 'physical' – that if two individuals are molecule for molecule identical in their physical constitution, then they must *also* be identical in their mental characteristics (for these are, *ex hypothesi*, themselves identical). This point is often made by way of 'Twin Earth' examples. In these examples, it is imagined that two individuals and their worlds are molecule for molecule identical, except for a single variant factor. Thus, it is imagined that Nigel-1 and Nigel-2 are twins in the strictest sense of having identical physical structures down to the finest details, and that they dwell on worlds that are also 'twins', alike in every minute respect such that they could both be called 'Earths' *except for* that single variant factor: the chemical composition of water is different. On Earth-1 (our world, where Nigel-1 lives), the chemical composition of water is H_2O but on Earth-2 (where Nigel-2 lives), its composition is XYZ. (We shall overlook the slight snag in this imaginary scenario as to how Nigel-1 and Nigel-2 can be 'molecule for molecule identical' when they are both made up in large part of 'water'.) The argument is then advanced that when Nigel-1 thinks of water he does not have the same thought, does not think the same thing, as Nigel-2, and that this is because the things they respectively think of are different in their natures. Thus, even though Nigel-1 and Nigel-2 are physically identical in every respect, they are, because of their different environments, different in their *psychological* attributes.

This gives Fodor's programme considerable trouble, for *if* the beliefs, thoughts, intentions, purposes, etc. which we use to explain (*causally* explain, in Fodorian dogma) people's bodily behaviour are not *intrinsic* to the individuals, then they fall outside the domain of psychological explanation *as Fodor has stipulated that domain*. In order to preserve the idea of a 'scientific psychology', Fodor is, then, compelled in important respects to sacrifice his initial conception of his subject-matter. He has to *redefine* his project in such a way as to preserve its central presuppositions. Thus, he adopts the strategy of what he calls 'methodological solipsism' (Fodor, 1981a, pp. 307–38). He does not deny that the identification of (the contents of) beliefs or thoughts depends upon circumstances, but he denies that this affects his fundamental conception of a 'cognitive science'. It means, rather, that he must make explicit a methodological implication of his fundamental assumptions, which is that his inquiry will dispense with *everything that depends upon contextual considerations* and that his projected psychology will continue to focus exclusively upon the intrinsic characteristics, attributes and properties of individuals: it is these intrinsic properties which alone can be construed as causal in the relevant (materialist) sense. Under pressure, however, from arguments about the essentially contextual *identification* of beliefs, thoughts, intentions, etc., he will have to redefine his subject-matter as that of 'narrow content'. The 'content' is that of the belief or thought, what it is we can say someone believes or thinks. As has been indicated, the 'content' arguments say that the content of a thought or belief is contextually sensitive. *Therefore*, Fodor concludes that a thought or belief is made up of *two* components, one which is intrinsic to the organism and one which is contextually dependent – it has both 'narrow' and 'broad' content. Thus, Nigel-1 and Nigel-2 have beliefs with different 'broad content', this difference being a function of the difference in the circumstances in which they live. The fact that the chemical composition of water differs between their worlds does not mean that the ways in which Nigel-1 and Nigel-2 behave differ, since each can think: 'I need a drink of water', and their subsequent conduct of turning on the tap, filling a glass, drinking it, etc. can be identical also, even though what they think about when they think they need a glass of water (and what they actually pour and drink) differs in its chemical composition. The chemical composition of the respective 'waters' plays *no causal role* in the behavioural sequence, from turning on the tap to the eventual drinking, therefore their thought/belief that they 'need a drink of water' has a comparable *causal* role in their behaviour and is, therefore, in important respects, the *same* belief even though what it is a belief about differs. If we could, then, so to speak, subtract the difference resulting from the varying nature of the 'water', we would be left with what was common to their beliefs and this would presumably qualify as what was the same and *intrinsic* to them as individuals. It would be that *part of* their belief which caused them to behave in the same way. Fodor proposes to decompose beliefs in this manner, to separate their 'broad content' (that which depends upon context) from their 'narrow content' (that which remains after we have abstracted out the contextually furnished element(s)). 'Narrow content' is thence the proper subject-matter for a Fodorian scientific psychology.

Just what *does* remain when 'narrow content' is abstracted from 'broad content'? In a masterpiece of understatement, Heil remarks:

> We are thus led to a conception of *narrow mental content*. It is not easy to say what such content is. Indeed, as Fodor points out, given that the meanings of terms in our language are largely externally fixed, those terms are particularly ill-suited for descriptions of the contents of narrow states of mind. (Heil, 1992, p. 54)

Stich, one of the sources of Fodor's difficulties in this realm, but one committed nonetheless to the same general conception of a 'cognitive' psychology, sees that there is a tension between retaining the 'solipsistic' approach and retaining the very concept of 'belief' (Stich, 1983). Like Fodor, Stich insists that there is a need for an explanatory psychology, and that it will require a defensible account of mind. In Stich's view, a properly scientific psychology will conceive of the mind in purely 'syntactic' terms, and will have no need for the 'representational' elements which were so important to Fodor's programme. The mind will be theoretically construed as comprising sequences of operations on forms which have a syntactical organisation, and it is an entirely open question as to whether in describing these we will need to invoke *any* notion of belief. Exactly what sorts of phenomena will be recognised within the kind of explanation Stich envisages he cannot say, just as he cannot precisely specify just what it is about behaviour that his system will explain. We shall require, he thinks, entirely new vocabularies with which to describe the structure and operations of mind, as well as to characterise the behaviour that is to be explained thereby. After all, something like the 'broad/narrow content' problem is *also* involved in the characterisation of human behaviour generally.

It is time to broaden our discussion here in order to develop the point that what we ordinarily refer to as 'human behaviour' is not adequately captured by referring to 'human bodily movements' (a designation shared by Fodor, Stich and most other advocates of scientific-psychological explanations of conduct). It has been argued that, 'narrowly construed', *all* of our activities are (ultimately) just instances of motions of our bodies or parts thereof, and it is only when given 'broad', contextual or, in Ryle's famous phrase, 'thick descriptions',[6] that problems of individuating them as *explananda* can arise. Let us consider, and at some length, the case of the advancing bear.

Suppose that Wayne is walking down a path and is confronted by a bear which advances on him. He runs away. Called upon to give a causal explanation of Wayne's behaviour, i.e., his running away, we should ordinarily say that what caused him to run away was – the bear! Or, perhaps, we should say that the cause was the bear's advancing on him. However, at this point, the fact that Fodor envisages a psychology becomes important. The fact that a bear is advancing on someone is not a *psychological* fact. Hence, the bear's advance would not, could not, appear in any psychological explanation. Psychology, as Fodor understands it, must explain behaviour only in terms of characteristics of the individual, and so, from such a psychological point of view – as Fodor stipulates what this amounts to – it must be the 'internal representation' of the bear in Wayne's mind/brain which causes him to run away. Furthermore, suppose that Dwayne is walking along a forest path and begins to hallucinate – he hallucinates a bear in front of him, one which is advancing on him, is overcome by fear, turns and runs away. From the point of view of any individual-centred psychology, there is no significant difference between Wayne and Dwayne. The hallucination of a bear must, presumably, be represented in Dwayne's mind/brain in a way (although perhaps not by the same 'mechanisms') that is identical to that in which an actual bear is represented, and since it is the representational state which causes behaviour then it is this representation of the bear which causes the running movements of both Wayne and Dwayne: in terms of 'bodily behaviour' there is no difference whatsoever in their locomotions.

What Fodor's psychology purports to explain, then, are the 'locomotions' of Wayne and Dwayne, and it does this by showing that they are the product of the same 'mental state', namely, a representation of an advancing bear. From the standpoint of this psychology,

6 Ryle, 'The Thinking of Thoughts', in Ryle, 1971a.

then, it does not matter whether or not there is a bear there. Indeed, it is outside the competence of psychology to establish whether there is or is not a bear there. It is not the psychologist's task to investigate whether there is a bear there, whether it is a real bear or an animated model of one, etc. It is an interesting account, then, which ends up positing no *psychological* difference between someone who has been frightened by a bear and someone who has hallucinated a bear! The explanatory business of psychology, as an envisaged 'scientific' discipline set up to produce specialist knowledge, differs from that explanatory work which we do in our ordinary relationships with one another: Fodor's 'explanation' neither rivals nor confirms the explanations that we would routinely give as lay people for Wayne's or Dwayne's behaviour. What we have to explain, after all, is *not* the 'same behaviour' in any sense we would ordinarily honour: someone who is running about under the influence of an hallucination is *not* behaving in the same way as someone who runs away from something frightening. They are, however, the same in Fodor's scheme, insofar as they are engaging in the same bodily behaviours; their arms are moving in the same pumping motions and their legs are taking the same running steps, etc. Since these are indeed bodily movements they can have only some (bodily) cause, and since they are the same (kind of) bodily movements they must have the same (kind of) cause, which, for Fodor, might be that a 'tokening' of a bear has appeared in the same place in their cognitive system, even though their respective tokenings had different sources, one caused by the physical appearance of a bear and the other caused by hallucinating one. Even if we were to accept Fodor's view that it is a 'tokening' of a bear within someone's head which causes his behaviour, it is certainly *not* the case that, for the requirements of explaining Wayne's or Dwayne's behaviour, this would obviate the explanation we should ordinarily be in a position to give, nor would it obviate the differences between the behaviours to be explained. Wayne is running away from something, but Dwayne is not – and Wayne is certainly not running away from a representation of a bear, but from the bear itself. Dwayne is certainly not running away from a bear, though that is what he imagines himself to be doing.

That there is, in Fodor's very narrow sense of psychology, no difference between Wayne and Dwayne does not mean that there *is* no difference, even no *psychological* difference, between the two. It is, for our mundane purposes of explanation, the bear (or the bear's advance) and not Wayne's inner representation of it which caused him to run away. Perhaps the approach of a bear does not count as a psychological cause but it is nonetheless the cause of Wayne's behaviour. Indeed, the notion that Wayne's running is caused by the 'tokening' of the bear is parasitic upon our ordinary explanation as to why anyone would run away from a bear – because they are dangerous animals, might attack you and so forth: it is facts about bears and what they might do which provide the explanation.

Much ado about nothing

The notion of 'belief' often serves as the primary example of 'intensional states' more generally, and it can continue to serve that role in this section of our discussion. Beliefs are certainly appealed to in our ordinary explanations of action and it is frequently alleged, though without much deliberation, that they are there invoked as causes of behaviour. As part of the so-called 'folk psychology' then, beliefs are up for scrutiny as candidates for inclusion in the envisaged scientific psychology (or cognitive science). This, however, places the notion of 'belief' in question. Are beliefs the sort of things that can be included in the 'ontology' of a *bona fide* scientific theory? In other words, are they the sort of things that a properly constructed scientific theory could recognise as existing? Are the kinds of explanations within which beliefs are invoked ones which will be *scientifically* valid? Suppose that these questions are answered in the negative. Since scientific theories are commonly taken as yardsticks for what there really is, then if the notion of 'belief' (or any other intensional/mental state) fails to qualify for inclusion within the theoretical apparatus of cognitive science, this would, to many, seem to suggest that there are no such things as beliefs. Insofar as the 'ontology' of scientific theories in this area is presumed to be a materialist one, then the decisive question as to whether or not beliefs could be included in the scientific apparatus would depend upon whether or not beliefs are realised in material states. If not, then, in these terms, there would be no such things as beliefs.

How are we to confront such proposals? 'There are no such things as beliefs.' What an astonishing claim to make! How could that be? How could we be mistaken in this way, and what would the determination that we have made such a mistake signify? What kind of difference could such a realisation actually make? Presumably it would be immense, so far-reaching that we cannot fully imagine its manifold ramifications. These, at least, are the kind of unguarded reactions one might have to the bold, bare statement that science has shown (or could in principle show) that there are no such things as beliefs and that they have no place in the explanation of our behaviour. These are, moreover, the kinds of reactions which are cultivated by those who foster the controversy over 'the reality of belief' by presenting the debate as one whose outcome will have momentous consequences for us all.

There are, it is claimed, arguments which should encourage us to take seriously the view that there are no such things as beliefs. Stich, for example, states that he, like Candide, embraces a 'reluctant scepticism' about beliefs:

> Much as I would like the story [that we have beliefs and act on their basis] to be true, I simply cannot get it to square with the facts. In the pages that follow my focus will be on the folk psychological concept of belief, and my central thesis will be that this concept *ought not* to play any significant role in a science aimed at explaining human cognition and behaviour. I shall also argue that, despite appearances to the contrary, the folk psychological notion of belief *does-not* play a role in the best and most sophisticated arguments put forward by contemporary cognitive scientists. (Stich, 1983, p. 5)

He is satisfied that arriving at such a conclusion will have a world-shaking, although not undesirable, impact:

> Deprived of its empirical underpinnings, our age-old conception of the universe within will crumble just as certainly as the venerable conception of the external universe crumbled during the Renaissance. But that analogy ultimately suggests an optimistic conclusion. The picture of the external universe which has emerged from the rubble of the geocentric view is more beautiful, more powerful, and more satisfying than anything Aristotle or Dante could imagine. (Stich, 1983, p. 246)

Fodor, likewise, is firmly convinced that very much is at stake here, and that if his 'realism' about beliefs were to be proved mistaken this would show that not just he, but all of us, had made an immense mistake. This would, he tells us, be the biggest boob in the history of human thought:

> if it isn't literally true that my wanting is causally responsible for my reaching, and my itching is causally responsible for my scratching, and my believing is causally responsible for my saying . . . if none of that is literally true, then practically everything I believe about anything is false and it's the end of the world. (Fodor, 1990, p. 156)

So strong are Fodor's philosophical convictions on this point that he cannot imagine that he (and, by the same token, the rest of us) are mistaken. He cannot, further, imagine what alternative there could possibly be to operating with 'folk psychological' notions such as 'belief' – to the extent that it seems that the impossibility of conceiving of an alternative indicates that there cannot be one. Eliminativists are not, however, deterred by such considerations and continue to maintain that science *will* show that talk of beliefs and explanations of actions in terms of them involve nothing but superstition, and that the practices which involve such things will become, like other superstitions before them, outdated.

There can be no doubt, then, that those involved in this controversy consider that there is a good deal at stake, and that its import has bearing not only upon the technical concerns of a 'cognitive science' but upon explanatory and ascriptive practices shared by all of us: progress in this envisaged 'cognitive science' will present a challenge to the 'commonsense' psychology to which we all (tacitly) subscribe and on the basis of which we conduct the affairs of our organised lives. And, of course, the casting of the debate in this form provides much room for blustering about those who are 'on the side of scientific progress' and those who are (suspiciously) resistant to this, about those who are 'philosophical reactionaries' and those who seek to decide scientific matters on *a priori* grounds, and similar irrelevancies.

Before reacting as though a profound challenge to life as we know it was before us, we should consider whether there really is very much at stake in all this, whether the challenge is *actually* one which could make any difference to anything. Consider Fodor's concern that, if it were true that there are no such things as beliefs then everything he thought he had known would turn out to be false. Yet if it were shown that there were no beliefs, then it would have been shown thereby that there *never were* any, and so, presumably, the world today would be just the same as it has always been. If science did indeed (*per impossibile*) show us that there were no beliefs, it is not as though something would have been *removed from the world,* or that something which had been there has ceased to be (as with dinosaurs and dodos). No, there are no beliefs now, and there were no beliefs then, nor will there ever be any. Presumably, the *only* respect in which the *world* is changed would be the respect in which the *idea* that there were beliefs has been eliminated. Nothing else would be changed and all of the things which had made it seem as though there *were* beliefs remain the same. We'll deny ourselves the cheap jibe that the main change brought about by the demonstration that there are no beliefs would be to show that the belief that there are such things as beliefs is false (but only because it has been made many times before).

As Dennett has perspicuously noted, the suggestion that there is a very great deal at stake with respect to the reality of belief is accompanied by a much less loudly trumpeted acknowledgement that nothing of much actual, practical consequence follows from it. In his 'Mid-Term Examination',[7] Dennett remarks that those contemporary philosophers who are *ostensibly* in disagreement about the reality of beliefs (and other referents of intensional idioms) (i.e., making use of 'belief', 'intention' and other 'mental' terms) are nonetheless in agreement upon the *indispensability* of such idioms, that there is a convergence upon what he terms 'Quine's double standard', to wit, that 'strictly speaking, there are no such things as beliefs, even if *speaking as if there were* is a practical necessity' (Dennett, 1987, p. 348). Confusing as it may seem, the prospect begins to loom that a difference which might seem to be immense, and immensely far-reaching – between a situation in which we do have beliefs, and in which these do cause our actions, and one in which there are no such things as beliefs, and the actual causes of our actions are things of which we are ignorant – may prove to be a difference *which makes no difference at all.*

Within the available space we cannot review the full scope of the contemporary dispute and must focus upon only a couple of pivotal points in the controversy. We will, therefore, take the opposition between Fodor and Dennett as providing such a pivotal issue, one whose assessment should, we hope, go a long way to *dissolving* the controversy within which it is, indeed, pivotal.

The intensity of Fodor's conviction that there *really are such things as beliefs* has been instantiated in the quotation given above. Fodor dubs himself an 'industrial strength realist', one who insists that beliefs do exist as material states of the mind/brain and are actually causes of behaviour. These *must* figure in the explanatory scheme of a cognitive science. Dennett is not, by any means, a polar opponent of Fodor's. He shares broadly the same materialist assumptions, especially the assumption that something has 'industrial strength reality' only if it exists as an identifiable physical state. Thus, both Fodor and Dennett are agreed that if beliefs, for example (or 'intensional states' more generally), are to be real, then they must be specific physical states (or, more technically, 'information-bearing neural structures') within the organism. Their disagreement is, however, over whether such states/structures do exist. Fodor insists that they must, while Dennett denies that they do.

7 Dennett, 'Mid-Term Examination: Compare and Contrast', in Dennett, 1987, pp. 339–50.

Fodor wants to assert that beliefs are real. Does Dennett want to deny that they are? Yes and no. He wants to deny that beliefs are real in the sense that Fodor wants to assert that they are, but he does not want to deny *all* reality to beliefs. He aims to defend a position about beliefs which is realist, but which is more 'moderate' than Fodor's 'industrial strength realism'. Thus, beliefs can be said to be real, but they are real in the sense in which 'the centre of gravity' or the 'North Pole' of the globe may be said to be real. You can walk to the top of the world and stand on it and inspect the ground around you and you will not find any particular bit of earth, ice, metal or anything else which is the 'North Pole'. Nonetheless, you can stand upon the earth there at a location which can be calculated as that point at which the magnetic lines of force converge. Similarly, you can examine the interior of a human body and you will find in it such organs as the spleen, the kidney, the small intestine and the heart, but you will not find there any comparable item which is its 'centre of gravity'. Nonetheless, you can apply appropriate calculations to identify a point within the organism around which its capacity for balance is structured. Human beings have beliefs in the same sense in which the earth has a North Pole and a human body has a centre of gravity. They do not have beliefs in the sense in which a body has a spleen, a heart and so on.

So, people *do* have beliefs after all? If only the issues were as simple as that. They do . . . and they don't. Well, it is *useful* and *effective* to treat them *as if* they do. Though, in fact, they don't.

Dennett, being a materialist like Fodor, is convinced that the business of a cognitive science will involve explanation on the basis of only those things which can act as *causes*, namely, physical states of the organism, and, of course, beliefs (and other intensional states, so-called) are not such states. Thus, *in this sense* people do *not* have beliefs, and their activities are *not* to be explained in terms of them. However, Dennett takes an 'instrumentalist' line with respect to explanation in terms of beliefs. Explaining people's behaviour by reference to their beliefs is something with a proven track record. If we *assume* (as Fodor and his contemporaries typically do) that what they term 'folk psychology' has a *central purpose*, and that purpose is to predict the behaviour of other human beings, then we can claim that 'folk psychology' has been very successful. Indeed, presumably 'folk psychology' has been a *necessity*: the prediction of the behaviour of other people (or of computing systems) on the basis of the actual material causes of their behaviour would be just too complex for us as a practical matter, and it is only in the terms of – or presumably something equivalent to – the 'intensional idiom' that we can comprehend such behaviour well enough to predict it. *Fortunately*, it is the case that the (intensional) terms which we can comprehend can elucidate the behaviour of others. People do act, and consistently so, *as if* they have beliefs. So, *do* they have beliefs?

Not in the sense that such 'intensional states' are, as Fodor (and Searle also) would say, *intrinsic* to the persons who are attributed with such beliefs. Whatever is causing people to behave in the ways they do are, *ex hypothesi*, material states of the mind/brain, and these states do not comprise realisations of beliefs, any more than material states of a body realise its centre of gravity. The 'centre of gravity' is something which, in a sense, we attribute to the body, something which we identify according to a system of co-ordinates via a process of calculation, but it is not a material part of the body itself. One's age may be computed in Gregorian calendar 'years' and lunar 'months', but neither the Gregorian convention nor the moon's periodicity of rotation comprise biological data about the ageing body. Nonetheless, someone's 'age' is a fact about *him*. In the same way, then, beliefs are things which we attribute to a person, on the basis of procedures for ascription. Thus, an individual to whom certain beliefs are ascribed does not *intrinsically* have those beliefs, but only the beliefs which someone else attributes to him or her. If the person making the attribution of the belief were to follow different ascriptive procedures, ones which would lead to a different outcome with respect to the belief ascribed, then the person's belief would be different. What a person's belief would be, then, would depend not upon him as an individual, but upon who was attributing the belief to him, and how the ascriber was doing so.

Dennett's is thus an 'instrumentalist' account of the notion of 'belief'. That is, the notion of 'belief' is one which we adopt because it is, as it has proved to be, useful. We have an objective, a purpose, which is the prediction of people's behaviour – including our own – and we have found that treating people *as if* they had beliefs, engaging in whatever practices we have for attributing beliefs to them, provides us with sufficiently satisfactory predictions of their behaviour for all practical purposes. Thus, it seems, *whatever 'folk psychology' may suppose*, 'beliefs' are not to be regarded as inner states, but, so to speak, convenient abstractions. They are practically indispensable because, on the one hand, they work and because, on the other, they are cognitively manageable, providing us with means for *simplifying* the complexities to the point at which we can comprehend them. Whatever the purposes of cognitive science, with its projected capacity to comprehend the full complexities of the actual causal situation, for the operating purposes of daily life the application of the 'intensional stance' will remain the only feasible way of keeping track of things.

We are, to use Dennett's favourite example, in possession of a full 'scientific' understanding of the inner, causal operations of the computer, in terms of programs running and of the ways in which these are 'realised' in the machine's electronics, but those who are attempting to make practical use of a chess-playing computer cannot possibly respond to its play in *those* terms but must, rather, work out its play *as if it were* another chess-playing person, in terms of ideas of chess strategy, beliefs about strategic intentions, etc. In other words, although we *possess* the scientific understanding of what goes on inside a computer, in using one for chess play (or any other purpose) we relate to it in terms of (or something closely related to) the 'intensional stance'. It is because of such arguments that Dennett figures that he can conclude (at least jocularly) that philosophers in general – with their agreement upon the *practical* indispensability of the 'intensional idiom' – 'are gradually being persuaded that Dennett is right. But that is no doubt an illusion of perspective' (Dennett, 1987, p. 350).

No doubt it is. But let us note that the disagreement between Fodor and Dennett might be regarded as one to be considered in terms of their characterisations of the so-called 'folk psychology' itself. Let us also note that the supposedly far-reaching implications of the controversy about the 'reality of belief' have to do with the upheaval that it promises for what we 'ordinarily believe', for our 'commonsense' or 'folk psychology'. Consider, now, that the differences between Fodor and Dennett can be construed as differences about the nature of that 'commonsense' or 'folk psychology'. These are not, however, differences which are made manifest *in the ways in which we ordinarily speak.* There is no specific difference to the kinds of remarks which follow in our ordinary uses of words such as 'believe' ('intend', 'think' and the rest of the 'intensional idiom') from whether or not we accept either realist or instrumentalist philosophical views. Philosophers of both persuasions talk, in their off-duty moments, in much the same way, using such words like the rest of us do, and, of course, it is the case that 'the rest of us', when we use such words in our ordinary discourse, do not *align ourselves thereby* with philosophers of one persuasion or the other. Fodor is certain that when we speak of 'beliefs' we are speaking of things which must exist as material states, and which do serve as causes of our bodily behaviours, but this is not because of any (if you will forgive our usage here) *intrinsic* properties of our utterances featuring the word 'belief' (or 'believes', etc.), but, rather, is a product of the terms on which Fodor approaches those utterances, of the very *preconceptions* (essential only to his metaphysical commitments) with which he reads them. Dennett, as we have seen, has a somewhat different set of preconceptions, and maintains that people behave and talk *as if* their behaviour was caused by their beliefs, and it is, therefore, within the very meaning of his proposal that people will speak and act *in the very same ways* as they would if Fodor's realist convictions were true. Thus, there would be *no* detectable difference in the conduct and discourse of persons *whichever* theory were correct. Perhaps, then, the conclusion to draw is that nothing in the practical conduct and discourse of people *hinges* upon the truth of materialist or instrumentalist conceptions of 'belief' (and other 'intensional states') and that it is the philosophical differences themselves which are immaterial.

Perhaps, indeed, the situation which arises with respect to 'beliefs' and other 'intensional states' is one which has arisen before, and which is characteristically involved in sceptical claims, wherein it *appears* that philosophers are straightforwardly and directly confronting something that we ordinarily say and, allegedly, believe, but wherein it transpires that the confrontation, if there actually is one, is by no means straight-forward. The classic case is, of course, scepticism about *knowledge*. The sceptic asserts that we cannot say we know anything, because we cannot have the requisite degree of certainty. This might sound like a direct challenge to our proclivity to say such things as 'I know Mike Ball's phone number' – if the sceptic is right, must such a mundane claim be false? Now, the sceptic does not contest such a claim directly, for that would be to say, flatly, 'You do not know Mike Ball's phone number' and to mean by that, say, that the claimant has got the number wrong, misidentified it as 061-445-1978 when, in fact, it is 061-445-1987. In the specific sense in which the claimant says he knows the number, the sceptic must concede that the claimant does know it – dialling this number will bring Mike Ball to the phone (if he is in). In the sense, then, in which we *ordinarily* claim to know such things, there are require-ments which, if satisfied, entitle us to say that we do indeed know such things, and the sceptic does not wish to contest *these* claims because, after all, this would involve him in finding out about, for example, Mike Ball's phone number, which is, of course, an utter irrelevance to the sceptic's concern. The sceptic wants to argue that, *even when someone does, in the ordinary sense, know something, it still cannot relevantly, for philosophical purposes, be said that he really knows something*. In short, the sceptic does not want to contest our 'ordinary' claims to know on the basis of the same standards against which they are offered; he wants, rather, to test such claims against some *other* standard, one which the sceptic will choose to view (typically without further justification) as 'higher' or 'stricter'. It is significant, therefore, that, as Dennett puts it, the Quinean 'double standard' involves the contention that *'strictly* speaking' [our italics] there are no such things as beliefs, 'even if *speaking as if there were* is a practical necessity [our italics]' (Dennett, 1987 p. 348). '*Strictly* speaking' seeks to *elevate* one claim above another while conceding that, of course, the supposedly rival claims are not made relative to the same requirements, while labelling this stance a 'double standard' indicates the extent to which it seeks to insinuate the disparaging contrast between 'true' and (merely) 'convenient'.

What this means is that by the standards according to which we make them, claims about people's beliefs are often simply *correct or true*. When we claim, for example, that Mrs Thatcher never really believed in free markets we are making a claim about *what Mrs Thatcher believed* and not claiming that *there are such things as beliefs*. The claim that Mrs Thatcher never really believed in free markets is the claim that, though Mrs Thatcher always insisted upon the virtue of unfettered market forces, it turned out that, in practice, she was not apt to leave such markets free if their operation portended results she did not like. This is, of course, a claim about what Mrs Thatcher did or did not believe, and there is evidence which can be cited for and against the claim. The point of the evidence is that it bears upon the issue of whether Mrs Thatcher *did or did not believe* the thing in question, whether she really believed in the virtues of unfettered markets or whether *she really believed something else*. As a matter of fact, the evidence with respect to this particular belief of Mrs Thatcher's might be ambiguous, but it is nonetheless the case that we can conceive the evidence on the relevant point being so unequivocal that it established, conclusively, that Mrs Thatcher did not actually believe what she said she believed (or that, indeed, she did). What counts as evidence for or against the proposition 'Mrs Thatcher did not – really – believe in free markets' is not something that hinges upon either realist or instrumentalist preconceptions. The *basis* on which we decide whether Mrs Thatcher believed one thing or the other is our scrutiny of the relevant aspects of *her record*, on the strength of the various things that she said and did and the degree of consistency between them. Establishing that Mrs Thatcher did indeed believe in the unfettered operations of free markets does not require or involve investigating *any internal states she may have been in*. The standards of correctness which we ordinarily invoke for correctly determining what Mrs Thatcher – or anyone else – believes are entirely *independent of* questions as to whether her holding such beliefs involves her having been in any particular state.

Stich, by contrast, seeks to give an account of 'belief' in this way: when someone attributes a belief to another person, he is claiming that this other person is in the same internal state as the attributor would be if he were caused to utter the same expressions of belief which the other has emitted. This is assuredly not what any speaker of the ordinary language is saying or means when he says that X believes Y. Saying that Smith believes that Jones is a murderer is simply saying – in any ordinary usage – that, as far as Smith is concerned, it is true that Jones is a murderer. Stich's account is not, then, an account of what anyone using his ordinary language means by saying 'Smith believes Jones is a murderer', and, consequently, it cannot be the case that the considerations in Stich's account of 'belief' can have any bearing upon what it would take to establish – according to our ordinary standards – whether Smith really does (or does not) hold the belief attributed to him. Establishing by those standards that Smith *does* hold the belief does not establish anything at all about the existence of hypothesised inner states of the sort postulated by Stich and his fellow cognitivists. The question of when we say that a person believes something (i.e., *on what bases*), and the question of what we mean when we say of someone that he believes something, are both very different questions from the one which these contemporary philosophers persist in debating, namely, 'What kinds of things could beliefs be, if indeed people can be said to have them?' The two prior questions can be given meaningful and correct answers in disregard of a resolution of this latter debating topic. It is, clearly, *the materialist premises of their argument alone* which make it seem as if there were something controversial at stake in the debate amongst contemporary philosophers of mind about beliefs.

The 'announcement' that there are no such things as beliefs for people to have appears newsworthy only on the supposition that people will 'ordinarily' disagree about this. In fact, in announcing this, the philosopher is merely reiterating, in a distorted form, a truth of the elementary grammar of things. We quite ordinarily recognise that someone's 'having a belief' is utterly dissimilar to his having some particular physical characteristic. We can see from inspecting someone's face that he has acne spots or that she has a scar, but we know very well that we cannot determine on the same basis whether someone has a particular belief – looking at someone's nose, eyes, skin, etc. does not tell us what he or she believes. The materialist philosopher makes 'having a physical characteristic' the hallmark for all legitimate talk about someone's having a characteristic, and it is only on the basis of this *stipulation* (for it is certainly no 'discovery') that it becomes possible to declare that 'there are no such things as beliefs'. This is not, however, in contradistinction to what we ordinarily understand, to wit, that having a belief is nothing like having a scar on your face or a lesion in your brain. Of course, in everyday life, we do not treat cases of 'having something' which are not cases of 'having a physical character-istic' as if they were, at best, secondary, inferior or diluted cases of 'having something', as though their actuality were somehow more doubtful or contestable than those in which 'having something' con-sisted in the possession of some physical mark, substance or attribute. Dennett gets caught up in wanting to insist that 'centres of gravity' are real, but *not quite as real as*, say, brain lesions – rather than simply acknowledging that the senses in which one may 'have something' are simply varied. Considering the restricted auspices under which ma-terialist philosophers declare that 'there are no such things as beliefs', we might answer that no speaker of the 'ordinary language', on the strength of his speaking that language, ever supposed that there were.

The *indispensability* of the 'intensional idioms' is perhaps now more intelligible, and the roles which such notions purport to play in the envisaged (fantasised) 'cognitive science' may be seen more perspicu-ously as *orthogonal* to those which they play in the 'ordinary language' which is their home. The temptation of those who argue for their *practical indispensability* is to suggest that this is due to the fact that these terms are used for many other purposes *besides* their psychological-explanatory ones, but we are suggesting here that such expressions do not play the part of a 'folk psychology' *at all*.

The concept of 'belief' is a very complex one. It can, for example, be used to contrast with 'know', but it can also be used to mean the same as 'know'. Thus, someone who says that he knows Smith to be a murderer might be asked whether he knows this or only believes it, and might concede that he only believes it. Someone who says he believes in God would not perhaps be challenged in quite the same way: to say that he believes in God is the same as saying (for him) that he *knows* He exists. Similarly, 'believes' can sometimes be used to express uncertainty, but also, on occasion, certainty. 'I believe you're planning to take a new job' can express the fact that one is repeating hearsay, is asking for confirmation about what one has previously – although less than entirely reliably – been told. This would be an expression of uncertainty. By contrast, a question of the form: 'Do you really believe it, or do you still have those doubts about it?' can be answered with a straightforward: 'No doubts remain. I believe it now', expressing certainty. Although we cannot explore its many dimensions here, we can offer a summary account of the reason why the notion of 'belief' is (so to speak) indispensable in our lives. This is primarily because the role of the expression 'belief' and the verb 'to believe' is very much bound up with the evaluation of information. These terms belong to a variety of *information-grading* expressions. Their import is not, then, with respect to (implied) claims about the physical states in which speakers are, but about the information which they (claim to) possess.

We should not normally say (to choose a random example) of Graham that he *believes* he has a job at the research laboratory in the circumstance in which Graham *does* have a job at the research laboratory. However, we might come to say of Graham that he believes he has a job at the research laboratory because of the situation he is in with respect to information about the laboratory's closure. He worked until late last night, then went home, after which the company officials came in, closed the lab, and installed the security personnel to prevent re-admission. Graham no longer has a job, but does not yet know this – his information is out of date, and so we say that he *believes* he has a job and, in so saying, carry the implication that he is mistaken *about his still having a job*. The interest is, of course (in such cases) in *what is the case*, whether what someone *says* is the case is *in fact the case*.

The ideal might be to check extensively whether what is said to be the case *is* the case, then we will know whether the information someone gives us is true, but, of course, it is a feature of our practical life that we often have to decide, solely on the basis of what someone says, whether what he says is the case or not. For example, we need to take the train home. When does the last train depart? We ask our host. He tells us that it leaves at midnight. We cannot ring the railway timetable service (it is closed) nor go down to the station and check: we have only the host's word. Should we rely on that? What is the information given by our host actually worth? We can only test this by going down to the station and checking for ourselves, but the reason for asking is precisely to decide whether we need to go down to the station yet. That the host *says* the train is at midnight does not ensure that it is. How good is the host's information? Well, one thing which the host can do is to give us an indication of what he thinks the information is worth – and words such as 'believe' and 'know' can figure in such an estimation. Thus, the host might say: 'I believe the last train leaves at midnight, but it's been a while since I used the trains myself.' The information that the host can provide is not perhaps entirely baseless, and to the best of his knowledge the train does leave at midnight, but he is far from certain about this, and so the information he is supplying is not to be entirely relied upon. Jones says: 'Smith, I am no murderer. Can't you believe me?' and Smith replies: 'Jones, I do believe you.' Jones claims that something is unequivocally the case, that he did not kill Brown, and asks whether Smith sets any store by what he tells him, whether Smith now agrees that it was not Jones who killed Brown. Smith has indicated his agreement, that he believes what Jones tells him. Had Smith said: 'I find it hard to believe what you tell me', this might have been a comment on the unconvincing character of the defence that Jones has been putting up, a complaint that there are flaws in the story, and an invitation for Jones to give other, and more convincing, details. Smith is not asserting that it is hard for him to perform a mental act – believing – one which, with more strenuous effort, he might accomplish, but is, rather, commenting on the quality of Jones' evidence, on the *credibility* of his defence against the charge made against him. (It should be borne in mind that by 'eliminating' such notions as 'belief' one would *also* be 'eliminating' notions like 'credibility', 'trustworthiness' and many others.)

We could continue to elaborate many more instances and arguments around these basic points, but would only conclude that there will be a continuing role for the family of 'information grading' expressions to which 'believe' belongs as long as *the evaluation of information* continues to figure as an important feature of our social lives. It is impossible to see how developments in cognitive science could obviate such needs and, therefore, impossible to see why such expressions should – let alone how they could – be eliminated from the language. If we were to continue to contrast cases in which the person who relayed information was wholly confident in it with those in which he was not (as with 'know' and 'believe'), and if we were to continue to distinguish between information whose factual status has been established and information which is only reasonably though not decisively well-founded, then we are going to continue to require a term like 'belief'. If we eliminated 'belief', we should simply need a 'functional equivalent' to it, and thus hostility towards the word 'belief' would prove merely to be another instance of the kind of animosity towards notations to which, as Wittgenstein noted, philosophers are prone.

The ways in which a notion like 'belief' is used are learned by speakers as a part of their acquisition of their ordinary language, and it is on this most fundamental issue – the nature of language learning – that we discern significant differences between proponents of cognitivism, such as Chomsky and Fodor, and ourselves. Fodor, for example, argues that the acquisition by a child of its native tongue is an accomplishment which requires us to postulate the *pre*-existence of *another* language – 'the language of thought' – which the learner uses to express for himself the 'meanings' of the words he is acquiring and the 'rules' governing their use. He calls this internal language 'mentalese', noting that its structure can only be recovered *by analysis* and not by interrogating the child who is depending upon it. His problem, then, is to show how such a pre-existing, 'internal' language can be intelligibly ascribed, not to the child as a person, but to its central nervous system (primarily the brain). The Chomskian roots of this doctrine are quite clear and explicitly acknowledged, but Fodor proffers a more 'radical' perspective than Chomsky's on the nature and 'richness' of the postulated 'cognitive apparatus' involved in learning how to talk, as we shall see.

The problems here ramify, and we shall begin by taking issue with Fodor's invocation of the computer analogy as a means of portraying what could possibly be meant by an 'internal language'. We shall then proceed to unpack the assumptions upon which he erected his theory of 'the language of thought', arguing that none of them are, as he appears to think, 'unavoidable'.

Who needs the 'language of thought'?

Fodor advances two main lines of argument. The first is that the computer is a good model for the mind on the grounds that it involves the material realisation of a set of representations; the very existence of the computer shows the possibility of a 'private language', one which is, so to speak, 'built in' and not learned. This is instantiated by 'machine language'. Fodor asserts that: 'whatever Wittgenstein proved, it cannot have been that it is impossible that a language should be private in whatever sense the machine language of a computer is, for there *are* such things as computers, and whatever is actual is possible' (Fodor, 1975, p. 68). Secondly, Fodor argues that the existence of the computational 'machine language' gives us an appropriate model for conceiving of how the mind/brain could represent or implement the postulated internal language 'mentalese' – thought to be necessary in the explanation of natural language acquisition.

Fodor argues that:

> Real computers characteristically use at least two different languages: an input/output language in which they communicate with their environment and a machine language in which they talk to themselves i.e. in which they run their computations. . . . My point is that, though the machine must have a compiler if it is to use the input/output language, it doesn't also need a compiler for the machine language. What avoids an infinite regression of compilers is the fact that the machine is *built* to use the machine language. Roughly, the machine language differs from the

input/output language in that its formulae directly correspond to computationally relevant physical states of the machine: The physics of the machine thus guarantees the sequences and operations it runs through in the course of its computations respect the semantic constraints on formulae of its internal language. (Fodor, 1975, p. 66)

Further,

The critical property of the machine language of computers is that its formulae can be paired directly with computationally relevant physical states of the machine in such a fashion that the operations the machine performs respect the semantic constraints on formulae in the machine code. Token machines states are, in this sense, interpretable as tokens of the formulae. Such a correspondence can *also* be effected between physical states of the machine and formulae of the input/output code, but only by first compiling these formulae i.e. only by first translating them into the machine language. This expresses the sense in which machines are 'built to use' their machine language and are *not* 'built to use' their input/output codes. . . . It also suggests an empirical theory: When you find a device using a language it was not built to use, assume the way it does this is by translating the formulae of that language into formulae which correspond directly to its computationally relevant states. (Fodor, 1975, p. 67)

The most striking thing about these remarks is the manner in which Fodor literalises the metaphoric expressions which are employed in talk about computers in order to make it sound as though there are some actual linguistic operations involved on the part of computers. Thus he speaks of the language which computers 'use', of computers 'talking to themselves' and of 'translation' between input/output codes and their machine language, thereby rather insidiously insinuating the impression that computers actually *possess* languages, thus permitting him to argue that the language computers possess cannot be one that they have learned, for computers don't learn – thus, if they have a language it can't be one they have learned, so it must, so to speak, have been 'built in'.

This is immensely strategic for Fodor, in allowing him to avoid the infinite regress argument which results from the conception that a language is something which is – necessarily – learned. The plausibility of the claim that languages are not necessarily learned is established if it can be claimed that there is a language which has not been learned, i.e. one which is built in. If a language can be 'built in' to the wirings of a computer then why cannot language – a system of representations – be 'built in' to the neural networks of the brain by, presumably, evolution?

It is hard to see why Fodor should think that these manoeuvrings serve in any way to counter Wittgenstein's arguments against a private language or actually has any bearing whatever on them. First of all, the computer 'languages' which Fodor talks about are not, of course, the languages *of the computer*, are not languages which have somehow acquired their character as a language through the development of the electronic wirings of the computer. These languages are, after all, the creations of a human *community*, and their actual character fits very closely with Wittgenstein's conceptions, insofar as their development has been interwoven with the developing activities and needs of social groups – those of computer designers and users. Furthermore, the representational powers of these languages are ones which obtain relative to the computer programmers and users, and it is through them that programmers and users can represent to themselves and each other the various states, functions and operations of the machines that they use – these languages are designed so that they can be understood, learned and used in programming by programmers, and also can be used by them to manipulate the machines to effect certain kinds of outputs. The capacity of these languages to represent is, then, of course, dependent upon their embeddedness within the relationships between people. These languages do not represent anything to, nor are they used to represent anything by, the computers themselves. Though a computer may run on one or other of these languages, in no sense does the computer *possess* the language upon which it runs. It does not, to put it another way, use the language as *a language*, does not use it to send messages, express thoughts, give instructions, etc. Thus, though we might concede that a computer is indeed 'built to use', in the sense of 'built to run on', a programming language this simply does not translate over into the suggestion that, therefore, somehow the computer possesses that programming language and can therefore instantiate the possibility of something possessing a language it has not learned. The computer hasn't learned a language because it does not have a language.

As we have said, the connection between the computer instance and the problem of 'private languages' and of 'innate ones' depends upon the literalising of idioms. Writing of computers as though they 'talk to themselves' is, of course, only to deploy a figure of speech, for computers do not, in any literal sense, talk to themselves – or anyone else – and so *computers* do not require a language in which to talk. Similarly, whilst we may – and quite happily – speak of the computer translating formulae from the input/output code into machine language, we should not make the mistake of thinking that we are thereby speaking of some *linguistic* operation in which the meaningful expressions of one language are translated into the meaningful expressions of another language. The operation is, in that connection, only metaphorically a translation for it is, of course, an entirely causal, electronic occurrence; electrical pulses are triggered, the pattern of causal connections being regulated by a system of conventions set up by computer engineers.

Of course, these supposed 'languages' are not themselves languages. The translation of something into machine code is no more a translation between two languages than is the translation of a message into Morse code. One can indeed be said to translate a message into Morse but one has not, therefore, transformed a statement in English into a statement in Morse – the statement translated into Morse remains, of course, a statement in English. This is why it would be pointless to translate an English statement into Morse in the hope of communicating with someone who understood Morse code, but spoke – say – only Russian. The transformation into and out of Morse is not, in that sense, a *linguistic* operation, for Morse itself is no language, though in it can be conveyed all the things which can be said in languages. Just as Morse is a device for relaying messages through telegraph wires, so computer languages are devices for manipulating the inner states of computers, using them, sometimes, to simulate linguistic and mathematical expressions and operations. Morse satisfies Fodor's requirement for matching 'the formulae' of an actual language with the operations a machine performs in such a way that the workings of the machine 'respect' the semantic constraints on the formulae but no one – except perhaps Fodor? – would imagine that, therefore, there must a language 'built in' to the telegraph wires (or, indeed, into the telephone lines to permit telephone conversations).

So far as we can see, then, the machine languages of computers comply far more closely with Wittgenstein's picture of language as something that develops along with and as integral parts of people's activities and do not tell at all against his arguments – these languages are, after all, the possession of computer programmers, not of the computers they program. It is not, after all, the case that programming languages are formed in the way they are because their designers have discovered that these were the languages already present in the computers, languages present there simply because of the way the hardware has, contingently, been configured. It is, rather, the case that the languages are designed to enable the planned and controlled configuration of the hardware, that the hardware is designed for computational and language-like operations.

The programmers have, of course, developed those programming languages in response to an immense variety of practical constraints, ranging from those set by the engineering characteristics of hardware development to the need for an expanding, less technically adept population of users to be able to program for themselves, and the 'languages' they have created are, of course, no less public, and no more private – in any sense relevant to Wittgenstein's work – than are the natural languages that they can be used to encode. The employment of such programs to manipulate computers does not therefore result in the endowment of computers to, for example, comply with the normative requirements of a language but involves, as Stuart Shanker (1987a) has effectively argued, the treatment of a set of causal, electro-mechanical operations as the *analogues* of normative relationships, a mapping or projection of these onto states of the machine. The activity of a computer programmer working in a programming language is a normative matter, whilst the machine's operation is not.

Fodor claims that an internal, human 'language of thought' is not only possible but necessary. There are two principal reasons for this claim, the first concerning the principles of language learning, and the second concerning properties of 'mental states' more generally. Let us consider, first, the argument from language learning.

The natural languages which we all speak cannot *themselves* be the 'language of thought', for these are languages which we learn. They are not themselves innate languages. However, to Fodor, primary language learning can only be undertaken if the learner is already in possession of a language, so natural languages, accordingly, could not be learned if we did not already have a language *to learn them with*. Learning a language is said to involve thought, specifically, the 'confirmation of hypotheses' about what words mean and about the ordering they are supposed to have in the stream of speech. The fact that we do learn to use natural languages is seen to attest to the 'fact' that we must possess some language that we have not in fact learned. Secondly, many if not all 'mental states' are, as noted before in this discussion, *intensional*: my 'intending' is characteristically an intending *to do something*, my 'thinking' is, necessarily, thinking *of* something, *about* something, or *that* something is the case, and my 'expecting' is expecting *that* something will happen, and so on. These 'mental states' are thus said to be comprised of 'propositional attitudes'. (This is a technical variant upon Brentano's 'intensionality thesis', although it is evidently a much more *regimented* version of this thesis than was propounded by its initiator.) To intend to do something is, according to this version, to stand in a certain kind of relationship (called an 'attitude') to a *proposition*: thus, if one 'intends to raise his arm', then he stands in a relationship of 'intending' to the proposition 'my arm goes up'. His intending to raise his arm is a matter of intending to make the proposition 'my arm goes up' a *true* proposition. Mental states which involve 'propositional attitudes', then, must involve a language within which one can express the propositions to which one adopts a given 'attitude' (wanting, expecting, intending, remembering and the rest). That some animals and most small children can also be said to possess certain 'mental states' (such as believing, intending, expecting, hoping, wanting, realising and, more contentiously, 'projecting hypotheses' about 'inputs' to their nervous systems) is itself grist to Fodor's mill. He appeals to the *lack* of a natural language on the part of animals and infants, in respect of these capacities, as evidence in favour of an innate language, one within which they can form the 'propositions' to which they can adopt the relevant array of 'attitudes'. The 'intellectualist' aspect of Fodor's Cartesian heritage thoroughly bewitches him here.[8] We have already remarked upon the propensity of naturalists to treat the 'intensional' verbs as if they could neatly be dichotomised into 'state' or 'process' verbs, and we have indicated at some length why this treatment violates their actual grammar of use. It was a major part of Wittgenstein's as well as Ryle's contribution to have shown the diversity, heterogeneity and complexity of the grammars of these terms. Fodor nowhere comes to grips with the range of their arguments about them. It is surely just a further mode of 'intellectualist' stipulation to introduce the idea of internally entertained 'propositions' ubiquitously into their analysis.

The brunt of Fodor's case, however, remains the learning of language. He seeks to demonstrate that one cannot learn a language unless one already has one. The essence of his reasoning is as follows:

> What, then, *is* being denied? Roughly, that one can learn a language whose expressive power is greater than that of a language that one already knows. Less roughly, that one can learn a language whose predicates express extensions not expressible by those of a previously available representational system. Still less roughly, that one can learn a language whose predicates express extensions not expressible by predicates of the representational system *whose employment mediates the learning*. (Fodor, 1975, p. 86)

On Fodor's account, the only apparent alternative to his proposal – that children learn the language in a piecemeal and progressive

---

8 The *locus classicus* for the rebuttal of the 'intellectualist legend' in respect of a wide range of human capacities, skills, powers and attributes routinely referred to as 'mental' is to be found in Ryle, 1973, p. 31 *et seq.*

fashion, using some of the language to learn more of it – is to be ruled out of court. He explains:

> One cannot use the definition D to understand the word W unless (a) 'W means D' is true and (b) one understands D. But if (a) is satisfied, D and W must be at least coextensive, and so if (b) is true, someone who learns W by learning that it means D must already understand at least one formula coextensive with W, viz., the one that D is couched in. In short, learning a word can be learning what a dictionary definition says about it *only for someone who understands the definition*. So appeals to dictionaries do not, after all, show that you can use your mastery of a part of a natural language to learn expressions you could not otherwise have mastered. (Fodor, 1975, pp. 86–7)

That Fodor can argue this way is a result of his conception of possessing/learning a language as learning a series of formulae for the truth conditions of word applications, as though one could conceive of human beings as creatures who did virtually nothing but speak and hear, and as though we could conceive of them as developing and using a language though doing precious little else, as not leading – in any other respect – an active life. From this vantage-point, it is presumed that the point of a dictionary definition is to present simply a formal equation, but this is not necessarily all that a dictionary definition does. It can, of course, convey information. It must, if it is to be at all useful, convey such information as it does in words that one can already understand, but that does not mean that *one already understood what those words convey*. In giving a definition of a word, one must, indeed, use words which are already familiar, but in using familiar words one is not merely providing an equivalent formulation but, rather, one is *giving an explanation* of the word in question. A random turn to page 548 of *The Shorter Oxford Dictionary* yields the fifth in a sequence of definitions of the word 'dignity': '*Astrology*: a situation of a planet in which its influence is heightened'. The explanation of this word involves its location relative to a discourse, that of astrology, with which we may have only a vague, but for this definition's purpose, sufficient, familiarity. It is only in terms of a grasp of the astrological notion of 'planetary influence' that we see what the term 'dignity' means here, and, moreover, the words 'planetary influence' would not have the meaning which they do to us for someone utterly ignorant of *astrology*, someone to whom *that* notion had not been explained. A person ignorant of astrology may well have the words 'planet' and 'influence' *already in his vocabulary*, but this alone would give him no basis for understanding the expression 'planetary influence' without some *additional explanation* of astrology's principles. For example, one would need to explain what 'influence' amounts to in this connection, and what 'planetary' might be used to cover in such a discourse. Having the words 'situation', 'planet' and 'influence' in our vocabularies would not suffice to enable us to formulate this concept of 'dignity' because we needed to see what role this concept, formulated in these terms, could play. Our expressive power, then, *can* be expanded, for such expressive power does not reside in the *vocabulary* we possess but in the uses we can make of that vocabulary, and such uses will depend, at the very least, upon the information that we have. As noted, without some information about astrology, the combination of words: 'planetary influence', would be a nonsense.

That one knows certain words and understands their meaning simply does not entail that one thereby understands the combinations that those words can be used to make. 'Greenwich mean time', for example, is made up of words which, assuredly, one might be familiar with, without being able to grasp the concept that they express in this combination. One can understand the English words but not, thereby, the concept. To know that 'Greenwich' is the name of a place, that 'mean' has to do with 'a mid-point location', and that the word 'time' has to do with such things as clocks and watches, etc., does not suffice to enable one to understand *how these words are being conjointly applied in this case*. That Greenwich is the name of a place which functions as the centre of a time-keeping system, or to understand just what 'mean time' is, would require a considerable amount of explanation, conveying a good deal of information about the practice of co-ordinating the global time-keeping system, to enable someone without this background information to grasp this concept.

It would be absurd to propose that no one who is given an explanation could learn anything from it, but Fodor's arguments point in that direction. Fodor's line of reasoning is as follows: (a) An explanation which enables someone to understand something he did not understand before must be an explanation which he can understand. (b) However, in that case, the explanation must be in terms he can *already* understand. (c) But in *that* case, the explanation cannot be telling him anything he did not know already. The absurdity is patent. Someone who understood the words in a definition does not, thereby, already know what the definition states. We understood the words in the definition of 'dignity' considered above, but did not, in consequence, already know that there was a use for a word which identifies the situation governing the degree of influence of the planets. Though we had the words already, we did not have the concept, and through the words have found out that there is such a concept. Explanation is a way of *extending* what people already know, of making use of the tools already in their possession, in order to comprehend things which they did not. This is one way in which the expressive power of the language learner can be expanded, and by which that language learner can continually exceed the things which he was previously capable of expressing.

Teaching someone the meaning of words in a language is not just a matter of giving them equivalent expressions in that language, nor of stating truth conditions. One of the things we do in teaching people language is to explain. Teaching does not *always* involve the provision of explicit explanations, however. A key to the most egregious error of the Chomsky school, including Fodor, is the claim that we do not really teach children language. We do not, we agree, *systematically* teach small children language in the way that, later, we might sit them down in a classroom and attempt systematically to instruct them in principles of grammar. But this does not mean that we do not teach our children language – only that we do not do this as a *specialised* task. Teaching children concepts, and the words that express them, is something that takes place as part of teaching them, and engaging with them in, other activities. Though we do not *systematically* explain things to our children, we do a lot of explaining to them as part of engaging in activities with them, correcting them, inculcating interests in them, giving them demonstrations, assisting them in practising, and the rest of the myriad of practices through which they come to learn a very great deal, including what words can be used to say and do.

What *'looks'* to Fodor as though it 'does sometimes happen', namely, 'using one part of one's language to learn another' (Fodor, 1975 p. 83) actually does happen. Fodor's effort to deny that anything conceptually novel is *genuinely* being learned depends, in part, upon his treatment of the dictionary as a mere supplier of definitions, overlooking the fact that, and the extent to which, definitions can be *explanations*. The case of the dictionary is, further, only an instance of the many ways in which explanation can figure in language learning. Explaining something to someone is surely a significant, if not unique or even primary, way of getting them to learn something. The contentiousness of Fodor's opposition to the apparently commonsense observation that children do, indeed, learn language, resides in his preoccupation with the fact that explanations are often (although not invariably) cast in language, and his insistence that children with no initial comprehension of language could not develop linguistic competence on the basis of such explanations.

Since we ourselves are not in search of any *general psychological theory* of 'concept learning', we do not have to suppose that all such learning takes place in the same way, and we certainly do not have to suppose that all such learning involves the formulation, testing and confirming of 'hypotheses' about word meanings and word order.[9] We wish to remind ourselves here of the simple facts of human nurturing: the small child learns to relate to other people in increasingly differentiated ways, particularly to those who raise it, before it has any language, and it develops an early understanding of them before it develops language, and it is into the communicative relationship between the adult and the child that the teaching of 'first words' is inserted, the words which are taught being those which are easily inserted into such situations and relationships, such as 'Mummy', 'Daddy', 'dolly', etc. In the early stages, children are given *demonstrations* not explicit explanations. The teaching and learning of language is, from this point of view, simply something continuous with the rest of the teaching and training of the small child that goes on with respect to its conduct, and its *beginning to talk* represents no more of a problematic transition from something it could not do before to something it can now do than does the transition from being immobile to beginning to crawl or from crawling to beginning to walk. In talking, as in much else in life, we *build upon* the child's reactions and explorations and then *build further* upon the patterns it has learned.

Fodor's tendentious claim that 'if there is such a process as learning a new concept, no one has the slightest idea of what it might be like' (Fodor, 1975, p. 96) is akin to Socrates' attempts to convince people that, because they could not adduce any *generalised* characterisation for diverse examples of 'justice', then they had no real idea of what justice was. To deny that there is such a thing as *the* process of learning a new concept is not *eo ipso* to deny that concept learning takes place (which is, of course, Fodor's implication) but is simply to reject the idea that there is *one* sort of way in which concepts can all be acquired. The world is teeming with what would, in anybody's normal vocabulary, be called not merely instances of people acquiring new concepts but even instances of their contriving new concepts. Why should anyone suppose that the acquisition/transmission of new concepts should proceed in any *uniform* manner? Consistently disengaging his discussion of these matters from any serious reflection on the nature of our ordinary, social procedures for acquiring and

---

9 Fodor writes: 'one can't learn a conceptual system richer than the conceptual system that one starts with, where *learning is construed as a process of hypothesis formation and confirmation* [our italics]' (Fodor, 1975, p. 97).

transmitting knowledge (of concepts, of beliefs, of information of all sorts), Fodor fails to acknowledge the sheer diversity of these procedures, and of their differential relationships to the very *different sorts* of concepts belonging to our language. How difficult mastery of any particular concept may be, for example, is clearly contingent upon the extent to which those who are to master it are prepared, the extent to which it is close to concepts already mastered, and the like. With mathematical novices, the route to further concepts is prepared for by extensive 'drilling'; in computing, by 'hands on' experience, and in psychiatry, by examining cases and 'walking the wards' with experienced clinicians. People have, in practice, very good understandings of how new concepts can be acquired.

Concluding remarks

We began this lengthy discussion and assessment of Fodor's (and related) conceptions of minds, machines and 'folk psychology'[10] by

10 As we go to press, Fodor's latest book, *The Elm and the Expert: Mentalese and Its Semantics* (1994), in which he makes further concessions to his critics on the issue of 'narrow' content, has appeared. There is, however, no alteration whatsoever in the fundamental framework of his thought. He adheres unswervingly to the Cartesian problematic: how can thoughts cause behaviour, behaviour which, furthermore, fits in with the way of the world such that it is, so to speak, typically successful? This apparently requires, once again, a perfunctory correction of Wittgenstein and Ryle, who misdiagnosed the problem of how thought 'could mediate between behaviour and the world. . . . The trouble isn't – anyhow, it isn't *solely* – thinking that thoughts are somehow immaterial. It's rather that thoughts need to be in more places than seems possible if they're to do the job that they're assigned to. They have to be, as it were, "out there" so that things in the world can interact with them, but they also have to be, as it were, "in here" so that they can proximately cause behaviour' (1994, 83). Nothing much changes. Fodor does, of course, disregard the fact that Wittgenstein and Ryle reject the problem, that they seek, in various and numerous ways, to show that the question of how thought 'mediates' between behaviour and the world is a spurious one – Wittgenstein, of course, eschews – in his later writings – what had in fact been the problematic of his early *Tractatus Logico-Philosophicus*, the very problem that Fodor insistently tries to solve. Again, both Wittgenstein and Ryle were resolutely attempting to erode the idea, which Fodor adamantly maintains, that thought is *any kind* of 'inner process', let alone a computational one. They sought to undermine the idea that thought must be located *somewhere*, to remove the idea that the contrast between 'in here' and 'out there' must provide the foundation for discussion – the claim that thought must be *both* 'in here' and 'out there' does not represent an improvement over the view that it must be either one or the other, but only the perpetuation of the same spurious problematic.

promising to review four major themes: the critique of so-called 'logical behaviourism'; the relationship between the sorts of explanations a cognitive science is called upon to provide and those which may ordinarily be given for our behaviour; the controversy over 'beliefs' as a case in point; and the characterisation of what is involved in 'learning a language', perhaps the major spur to the postulation of the 'internal language of thought' hypothesis. In the course of arguing about these matters, we have had recourse to many of the seminal contributions made by Ryle and Wittgenstein some fifty years ago, and yet it appears that much of the influential work in the contemporary philosophy of mind either ignores or misrepresents their views. If we have achieved anything here, then, it will have been to rehabilitate both thinkers as significant, if posthumous, participants in the debate.

Some theorists believe that certain very recent technical innovations in computation enable them to circumvent what they take to be the core criticisms advanced by the likes of us. 'Parallel-distributed processing' computation appears to operate without running rule-based programs, and without reliance upon the kind of electronic system depicted in 'machine code' for serial-digital computing systems. These theorists propose that such a development can, in principle, obviate reference to an 'internal language of thought' in Fodor's sense, and can meet at least some of the objections which they assume to be at the centre of the Wittgensteinian opposition to their theorising: the argument against the proposition that 'rules' of behaviour are 'causes' of behaviour via their material instantiation in the 'mind/brain', and the argument against the proposition that 'mental states' themselves are intrinsic to certain particular (computational) properties of the mind/brain rather than ascribable to its 'global' operations and achievements. Although these theorists evade many of the more fundamental conceptual problems we have been concerned to lay bare here, and still maintain the computer analogy as their model for what they persist in calling the 'mind/brain', we turn next to address their claims directly.

4

Connectionist Theory and Cognitive Science

For many theorists, the advent of parallel-distributed processing models ('connectionist' models) marks a decisive transformation in the conceptual structure of cognitive science. It has been argued quite widely of late that connectionist systems can serve as better models for 'our view of the nature of mind and its relationship to brain' (Rumelhart, 1991), and that many of the theoretical and philosophical difficulties besetting 'classical' cognitivism may be avoided either in part or altogether by a close consideration of the new connectionist alternative. In what follows, we shall describe the historical roots and major parameters of contemporary connectionist theorising in order to reveal the many commonalities of philosophical presupposition with the more traditional frameworks we have been discussing here. We shall also be concerned to isolate the genuinely technical, computational achievements of network modelling from the contentious philosophical glosses superimposed upon them by many modern philosophers of mind and cognitive theorists. If we are correct in our arguments, it will turn out that connectionist theory *cannot* be used as a resource for settling any of the philosophical questions which we have been raising in this book. Fundamentally, the move from classical to connectionist theorising about human conduct in the psychological and philosophical literature sustains the same (and similarly misplaced) explanatory objectives, and the disputes between their respective proponents merely engage questions about the manner in which these objectives are to be fulfilled.

Historical roots of connectionism

In 1943, Warren S. McCulloch and Walter H. Pitts published a paper entitled 'A Logical Calculus of the Ideas Immanent in Nervous Activity' (McCulloch and Pitts, 1943). Their *mathematical* achievement was to have proved a version of Turing's effective-computability thesis for the domain of an array of hypothetical neurons having the following properties: (1) all or nothing activation; (2) a fixed number of synapses must be excited within a specific critical period to fire any given neuron; (3) the only significant delay is synaptic delay; (4) the activity of any inhibitory synapse absolutely prevents excitation of a given neuron at that time; and (5) the structure of the interconnections between neurons does not change (Quinlan, 1991, p. 10). McCulloch and Pitts claimed to have shown that 'all processes that can be described with a finite number of symbolic expressions (e.g., simple arithmetic, classifying, storing and retrieving finite sets of data, and recursive application of logical rules) can be embodied in nets of what [McCulloch and Pitts called] "formal neurons"' (Cowan and Sharp, 1988). Cowan and Sharp cite Donald MacKay's specification of the capacity of McCulloch–Pitts' 'formal neurons' which is, in general terms,[1] as follows:

> if you assert that there is a certain process that a computer cannot go through, and if you can describe in words exactly what constitutes such a process, then at least one McCulloch–Pitts net that can carry out the process exists. McCulloch and Pitts thus proved that formal neural nets, if supplemented with indefinitely large memory stores, are equivalent to a class of computing machines that Alan M. Turing has shown to be computationally universal. (Cowan and Sharp, 1988, p. 87)

The general idea which relates McCulloch's and Pitts' 'formal neurons' to computational theorising was the claim that neurons could be thought of as 'binary threshold logic units' (Quinlan, 1991, p. 10). They had set out to demonstrate that the operating characteristics of interconnected formal neurons might capture (formally represent) aspects of propositional logical relations. In effect, their argument amounted to showing that, in theory, neural nets could instantiate *logic circuits* of the sort characterised in standard computer engineering.[2] Cowan and Sharp note that von Neumann himself took an interest in the McCulloch–Pitts model, and sought to show that:

1 For a description in less general terms, see MacKay, 1954.
2 See, *inter alia*, 'Logic Circuits' in Millman and Taub, 1965.

By using redundancy – using many neurons to do the job of one – [it was possible to solve] the problem of making McCulloch–Pitts nets function reliably. In such nets one bit of information (the choice between one and zero) is signaled by the synchronous activation of many neurons rather than by the all-or-nothing activation of one formal neuron: one obtains whenever more than half are activated, zero otherwise. Von Neumann proved that redundant McCulloch–Pitts nets operating in such a fashion can be designed to carry out arithmetical calculations with high reliability. (Cowan and Sharp, 1988, p. 87)

So far, the story is primarily a mathematical one: McCulloch and Pitts were describing networks of 'formal' neurons, not real ones, and the operations which they could theoretically be made to carry out. The connection with neurophysiology proper, however, is instructive. Hughlings Jackson had, on the basis of studies of brain-damaged human patients, shown that although different regions of the human cortex are specialised for differing functions, the scale of such localisation of functions does not extend to single neurons. The stage was set for the development of a conception of massively *distributed* functional architectures as models of neural functioning, coeval with the von Neumann/McCulloch–Pitts view of the formal neuron network. In 1949, the great neuropsychologist Donald Hebb had argued in his major work *The Organisation of Behavior* (Hebb, 1949) that Karl Lashley's neurophysiological model of the 'equipotentiality' of cortical regions for diverse 'functions' can be accommodated theoretically in the idea that 'the brain is continually changing as an organism learns differing functional tasks and that *cell assemblies* are created by such changes' (Cowan and Sharp, 1988, p. 88). Ramon y Cajal, the discoverer of the neuron (y Cajal, 1972), had earlier argued that the repeated activation of one neuron by another through synaptic contact might increase its conductance. This together with Hebb's theory, McCulloch and Pitts' model and von Neumann's proof of its computational capacity, meant that the stage was set for a conception of the cortex as a distributed-representational, information-processing system.

Ten years or so after the publication of the paper by McCulloch and Pitts, Frank Rosenblatt sought to show 'how McCulloch–Pitts neuronal nets with modifiable connections could be "trained" to classify certain patterns as similar or distinct' (Cowan and Sharp, 1988, p. 89). He called such nets 'perceptrons'.

An elementary perceptron is any perceptron that possesses one layer of sensory or S-units, one layer of association or A-units and just one response or R-unit. S-units receive input directly from the environment;

indeed it is normally assumed that the mosaic of S-units corresponds to the perceptron's retina. The R-unit interfaces with the environment at the other end of the system and emits an identifiable response. The A-units simply intervene between the S- and R-units. In the elementary perceptron under consideration, all the A-units connect to the R-unit. Another important aspect of the system is that the A- and R-units all possess a threshold and all compute a weighted sum of their inputs. Each connection in the net had a coefficient or a weight associated with it. In other words, activity from a unit was weighted according to which connection it was spreading along. (Quinlan, 1991, p. 20)

Here, then, we find the basic conceptual framework for what was to become 'connectionism'. However, this early work was seriously attacked by artificial intelligence researchers Papert and Minsky of MIT. They argued that elementary perceptrons of the kind constructed by Rosenblatt could not distinguish between such simple patterns as 'T' and 'C' (Minsky and Papert, 1969). They also advanced a variety of other technical objections, and perceptron research was gradually deprived of funding as a result. However, with the work of Rumelhart and McClelland in the late 1980s, 'connectionism' (re-)emerged as a major challenge to artificial intelligence models based primarily upon programs employing stored symbolic representations and soft-and-hard-wired algorithms (the so-called 'rules and representations' approach). It is to an outline of the basic tenets of modern connectionist theory that we now turn.

Network or 'parallel-distributed' computation

Computation employing networks of interconnected microprocessors has become the major theoretical alternative to the standard digital type employing programs (rules, algorithms) and stored data structures (internal, symbolic 'representations'). The primary interest in this alternative mode of computation amongst cognitive scientists and their philosophical protagonists has been the 'biological analogy': connectionist computation is frequently construed as using 'neuron-like' networks. Simple processing units or 'nodes' (typically compared to neurons) are connected to each other 'synaptically'. The original work of McCulloch and Pitts is generally invoked or presupposed in such a formulation, but quite often the distinctions between a McCulloch–Pitts 'formal' neuron and an actual biological neuron are glossed over. We shall consider this (and related) issues raised by the 'biological analogy' further on.

Associated with each connection is a 'weight' which determines the strength of the connection. A positive weight is an excitatory influence, a negative weight an inhibitory one, and a weight with a value of zero signifies that no connection is present. A node (in deterministic models) will transmit activation ('output') to other units (nodes) if and only if its threshold function has been attained, i.e., if the weights of its connections are sufficient to trigger a state of excitation.[3]

A connectionist system is organised into layers of processing units with their connections, usually with input, output and 'hidden' units (units which are not accessible externally, or which do not interface with the environment of actual use). Input values are transmitted to the input units (a procedure often referred to as 'clamping' certain activation values) and the network's output is generated by the output units. Networks of this sort are simulated on digital computers, so what we are calling the 'nodes' or 'processing units' are in fact computational abstractions rather than actual bits of hardware. Indeed, it is important to bear in mind throughout this discussion that many features of standard, serial-digital computation are exploited in parallel-distributed processing models (especially the 'memory' capacity in which prior connection strengths or activation distributions attained in trials are registered/stored).

How, then, do 'processing units' operate in connectionist models?

A unit adjusts its own activation level in response to the input it receives from other units through incoming connections. How a unit does this is described by an *activation function*. Almost always the input to a unit is determined by a *sigma-pi* computation, that is, by summing up individual incoming signals, each of which is the output produced by the unit on the other side of a connection scaled down by the weight of the incoming connection. Activation functions vary from one connectionist model to another. Very often a *sigmoid* function is used to squish the activation down to fit in a range from 0 to 1. Often the activation function will take the previous activation of the unit into account such that, for instance, if the input signal drops the activation of the unit will only gradually *decay*. Often some kind of *bias* is added to influence the value of the activation function. (Dinsmore, 1992, p. 7)

Connectionist networks as technical, computational systems, are *not* intended to be models of actual neural systems, even though the descriptive vocabulary conventionally applied to their structural features and facets of their operation is derived from neurophysiology. Perhaps

3 See Morelli and Brown, 1992, pp. 18–28.

the reason for this derivation is the historical confluence of Ramon y Cajal's claims about the all-or-nothing firing of neurons and Turing's (and others') determination that alphanumeric information can be encoded into digital form, stored, transformed, retrieved, etc. As Rumelhart and McClelland remarked, 'we have not focused on neural modeling but rather we have focused on neurally *inspired* modeling of cognitive processes [our italics]' (Rumelhart and McClelland, 1986, p. 130). By 'cognitive processes', Rumelhart and McClelland mean to include a range of functions, some of which are not best construed as 'processes' but rather as 'capacities', but, leaving that issue aside, it is clear that their models are only rather distantly similar to neurophysiological ones. Having noted this, however, it should immediately be added that many philosophers of mind *do* treat parallel-distributed processing systems as bases for thinking about so-called 'mind–brain relations', and we cited earlier in this chapter a recent comment by Rumelhart himself to that effect. We shall postpone a more detailed consideration of this issue until we have further explored the structure of connectionist theory. The fact remains that the chief function of connectionist networks is the computationally achieved discrimination of patterns, or artificial 'pattern recognition'. Other putatively 'cognitive' achievements which cannot be decomposed in some manner into pattern detection or feature discrimination problems generally lie beyond the effective scope of actual connectionist computation, although theoretical models of varying complexity exist defining possible computational solutions to problems of simulating the achievement of valid inferences in propositional logic. It is also worth observing that the recurrent conflation of 'mental' with 'neural' properties is a characteristic of many cognitivist claims made on behalf of connectionist theorising, and it is subject to the same order of criticisms we have advanced with respect to the 'classical' neo-Cartesian versions of cognitive science.

'Learning' in a connectionist network

A network is (usually) assigned initially random connection weights. An input pattern is presented (clamped on) to the system, and it generates an output pattern which is compared to the desired target pattern. If the target and actual output patterns differ, the connection weights are adjusted (according to a mathematical formula or algorithm) which reduces the difference between them. Weight changes needed to correct errors in output are 'back-propagated' through the network until the output units deliver the correct output.

A learning algorithm such as back-propagation ... can be repeatedly applied to the network, enabling it to learn to associate arbitrary pairs of input and output patterns by gradually adjusting the weights on the connections between units. These input–output patterns can be interpreted as representing information received from and sent to the network's surrounding environment. As a result of this training process, the network learns to recode each of the input patterns into different patterns of activation at each successive layer of units (called hidden units), so that the appropriate output pattern may be successfully generated at the output layer. (Blank, Meeden and Marshall, 1992, p. 119)

'Training' a net, then, involves presenting target pattern inputs repeatedly until the system settles into a configuration of connection strengths sufficient to determine a satisfactory output which yields the target pattern. This is achieved by comparing the activity of output units with the desired activity (which generates the desired output). Errors are calculated (an error being the square of the difference between actual and desired activation), and connection weights are changed so as to reduce them. To facilitate this process, an algorithm developed in 1974 by Werbos is available (the 'back-propagation' algorithm) which enables error-compensating adjustments to be made across an entire system of output and hidden layers.[4]

In this domain – automated pattern/feature discrimination – problems can arise which frustrate efforts to relate the achievements of connectionist systems to human capacities to recognise phenomena in natural environments. Dreyfus provides an interesting – and amusing – example of such a problem:

In the early days of this work [on connectionist networks] the army tried to train an artificial neural network to recognise tanks in a forest. They took a number of pictures of a forest without tanks and then, on a later day, with tanks clearly sticking out from behind trees, and they trained a net to discriminate the two classes of pictures. The results were impressive, and the army was even more impressed when it turned out that the net could generalise its knowledge to pictures that had not been part of the training set. Just to make sure that the net was indeed recognising partially hidden tanks, however, the researchers took more pictures in the same forest and showed them to the trained net. (Dreyfus, 1993, p. xxxvi)

It turned out that the net failed to discriminate between the new batches of pictures consisting of (1) trees with tanks behind them and

4 A more technical discussion of back-propagation is to be found in Rumelhart, Hinton and Williams, 1986.

(2) plain trees. As Dreyfus records, the mystery was solved only when it was noticed that 'the original pictures of the forest without tanks were taken on a cloudy day and those with tanks were taken on a sunny day. The net had apparently learned to recognise and generalise the difference between a forest with and without shadows!'.

Dreyfus goes on to make the point that network modellers could no longer allow their systems to be 'trained' without prespecifying, and thereby restricting, the class of allowable generalisations appropriate to the problem (or 'hypothesis space'). The architecture of the networks is thus designed so as to transform inputs into outputs 'only in ways that are in the hypothesis space' (Dreyfus, 1993, p. xxxviii). This entails that if a designer restricts a network to a predefined class of appropriate responses, 'the network will exhibit the intelligence built into it by the designer *for that context* but will *not* have the common sense that would enable it to adapt to other contexts [our italics]' (Dreyfus, 1993, p. xxxviii).

Connectionist architectures and genuine neural 'networks'

There are, as we remarked above, many reasons to refrain from according to extant connectionist models the status of plausible representations of neurophysiological phenomena. Grossberg, for example, in a well-known study, attacked the biological plausibility of 'back-propagation' (Grossberg, 1987) and Hinton has sought to demonstrate that there is no evidence that synapses can be used in the reverse direction (Hinton, 1989).[5] Reeke has argued that, amongst the constraints against accepting connectionist (virtual) architectures as viable models of actual neural functioning, the following parallels do not hold good: (1) back-propagation of weight adjustments contingent upon an error signal; (2) relaxation to stable states under constant input; (3) symmetrical relations between neuron-like nodes; (4) systematic connectivities; and, crucially, (5) the requirement (for modifiable networks) of 'lengthy presentations of an extensive sample or even the complete set of correct input–output pairs by an omniscient agent' (Reeke, 1989, p. 136). Schwartz considers the significance of connectionist virtual archi-

5 Hinton has argued that the most serious objection to back-propagation as a model of 'neuronal learning' 'is that it requires a teacher to supply the desired output for each training example. In contrast, people learn most things without the help of a teacher. . . . We learn to understand sentences or visual scenes without any direct instructions' (Hinton, 1992, p. 148).

tectures and the achievements of connectionist systems to date in the light of current neuroscientific research and theory and, although somewhat more impressed than Reeke and his colleagues with parallel-distributed processing as a very general thought-model for conceptualising some facets of neuronal and synaptic behaviour in the cortex, he offers the following caveats:

> The logical activity of each neuron can . . . be regarded as a process that combines approximately 10 thousand input bytes with roughly 40 thousand synapse status bytes at a rate of 100 times each second. The amount of analog arithmetic required for this estimate is (again very roughly) 10 million elementary operations per neuron per second, suggesting that the computing rate needed to emulate the entire brain on a neuron-by-neuron basis may be as high as 1,000,000 trillion arithmetic operations per second. (Of course, computation rates many orders of magnitude lower might suffice to represent the logical content of the brain's activity *if it could be discovered what that is* [our italics].) (Schwartz, 1988, p. 126)

Note that, despite the form in which Schwartz casts his speculative projections, he leaves open the question as to whether or not the brain's activity will be found to exhibit a logic best defined in computational terms. On this issue, Hilary Putnam has suggested that '[t]he claim that the brain can be modeled as a computer is . . . in one way, *trivial* [our italics]', and he buttresses this apparently heretical view with the following illuminating comment:

> in one sense, any physical system can be modeled as a computer. [More precisely, if we are interested in the behavior of a physical system that is finite in space and time and we wish to predict that behavior only up to some specified level of accuracy, then (assuming that the laws of motion are themselves continuous functions) it is trivial to show that a step function will give the prediction to the specified level of accuracy. If the possible values of the boundary parameters are restricted to a finite range, then a finite set of such step functions will give the behavior of the system under all possible conditions in the specified range to within the desired accuracy. But if that is the case, the behavior of the system is described by a recursive function and hence the system can be simulated by an automaton.][6]

Even a rudimentary version of such a simulation of neural operations will depend upon advances within empirical neurophysiology,

6 Putnam, 1988, p. 271. The text in brackets is taken from p. 280, note 7.

but this is not the project envisaged by most philosophical interpreters of connectionism. For them, the promise is that connectionist modelling will pave the way for a better understanding of brain–behaviour (or, more contentiously, brain–'mind') relationships. This project, which we have been claiming is incoherent, motivates a major dispute within cognitive science, perhaps best represented by the Fodor–Pylyshyn/Smolensky debate.

The Fodor–Pylyshyn/Smolensky debate

Classical cognitive science, as we have seen, treats the human mind in functionalist terms as a program operating within the hardware of the human brain. The brain is construed as processing 'information'[7] attained through the sensory organs, and so-called 'mental' states and processes are construed as computational states and operations utilising the wired-in resources of the neural system along with the acquired data structures stored in the memory. As we saw in our earlier discussion of Fodor's influential theorising, the computer analogy services this way of thinking by providing an empirical exemplar of a physical–symbol–system manipulation device. However, under pressure from a growing number of critics (both technical and philosophical) who have argued that conceptual confusions plague such a framework for conceptualising *human* conduct and capacities, many cognitive scientists have leapt onto the connectionist bandwagon in order to save the general project of a causal, materialist theory of the putative mind–brain–conduct nexus. This conversion has not been smooth, however. Fodor and Pylyshyn, two major figures in the classical cognitivist camp, have mounted an extensive critique of connectionist-inspired theoretical and philosophical claims. Little in this dispute turns upon the issue of the authenticity of connectionist theory with respect to neurophysiological phenomena: rather, the central points of dispute hinge upon arguments about how best to construe models of *mind* and 'mental representations'. The major contending figure in this (essentially philosophical) battle is Paul Smolensky. It is to the debate between these theorists that we now turn our attention.

The dispute between Fodor and Pylyshyn on the one side and Smolensky on the other is only tangentially a technical one. All sides

---

7 For a detailed analysis of the conceptual problems inherent in 'information-processing' theories using conceptions of information drawn from computer science and communications engineering, see Coulter, 1991b.

are familiar with the achievements and structure of connectionist work within the computing sciences. The nub of the issue between these contenders exclusively concerns the claim by connectionism's philosophical champions that it can provide a satisfactory account *in principle* of human conduct which avoids the controversial postulation of *symbolic representations* in the human cortex. We shall, in due course, challenge *both* sides of this dispute. For the moment, however, let us survey the lineaments of their argument with each other, which is essentially *internal* to the general assumptions of the programme of cognitive science.

The central objection mounted by Fodor and Pylyshyn against connectionism's philosophical claims is this: connectionist architectures recognise no *combinatorial structure* in their representational repertoire (e.g., in their node labels, connection strengths and vectors). Viewed as a contribution to our speculative understanding of the relationship between human conduct competences and the structures and processes of the central nervous system, then:

> What's deeply wrong with Connectionist architecture is this: Because it acknowledges neither syntactic nor semantic structure in mental representations, it perforce treats them not as a generated set but as a list. But lists, *qua* lists, have no structure; any collection of items is a possible list. And, correspondingly, on Connectionist principles, any collection of (causally connected) representational states is a possible mind. So, as far as Connectionist architecture is concerned, there is nothing to prevent minds that are arbitrarily un-systematic. But that result is *preposterous*. Cognitive capacities come in structurally related clusters; their systematicity is pervasive. All the evidence suggests that *punctate minds can't happen*. This argument seemed conclusive against the Connectionism of Hebb, Osgood and Hull twenty or thirty years ago. (Fodor and Pylyshyn, 1988)

This quotation reveals a great deal about the *metaphysics* tacitly embraced by Fodor and Pylyshyn (much of which, it appears, is shared by their connectionist rivals). The notion that a collection of '(causally connected) representational states is a possible mind' is actually one which Fodor himself *endorsed* in earlier work (which we have analysed and criticised at some length). Despite whatever differences may obtain between the respective metaphysics of the mental in classical and connectionist theories, all appear to share a proclivity to reify 'the mind' in a manner which serves the purpose of enunciating (although never demonstrating) the existence of a 'phenomenon' for study by scientific psychology (the mind). Talk about 'minds' as either 'systematic' or 'punctate' begs so many philosophical and logical questions that are totally neglected by these theorists that we are at a loss to take such claims seriously. After all, what is missing from all of their accounts is a rigorous and credible defence of the idea that 'the mind' is, in fact, an *entity* susceptible to characterisations of such a kind. Now, this does *not* mean that there is no sense to describing (someone's) mind as 'systematic', 'unsystematic' or 'punctate'. But we must be clear as to what such expressions could mean.

Let us consider the logical conditions of ascription of 'systematicity' to someone's 'mind'. Of what could we be speaking intelligibly if or when we assign this characteristic to someone's 'mind'? Well, it seems clear that such an expression could be used to remark upon a person's adherence to rigour and consistency in his or her thinking (as this is displayed in what he or she says or does). Someone of whom it may be said that he/she has a 'punctate' mind may be someone whose conduct exhibits occasional flashes of insight interspersed with lapses of clarity or incisiveness. (We would venture to propose that *many* people, on this account, have 'punctate' minds.) So why can't 'punctate minds' happen? The assumption that 'minds' are *empirical phenomena* reducible to description in neurofunctional terms is the basic common postulate here. Smolensky's reply is not encouraging in this respect, since he proffers an alternative ('connectionist') *theory* for the putative 'phenomenon' in question.

Additionally, we encounter in this dispute the familiar problem set by the Chomskian tradition (from which much of Fodor's metaphysics is derived) concerning the putative 'compositionality' and 'generativity' of human language use (and associated 'cognitive' capacities). All of this is *assumed* by Smolensky to constitute a genuine problem for cognitive studies. Before we consider the *philosophical* problems with generative conceptions of language, we shall report Smolensky's valiant technical-connectionist response to this (pseudo-) problem.

Smolensky argues extensively against Fodor and Pylyshyn (Smolensky, 1987; 1988a; and 1988b) that, *inter alia*, their critique of connectionist models holds only for *'ultralocal'* connectionist representational systems in which 'entire propositions are represented by individual nodes' (Smolensky, 1987, p. 9). In contrast to ultralocal cases, 'with *distributed* representations, complex representations are composed of representations of constituents' (Smolensky, 1987, p. 13) and *can* sustain structure-sensitive combinatorial operations. In Smolensky's account, connectionist models afford a view of 'mind' as a *'statistics-sensitive engine operating on structure-sensitive (numerical) representations'* (Smolensky, 1987, p. 14).[8] There is no internal system of represented symbols with semantic content (e.g., a bit-string representing a number or word) in connectionist models, so the form of representations which encode structures sufficient to permit combinatorial operations on their constituents are 'tensor product representations' based upon *vectors* of distributed activation (Smolensky, 1989, p. 15).[9] He illustrates the issue with the example of specifying the (distributed, non-classical) representation (in a connectionist model) of 'cup with coffee' without employing the classical 'symbolic language(s)' of Turing machines (binary encoding).

Beginning with a set of microfeatures of the sort employed in a pattern recognition device (e.g., 'hot liquid', 'upright container', 'container with handle', 'brown liquid', 'oblong silver object', 'glass contacting wood', 'porcelain curved surface', etc., down to a level of microstructurally specifiable detail), Smolensky notes that, in a properly functioning connectionist system, a pattern of activity in which *only* those units that are active are those that correspond to *only* those particular microfeatures present in the description of the cup containing coffee. Such an activation distribution will constitute a (distributed) representation of 'cup with coffee'. (Thus, a unit labelled as, sensitive to, or 'representing', say, 'glass contacting wood', would *not* figure among the activated units.) From this, he argues, we can see that 'the pattern or *vector* representing *cup with coffee* is composed of a *vector* that can be identified as a distributed representation of *cup without coffee* together with a *vector* that can be identified as a distributed representation of *coffee'* (Smolensky, 1989, p. 13). Smolensky then proceeds to provide a mathematical account which serves to show how a *tensor product* representation is a vector which meets Fodor's and Pylyshyn's 'formal requirements for a representation of combinatorial structure' (Smolensky, 1989, p. 18), thus transcending the pure 'associationism' imputed by them to all connectionist models in their original critique and yet *avoiding* the (classical) postulation of 'symbolic structures' by

8 The phrase 'statistics-sensitive' requires some explanation. Often, the output of a node in a connectionist network will be a non-deterministic or *stochastic* function of the activation value, such that, for example, a higher activation level will make it more likely (*probable*) that at a given time the output will be 1 rather than 0. For a discussion of stochastically operative Boltzmann machines, see Hinton and Sejnowski, 1986.

9 With this innovation, Smolensky believes himself to have solved a problem besetting connectionist theory for a long time, namely, how to take a distributed pattern of activation representing some variable and another pattern representing a value and generate a representation of their binding that has the correct computational properties.

replacing their functional roles with *sets of vectors*. Although susceptible of 'higher level' *interpretation* in terms of classical rules and data structures, vector sets defining distributed activation patterns across units do not *implement* either classical programs or sets of explicit symbols (0s or 1s, say, or atomic expressions in a program such as LISP) in any strict (mathematically precise) sense of 'implementation'. Outputs are orderly *emergent* products of operations describable in terms of *sub*symbolic properties. Thus, for Smolensky, there is no symbolic representation within connectionist theory, only vector representation, which may be construed as basically subsymbolic. He is, however, still wedded to the notion that the production of linguistic behaviour requires some sort of formal notion of combinatorial structure. Let us consider this assumption, shared by most cognitive theorists interested in linguistic phenomena.

Whatever may be the requirements of a computational system for the production of linguistic output, or the requirements of an effort mathematically to model abstracted features of a natural language (e.g., 'syntax'), the fact remains that the postulation of a generative system of elementary components and combinatorial rules underlying actual human linguistic behaviour remains a philosophical premiss with which we take issue. We do so on a number of grounds. First, the putative 'units' of a natural language upon which 'generative systems' are to be constructed by the theorist consist variously in *orthographically* defined features (such as 'word', 'noun', 'adjective', 'verb phrase' and the like). There is simply no sense to the proposal that linguistic neophytes acquire their first natural language by anything resembling a grammatical analysis of its parts, and the idea that they do (absurdly) presupposes that they could have access, prior to linguistic competence, to the correct identification of relevant grammatically defined objects like 'nouns', 'verbs', 'prepositions' and the rest of the analytical apparatus developed over the centuries by grammarians and logicians for the (primary) purpose of parsing texts. Moreover, the postulation of discretely identifiable levels of natural languages such as their 'syntax', 'semantics' and 'pragmatics' (distinctions elaborated by semioticians such as C. W. Morris) is indefensible. One cannot tell what a word actually means *in speech* independently of an utterance and a context, and, further, one cannot identify a proper 'part of speech' or syntactical category for any given word or string of words apart from a consideration of their meaning(s). Thus, to be able to tell that the word 'time' in the expression 'Time flies' is a noun and not an adjective presupposes that there are no such creatures as time flies as there are, for example, fruit flies, and that therefore the *sense* of the words yields a distinct set of syntactical possibilities from that which it may otherwise have yielded. Finally, although there is much more which could be said,[10] generative compositional/combinatorial models of language production and comprehension posit processes of encoding and decoding *pre*-linguistic 'messages' into and from unit linguistic elements combined into strings according to rules, by (crude) analogy with compiling processes in digital computers. This assumption leaves unaddressed the vexed question of the form(s) in which the putatively mental messages are themselves expressed, if not in a system of linguistic symbols,[11] as well as begging the further question of whether or not it makes sense generically to ascribe mental 'messages' of *any* kind to the minds of speakers prior to their actually saying something or as a necessary part of their understanding something said.[12]

We have taken stock of the fact that connectionist models do not (in principle) operate on programming systems and hard-wired algorithms (even though, as noted, since they are implemented in serial-digital computing systems, they actually must, at present, exploit such resources at a deeper level of operation). This has given rise to the claim that a system capable of simulating 'intelligent human performances' can operate *without* explicit rules.

The ideally defined capacity of a connectionist system when it computes, say, what occurs at point P if voltage is increased at location L, may be described by symbolically formulable rules, or 'hard' constraints, including Ohm's Law ($V = C \cdot R$).

> It's as though the model had those laws written down inside it [programmed into it, as in a Turing machine]. However, as in all subsymbolic systems, the performance of the system is achieved by satisfying a large set of soft constraints. What this means is that if we depart from the ideal conditions under which hard [e.g., explicitly programmed] constraints seem to be obeyed, the illusion that the system has hard constraints inside is quickly dispelled. The system can violate Ohm's Law if it has to, but if it needn't violate the law, it won't. (Smolensky, 1988a, p. 20)

The performance of a good connectionist model is thus not 'brittle' in the way that the performance of a classical computational one is: thus,

10 Perhaps the best treatment of this issue, in which a great deal more is said in criticism of generative theories of linguistic behaviour, is to be found in Baker and Hacker, 1984b, *passim*.

11 If these 'messages' *are* claimed to be expressed in linguistic symbols, an infinite regress sets in: how, unless by further decodings, are *these* expressions themselves to be understood? And if they are said to be decoded into deeper messages, how are *these* to be understood, *ad infinitum*?

12 Further arguments on this topic are presented in Coulter, 1991a.

if faced with ill-formed problems, inconsistent information or insuffi-
cient information, the connectionist network doesn't just fall flat, de-
duce nothing or operate randomly. It satisfies as many (soft) constraints
as possible. Moreover, its performance can 'degrade gracefully' in a
manner alien to a classical Turing machine model whose performance,
when hampered by the above adverse conditions, amounts to gross
malfunction or even 'crashing'. However, as Clarke points out, these
advantages of networks must be offset against a significant disadvan-
tage: presented with wholly *transposed* forms of initially posed problems, a network must be massively retrained, whereas a Turing
machine can be (relatively) easily adjusted (e.g., by changing its data
pointers or reconstructing its data structures) (Clarke, 1991, p. 118 *et
seq.*). As Reeke and his colleagues have commented, for some problems,
'tens of thousands of iterations' are required for a network to 'learn'
very simple problems such as symmetry detection in an array of six
cells (Reeke, 1989, p. 134). That should count, at least, as a constraint
against simple-minded efforts to use the results of connectionist work
as a model for thinking about human conduct and capacities. On this,
for us *central*, issue, however, there is much more to be said.

Does 'connectionism' provide answers to Wittgensteinian objections to cognitivist theory?

The purely *technical* details of connectionist models within artificial
intelligence (the study of computational systems which can successfully *simulate* human achievements), then, can be meaningfully discussed and assessed quite independently of considerations arising
from the empirical and logical study of authentic *human* conduct and
central nervous system functioning. The linkage to studies of human
phenomena actually argued for by cognitive theorists is intelligible
only when seen against the background of essentially *in-house* controversies generated by the original 'inner rules and symbolic representations' conception of human cognitive capacities advanced by Newell,
Fodor and many others as fundamental components of a 'computational theory of mind'. In considering this (vexed) question, let us
review these latter-day developments in the light of our critical perspective on these matters.

In this work, we have insisted upon a distinction between
simulations of human achievements and explanatory theories of these.
The attempt to produce a version of simulation (primarily of the
iterable detection of visible patterns or features in an environment)
without rule-based programs and stored data structures has, to some,

been construed as an advance and, moreover, as one which should silence critics such as ourselves. Stanley Munsat, for example, has said of connectionism that it is 'AI [artificial intelligence] for Wittgensteinians'.[13] This presupposes a very narrow construal of the wide range of objections to cognitivist theory which have been developed in large part from Wittgenstein's assault on Cartesianism, and it confuses varieties of cognitivist theorising with purely technical research and theoretical advances in the artificial simulation of selective human achievements (artificial intelligence) which, in themselves, pose no philosophical problems.

Of course, if all that had been involved in the Wittgensteinian criticisms of theoretical cognitive science was a principled repugnance for ascribing explicit rules and symbols to the human central nervous system, perhaps Munsat's observation would have some merit. However, as we have seen throughout these pages, there was, and remains, much more to it than this. Bearing in mind the (philosophical) *indifference* to conventional and contemporary work on 'artificially intelligent systems' *per se*, and to computational theory in general, proclaimed by Wittgensteinian commentators (an indifference perhaps not universally shared by *all* critics of cognitivism, e.g., Hubert Dreyfus), it seems odd that we are now being urged to embrace one computational system for (for example) pattern discrimination (connectionist) over another (classical programming). From a strictly philosophical and logical interest in the study of human cognitive capacities, achievements and conduct, such in-house divergencies in technological implementations of artificial intelligence objectives are simply *irrelevant*. If connectionist networks operate more effectively than classical architectures alone to accomplish the iterative discrimination of patterns, all well and good. And the same would hold true for us if the reverse were the case. Hardware and software engineering advances in the computing sciences are none of a Wittgensteinian's or a behavioural scientist's professional business. What we wish to insist upon here, however, is the *complement* of this: we insist on the claim that theoretical analyses of human conduct are not facilitated by borrowing from technologies produced in computing; indeed, the uncritical importation into the human sciences of models and conceptual frameworks initially and cogently deployed in the development of computational artifacts is more of a hindrance than a help. That has been one major basis of the current confused state of cognitive theorising in the human sciences against which we have been concerned to argue. Nothing has been

13 Cited in Lycan, 1991, p. 269.

truly learned about human abilities and their exercise from the study of these (rival) systems alone. It may well be the case that the success to date of connectionist and related neural-network systems over classical Turing/von Neumann serial-digital computing systems in some domains will erode the view that one must necessarily posit internal rules and symbolic representations to anything that can be said, in some sense, to 'discriminate a pattern' or to 'compute a move in chess', etc. This alone is not enough, however, to eliminate the grip on so many theorists of the underlying *philosophical* conception we seek to replace: the mechanistic and distorted view of real-time human 'cognitive' achievements and intelligent conduct, and the tendency to embrace one or another version of 'neural Cartesianism' within which mental and intensional predicates are assigned to brains and nervous systems rather than to *persons*.[14]

In contrast to our claims, some theorists are trying to reconcile specific aspects of the Wittgensteinian critique to current cognitivist thinking in the post-connectionist phase, or are suggesting that certain alignments are already available. It is to a consideration of arguments proposed by two of these theorists, Martin Davies and Stephen Mills, that we now turn.

Davies maintains that connectionist models constitute a resource for the development of a theoretical position which is amicable to what he calls the Wittgensteinian 'position' on 'mental' phenomena (Davies, 1991) (with which, however, he seems ultimately to disagree). In his posthumously published collection of notes entitled *Zettel*, Wittgenstein appealed to the nature of the logical disjuncture between, for example, 'thinking' and 'brain processes', arguing that the order of a spate of reflective thought is *emergent from* and not analysable into any isomorphic structure of neural events putatively *comprising* such a course of thinking:

> No supposition seems to me more natural than that there is no process in the brain correlated with associating or with thinking; so that it would be impossible to read off thought-processes from brain-processes. I mean this: if I talk or write there is, I assume, a system of impulses going out from my brain and correlated with my spoken or written thoughts. But why should the *system* continue further in the direction of the centre? Why should this order not proceed, so to speak, from chaos?
>
> It is thus perfectly possible that certain psychological phenomena *cannot* be investigated physiologically because physiologically nothing corresponds to them (Wittgenstein, 1967, paragraphs 608–9).

14 See, *inter alia*, Coulter, 1979; Coulter, 1993c; Kenny, 1985.

A thought and its expression (the latter being the best candidate for correlation with neural phenomena) are *not* identical (since in changed contexts the same expression can express *different* thoughts, and the *same* thought can be expressed by different expressions), even though no thought can 'exist' independently of *any* expression, and we can often explain the same thought in many different ways, with different examples and at different rates of speed; 'but no-one would care to say that all the ways in which he could honestly explain a thought have run through his head, and few would care to say that any of them did' (Hunter, 1977, pp. 518–19). Davies misses these more basic obstacles to neural correlationism, claiming only that connectionist models can capture 'the idea of order proceeding, so to speak, out of chaos' (Davies, 1991, p. 230) which he treats as Wittgenstein's central theme here, although he proceeds to endorse a conception of 'thoughts' as either (a) 'thought contents' or (b) 'states' of a thinking person, asserting that such 'states' may best be characterised as computational states involving tokens of a Fodorian internal 'language of thought'. Quite how Davies can read Wittgenstein and come to the conclusion that the grammar of 'thought' establishes its logical status as a 'state' concept of *any* kind is left unclear and the claim left unjustified, even though it is (merely) alleged that the notion of a 'thought state' captures one sense of the ordinary word 'thought' (Davies, 1991, p. 240).

Whether or not connectionist models can be considered as generating orderly outputs from relatively chaotic events (such as changing activation distributions throughout a network) is quite beside the point. 'Thinking' is not even a determinable process in itself, since the verb 'to think' is *polymorphous*, comparable in this logical category to the verb 'to work'. If I am told of someone only that he or she is 'thinking', I do not, context apart, yet know what he or she is actually *doing*. Is he/she trying to recollect a date? Figuring out which horse to bet on in the 4.15? Calculating his/her tax bill? Or something else entirely? Neither connectionist nor classical computational concepts assist us in illuminating the grammar – the nature – of *thinking*.

Mills, on the other hand, is sympathetic to Smolensky-style connectionist theorising and seeks to show to what extent Wittgenstein's writings on language mastery exhibit a 'complementarity' to Smolensky's connection-theoretic viewpoint (Mills, 1993). Mills argues that, just as the rejection of a conception of language as a symbolic calculus played a significant role in Wittgenstein's later writings on language, language learning and meaning, so also does such a rejection play a part in connectionist theorists' eschewal of the traditional cognitivist paradigm. Within non-localist connectionist models, which subserve what Pinker and Prince referred to as 'eliminativist connectionism' (Pinker and Prince, 1988),[15] there are no classical 'symbols' and no 'rules' represented explicitly within the processing system.

Wittgenstein's famous 'family resemblances' argument (against the essentialist claim that for a 'mass' noun or 'count' noun to have a sense there must be a set of properties common to all and only all of the instances properly named by the noun) is invoked by Mills in order to identify a further 'commonality': there is a (superficial) similarity between Smolensky's notion of a 'distributed (vector) representation' of, say, *coffee* in a connectionist model, and the avoidance of essentialist 'common feature' or 'definitional' accounts of its proper use. Two additional parallels are noted:

> One of these is where usage is unproblematically extended to a genuinely new kind of case on the basis of similarities to one or more existing kinds. Here the resemblance is to the much stressed capacity of connectionist systems to recognise examples of a type which differ significantly from those employed in the training set. Lack of precise limits in a word's usage is also displayed in the fact that '[t]he more abnormal the case, the more doubtful it becomes what we are to say' (Wittgenstein, *Philosophical Investigations*, para. 142). Arguably, this gradual increase in uncertainty is resembled by the way in which, in connectionist networks, there is gradual deviation from the desired output vector as examples become increasingly abnormal relative to the training set (Mills, 1993, p. 141).

These proposed parallels turn upon a common theme in connectionist theorists' writings about the acquisition of language: its dependence upon recognitional capacities. This is, of course, largely motivated by the fact that connectionist models were developed from, and continue to be primarily used in, feature detection and pattern discrimination. (Hinton gives a good example of this in his detailed discussion of a relatively successful handwritten-digit discriminating parallel-distributed processing system consisting of 256 input units, 9 hidden units and 10 output units (Hinton, 1992, p. 147).) The link to language learning is essentially *speculative*. But is it coherent? Its chief defect is its excessive dependence upon the learning-by-ostension

---

15 For a useful discussion of the idea of 'learning rules' within connectionist theory, and the difference between prescriptive programming rules (in serial-digital computation) and descriptive learning formulae (in connectionist computation), see Place, 1992. Of course, as Place remarks, this distinction is sometimes obscured by the fact that parallel-distributed processors are implemented in serial-digital systems employing conventional programming formats (Place, 1992, p. 25).

model, and its misplaced emphasis upon the role of (visual and acoustic) 'recognition' in human learning more generally.

It is perfectly true that Wittgenstein was aware of the important role of 'examples' in the acquisition of various (kinds of) concepts. He also understood the importance of ostensive definition for some forms of training in specific types of language use, although he is best known in this respect for his insight into the necessity of 'stage-setting' (including some background linguistic capacity) for ostensive definition to be able to work as a guide to language use. As he put it, 'the ostensive definition explains the use – the meaning – of the word when the overall role of the word in language is clear. . . . One has *already to know* (or to be able to do) something in order to be capable of asking for a thing's name [our italics]' (Wittgenstein, 1958, paragraph 30).[16] The role of 'examples' is also very different from that envisaged in the connectionist version, according to which being presented with a set of concrete particulars iteratively is sufficient to inculcate the appropriate knowledge. Giving someone an example, however, varies in its form and consequence(s) depending upon the language game in which this practice is embedded. Considering what may be involved in teaching a person who has not yet mastered the concepts of 'sameness' or 'uniformity', Wittgenstein comments:

> I shall teach him to use the words by means of *examples* and by *practice*. . . . In the course of this teaching I shall show him the same colours, the same lengths, the same shapes, I shall make him find them and produce them, and so on. I shall, for instance, get him to continue an ornamental pattern uniformly when told to do so. – And also to continue progressions . . . I do it, he does it after me; and I encourage him by expressions of agreement, rejection, expectation, encouragement. I let him go his way, or hold him back; and so on (Wittgenstein, 1958, paragraph 208).

From this passage it is clear that for Wittgenstein, 'exemplifying' a concept can take many forms, and involves a variety of (sometimes quite diverse) *practices*. There is no *uniform* phenomenon called 'learning from examples' (e.g., being presented with many cases of the same kind of phenomenon until it can be correctly reproduced or simply named). And we must remember that what is being trained is not a brain but a human being; what a human being is being trained *to do* under the rubric of 'learning what a word means' (even a referentially usable one) is far more than correctly to repeat it in the presence of an

16 See also paragraph 257: 'one forgets that a great deal of stage-setting in the language is presupposed if the mere act of naming is to make sense'.

instance of the named phenomenon; and what is doing the 'learning' is a person, not his brain. Conflating the technical concept of 'training' (as in 'training the net') with its non-technical, ordinary and human-level applications, as in, for example, 'training a marine recruit', 'training a child in hygienic habits' or 'training an infant in the multiplication table', results, not in better scientific theories, but in rampant confusion. Neurons are not being trained, and are not learning, to *do* anything. If some version of neural network theory in the neurosciences turns out to be right, we may well decide to refer to neural processes as 'neural-network training' in the same (or a similar) sense in which we presently speak of training a parallel-distributed processing network, but not in the sense(s) in which we speak of training people to do things (e.g., to speak intelligently), training them in certain things, etc. Therefore, this new usage would not license any claims on behalf of a *psychological* 'learning theory' pertinent to human language acquisition (or to anything else).

Let us, finally, consider at some length the most central concept within connectionist computational work and its philosophical interpretation: *recognition*. It would appear that at least one claim made on behalf of successful connectionist systems is that they can 'recognise' (within fixed parameters) specific sorts of perceptible features or patterns, even being capable of identifying objects which differ in some way(s) from the original target class. Classical theoretical approaches to recognition within cognitive science were developed on the basis of assumptions drawn from (contrastive) *representational* theories of the mind, as Marr makes clear in his celebrated work on this topic, *Vision*:

> Modern representational theories conceive of the mind as having access to systems of internal representations; mental states are characterised by asserting what the internal representations currently specify, and mental processes by how such internal representations are obtained and how they interact. This scheme affords a comfortable framework for our study of visual perception, and I am content to let it form the point of departure (Marr, 1980, p. 5).

Connectionist versions of the 'problem of recognition', in disagreement, dispense with the problematic notion of 'internal representations'[17] (except for 'ultralocal' models, as Smolensky has remarked)

17 It is worth observing here that Marr's usage is ambiguous throughout his treatment in respect of two meanings of 'system of representation': one signifies something akin to a description one has in mind, and the other signifies a method or rule for representing something. This conflation has disastrous consequences for the coherence of his theorising. See Hacker, forthcoming.

and postulate in their place *distributed electrical activations* best described in the language of *vectors* rather than the language of programming symbols and machine code. As we have repeatedly stressed, there is no (philosophical) issue to be taken with any technical enterprise in the computing sciences: problems arise when computational systems are thought to embody adequate models of *human* functions, or *to supply the right conceptual apparatus for depicting such functions.* In other words, *our* complaints are addressed to those who see psychological, explanatory significance for human conduct and capacities in the operation of such computational systems.

If we consider the logic of human recognition (and are not bound by attempts to distort or 'operationalise' its meaning so as to favour an *a priori* theory, whether of a computational nature or some other variety), several properties come into view which do not sit well with current psychological (cognitivist) (pre)conceptions. The first is that to recognise something is, often though not always, to be *correct* about what it is (in some specific way relevant to one's purposes, and according to the relevant conventions of identification). One can also recognise some specific thing without ever having seen it before if one recognises it *as* a token of a known type of phenomenon (e.g., *that* fish *there* is a 'trout'), and one can recognise something as having been seen before without knowing *exactly* what it is. ('There it is again! What on earth *is* it?') Further, one can claim sincerely to recognise, genuinely to think that one has recognised, something or someone, and be *mistaken*: the object or person *appeared to have been* such-and-such but *was* in fact so-and-so. This is especially important when considering claims about the constitutive role of neural events and operations (whether modelled classically or in terms of parallel-distributed processing).

Notice, as we have observed earlier, that recognising is *not* a process, but rather an achievement. (We can, and do, contrast *thinking that* one recognised X with *actually* having recognised X, with having succeeded in recognising X.) And now consider the following scenario. One is confronted with an absolutely life-like model of an object or animal in a given environment where one might expect to encounter such a thing. One claims to have recognised it (as an X). One's neural processes are, *ex hypothesi*, identical to what they would be if one was actually in the presence of a genuine case or instance of such a thing, since all of the features relevant to sensory neurophysiology, such as the pattern of retinal irradiation, photoreceptor transduction, ionic discharges, neural firings and so forth, are *indistinguishable* from what they would be in that circumstance. And yet one has *not* recognised the phenomenon at all, but has, rather, been fooled by its simulacrum. Same neural processes, but no genuine recognition. Consequently, recognising something cannot be *explained* neurophysiologically, whatever the preferred form of the 'cognitive' neurophysiological account (e.g., computationally classical or connectionist).

Of course, neural events and processes may well be cited which *subserve* visual accomplishments, but they do not explain them. Brains themselves recognise nothing: people do. A computational system, then, in the human sense of 'recognise', itself recognises nothing: it is those of us who use them who can recognise what it is we want the computer to 'recognise' in the specifically *technical* sense of producing the 'output' *which we desire from it,* and which *we* can recognise as the *correct* output given the circumstances. Neural-Cartesian misconceptions of human achievements are not made coherent by contemplating computational achievements.

5

Can a Machine Think?

The original question which motivated the philosophical interest in computing machinery – can a machine *think*? – is still a point of entry into the disputes surrounding cognitive science, and its relationship to materialist theories of the 'mind/body' problem is quite clear. If a machine can think, then explanations of the human capacity for thought, it is argued, need not require the postulation of anything other than purely 'mechanistic' principles of structure and operation. This initial query, however, was once answered by Wittgenstein in a manner deemed unsatisfactory to many. He wrote: 'But a machine surely cannot think! – Is that an empirical statement? No. We only say of a human being and what is like one that it thinks' (Wittgenstein, 1958, paragraph 360).

Our aim here is to show that Wittgenstein's approach to the problem was correct: it is *not* an empirical question as to whether a machine might (be said to) think. As we have argued earlier, conceptual questions such as this often appear to be empirical in kind, decidable with reference only to advances in, for example, computational technologies. In what follows, we shall try to unravel this prejudice and to provide some argumentative resources for showing (1) why the question, as posed by philosophers, and by those who are persuaded by them, is resoluble by *logical* means and (2) why the correct answer to it is, as Wittgenstein asserted: 'No'. In the ensuing discussion, then, we locate the *heart* of our disagreement with the entire project here in dispute.

In the background, the CD is playing the music of Morton Feldman. In the concert hall, the Kronos Quartet is playing the music of Morton

Feldman. Does this mean that the CD player can do what the Kronos Quartet can do? Suppose that someone were to listen outside a room and were to hear the musical sounds produced, in turn, by both the Kronos Quartet itself and by a supremely high-quality recording of the quartet's performance. Note for note, and in terms of quality, the two are indistinguishable, and the person outside the room cannot tell the difference between them. The person is led to believe that he is hearing only a recording; he cannot believe that the Kronos Quartet is actually playing in the room. Many people are put through this test, and they all reach the same conclusion; that they are listening only to recordings. Does this, then, prove that there is *no difference* between a live performance and a recorded one? Since the Kronos Quartet performance is one which we should normally regard as the product of a highly skilled group, certainly one which we could not ourselves duplicate even if presented with the instruments, and since the recorded version is notefor-note and in terms of sound quality *identical* with that performance, must we not, therefore, say that the CD player is capable of a performance which is every bit as skilled as that which the Kronos Quartet can produce? The CD player is obviously a match for the performance of at least four highly skilled human players, and it is vastly superior in musical talent to persons like the authors of this book. Should we not, now, become deeply depressed because it can be proved that compactdisc-playing machines can surpass human beings in their musical/ artistic capacities, capacities which we had previously regarded as distinctive to human beings and something which testified to their superiority over, for example, mere machines?

We trust that our readers will regard the reasoning of the previous paragraph as indefensible, even ludicrous, and that they will give a firm 'No' to the last question. If, however, one was to remodel this paragraph slightly and to substitute the word 'computer' for CD player, and to characterise the performances as being of the type produced by computer, we would be less confident about the response, for it is an argument of basically similar structure made on behalf of computers that has led many people to accept that 'machines can think' and that the truth of this proposition carries a diminishing truth for us human beings: that we are not so special as we thought we were, and that we are not, in fact, superior to machines.

The 'test' through which we put our hypothetical listeners in the above example was one which is essentially similar to that provided in the case of the Chinese Room, which was itself an implementation of the kind of test now known as the 'Turing test' devised by Alan Turing as a way of showing that machines can think. Anyone familiar with the writings in which Turing proposed his test might object that Turing did not believe that his test could prove whether or not machines can think and that he regarded this question as being too imprecise to answer, but this, as with so much else in Turing's arguments on this matter, is spurious. Turing *did* believe that his test would prove that machines can think. In chapter 1, we have discussed his test and the Chinese Room 'proxy' of it, presenting there a very sceptical account, but we have not, we think, yet disposed of the problem. The determination to insist that a machine *can* think is hard indeed to discourage, and the Chinese Room case was not meant to counter the whole panoply of confusions which have developed around the idea of 'machine intelligence'. Hence, we shall pay more thorough and detailed attention to the problem here, and we will attempt to substantiate our argument that the basic claim for machine intelligence is indeed as foolish as that for the musically skilled CD player.

The logic of Turing's position is as follows: it is possible to show that any computation, however complex, can be broken down into a series of extremely simple operations. The operations are so very simple that pretty well anyone could undertake to perform them, so very simple that they could, in fact, be reproduced on a simple tape-moving and tape-printing/erasing device. The operations are so elementary that the operations necessary to carry out some really large computations would be very numerous indeed, and so, in imagining a very simple tape device which could be used to reproduce those operations, we have to accept that these computations would take a very, very long time.

Turing's achievement was, in the first place, a mathematical one, for it was the *mathematical* demonstration that this must be true of computations that was the prodigious feat. It was, in the second place, to give great viability to the idea of a computing machine. The capacity of electronic machinery, which could carry out the kind of reproductive operations carried out by the imaginary tape-reading device, could be bolstered to do this very, very rapidly indeed, such that a machine organised to work on the basis of such decompositions of mathematical operations into these inordinately simple steps, but at tremendous speed, would be able to deliver on tremendously complex calculations.

Before we proceed further, let us see what Turing's mathematical achievement has shown. It has shown that complex calculations can be done not through mastery of a series of complex procedures for calculation but can, *instead*, be broken down into a series of very simple operations, ones which could be followed by almost anyone, which could be carried through *by someone who knows little or nothing of math-*

ematics. Indeed, they are so simple that they can be reproduced through the back and forth movement of a tape, coupled to the inscribing and erasing of simple symbols. As we remarked in chapter 1, Turing has contrived a way of getting mathematics done by those who have little or no idea of mathematics, such that the essential operations could be carried out by those who had no idea of what the purposes of such operations are. Someone could carry out the computations at the behest of another by being given instructions such as 'take two steps to the left, and write down a one; now, take three steps to the right and rub out the one you find written there'. The person carrying out these instructions need know no more about mathematics than how to tell the difference between '1' and '0', but he could, by following the instructions precisely, carry out an enormously large multiplication. We might note, too, that the tape operations are analogised to the situation of instruction-giving: the tape is, so to speak, instructed to move to the left and right, to enter and erase figures.

Turing's reflections on his achievement did not, however, lead him to see them in quite this way. As we have summarised them, Turing found a way to carry out calculations via instructions which did not require much intelligence on the part of those actually carrying them out. Persons carrying out such 'Turing instructions' could even do so without needing *any* mathematics whatsoever: they could, for example, be shown the figures '1' and '0' and be told that these were to be identified as the 'A' and 'B' shapes respectively, such that their instructions could thence be given only in the form of 'Write in an "A" shape'. Such calculations could be carried through by those having no understanding of mathematics, but only an understanding of English (or some other natural language) enabling them to follow such simple English instructions as 'Move to the left' and 'Write in an "A" shape'. People doing these things need have no idea at all of what, *mathematically speaking*, they were doing. There is no paradox or puzzle in this. These people are not 'doing mathematics' in the sense that someone who sits down at a desk and works out some sums on a piece of paper does mathematics. These individuals who are carrying out the calculation are not, themselves, *calculating*. Their activities are not those of persons calculating. They are simply following instructions, moving back and forth, writing in and erasing A and B shapes as they have been instructed to. Their role is akin to that of the labourers who, on a life-size chess board, might have the task of picking up and putting down the chess pieces in accordance with the commands of those who were actually playing the game. The persons carrying the pieces about the board need understand no chess. They could be told things like

'Move the piece with the horse's head' and thus they need not even know that this was a knight. They do not even need to be able to identify *any* pieces as *chess* pieces, let alone possess knowledge of the rules of the game. Their activities would, of course, be contributory to the playing of chess, but they could not themselves be described as playing chess, nor could they even begin to describe what they were doing in chess terms. They could not say, for example, 'I am moving a pawn to queen four'. What makes their activities moves in a chess game is their relationship to the actual players who are instructing them. Those players can translate 'the pawn is going onto queen four' into 'move the smallest black piece in the fifth column two spaces ahead' (and back again). Indeed, one can replace human beings in this situation with other devices; an automated lifter could carry the chess pieces, directed by a radio signal, just as the human agents can be eliminated from the calculating operations which can themselves be carried out by mechanically tugging a piece of tape back and forth and mechanically stamping signs onto it or erasing signs from it.

In neither case, then, does the mechanisation of the operation suggest that it is possible to do it because the lifting device or the tape device can acquire at least the same level of intelligence as the human beings who were doing the carrying and moving beforehand. It may only require a miniscule amount of intelligence for someone to lift life-size chess pieces and move them about: strength, not brains, is needed here. *Lifting* abilities are not *chess* skills: pieces must be lifted up and put down when one is playing with pieces on a board, but one can dispense with lifting altogether when one plays chess by correspondence, for example. Thus, in the case of moving life-size chess pieces around, the only intelligence that a labourer needs is enough to obey the simplest of instructions: if the lifting can be mechanised and controlled with a radio signal, then a way of lifting has been found which can be controlled without *any requirement* that even such simple instructions be understood. Intelligence can be eliminated completely from the lifting operation. In mechanising, one has not endowed mechanical lifter or tape device with intelligence, *one has substituted for intelligence altogether*. The mechanical chess piece lifter carries out the operations of playing chess, and the fact that its liftings up and settings down forward the game of chess carries no implication that the piece lifter knows what it is doing, that it understands the game of chess or is, itself, in any way engaged in playing chess.

Turing, then, had explained how complex mathematical calculations could be carried out *entirely without intelligence*. However, and we do not hesitate to say this, Turing misunderstood his own achievement.

He made the mistake of supposing that the substitution of a mechanical tape device for an intelligent operator achieved the transfer of intelligence to the tape device. His reasoning was simple and *patently* erroneous. The carrying out of a complex mathematical calculation requires considerable intelligence – on that we can all agree. The computing device carries out a complex mathematical calculation and, since we say that, in the case of human beings, the carrying out of a complex computation *requires* considerable intelligence, do we not also have to say that, in the case of the machine, the same operation *requires* considerable intelligence? Thus, when the device does the computations which a mathematician does then it too is showing intelligence. . . . One might as well say, however, that in the case of human beings, the carrying out of mathematical calculations requires *life* for, of course, when human beings are dead they cannot carry out calculations: thus, by the same token, the fact that the mechanical device carries out computations shows that it, too, must be alive. In this latter case, one might as well say that since digging ditches requires life when done by human beings, and digging ditches can be done by mechanical digging machines, then ditch-digging machines must be alive.

It is, indeed, true that when a mathematician carries out a piece of advanced mathematical work we regard this as requiring considerable mathematical knowledge as well as mathematical skill. The mathematician must have a good deal of mathematical intelligence. However, Turing has not shown us that the mathematician's *actual calculations* consist of very simple operations carried out in sequence. Turing has *not* given us a description of how *mathematicians* compute, but has provided us with a method for *decomposing* computations into very elementary tasks – has, in effect, provided *a new way of doing calculations*. He has shown us a new way of doing calculations that mathematicians have always done. Hence, it now appears, it was not the calculations themselves which required intelligence but the way of doing them, for what Turing has actually provided is a way of working through the calculations which requires nothing much at all (if anything) in the way of either mathematical knowledge or skill. Just as pressing the buttons on your calculator requires nothing like the mathematical skill that doing the sums for yourself involves, so proceeding through Turing's (mechanisable) instruction sequences does not require any specifically mathematical skill. We can detect the parallel with the Kronos Quartet case because, of course, prior to the invention of the recording device, the only way in which to generate musical sounds was through the application of musical skills. The progress of mechanisation involved, amongst other things, the mechanisation of music-making, and the devising of machines which could play tunes. The concern for musicians, when confronted with such devices, was not for their own standing *vis-à-vis* machines in that they had now encountered machines which had musical skills of their own, skills which matched and even surpassed the musicians' skills: rather, and more correctly, they perceived prospects for the deskilling of musical work due to the fact that musical sounds could now be produced which required only mechanical operations and that this greatly reduced or eliminated musical skills as such. The recording device presented another threat in that it provided for the reproduction of musical sounds that were produced through the exercise of musical capacities in the first place: the worries were not that musical skills or capacities had been endowed upon the recording device, but rather that once a musical sound was recorded it could then be reproduced on a massive scale without any further necessity for music-making skills. Such musical skills might be needed in quality control, for example, but no longer anywhere else in the industrial process for the mechanical reproduction or even generation of music. The CD player reproduces musical sounds, but without any skills on its own part. The operation is 'purely mechanical' (or 'purely electro-magnetic'), entirely divested of music-making skills. One can arrive at the same result by two different routes, as was patently shown by Turing's achievements.

Turing pressed on. He imagined that his mathematical proofs and their applications to the creation of computing machinery had provided a basis for thinking that machines could be intelligent. He could further envisage that the development of the electronic computer would permit programming not only for the carrying out of mathematical operations but for many other things too, to the extent that one could build machines which could produce contributions to dialogue to the standard already described in the Chinese Room scenario, dialogue so fluently reciprocal, so well-adapted to the conversational partner, that it would be indiscriminable from the participation of a human interlocutor. *That*, surely, would establish that a machine could be no less intelligent than a human being.

Can a machine think? This, Turing declared, was an imprecise question and could not be satisfactorily answered as it stood. What was required was a question which *could* be precisely answered. A question which could be precisely answered was, in his view, one which could be responded to with a statement of frequency, and it was this question that Turing proposed to ask. It was: with what frequency would people be able to discriminate between the conversational output of a computing machine and that of a human being? This was the basis for the Turing test. If we took Turing's own explicit eschewal of the question 'Can a machine think?' we would wonder why it is that so many have subsequently taken the prospect that a machine could pass the Turing test as a demonstration that a machine can think. However, Turing did not in fact eschew the question of whether a machine can think, for the contriving of the Turing test was in fact his way of trying to provide an unequivocal answer to this question. The unequivocal answer to this question would be, in his estimation, 'Yes!' After all, if Turing's test is not linked to the question 'Can a machine think?' then why should he even raise the prospect of answering that question as a preface to his own test? Indeed, it becomes difficult to see why Turing should have thought that his test provided the possibility of a more precise answer. We can report, for example, that 73 per cent of the subjects in our test could not tell the difference between the output from a computing machine and that from a human being (or 48 per cent, or whatever proportion should transpire). The appearance of precision is, however, merely in respect of the numerical distribution of responses, but there is no clarity with respect to what such figures show (beyond the fact that 10 per cent, 70 per cent or even 100 per cent of the experimental subjects could not discriminate). What does the fact that, say, a majority of subjects cannot tell the difference signify? Is the suggestion to be that it is, say, 70 per cent probable that a machine can think? Or is it the case that the decision as to whether a machine can think is a suitable matter for a majority vote, in which case the fact that 70 per cent of the experimental subjects cannot discriminate human from machine output establishes conclusively that a machine can think? Or is it the case that all that the test tells us is that (say) 70 per cent of subjects cannot discriminate human from machine output, *period*? What is the Turing test actually testing *for*? It is *intended* to test for intelligence in machines, but it might equally well be seen as testing the discriminatory powers of the experimental subjects. The alleged 'precision' of the Turing test is superficial, and that precision is entirely irrelevant to the question of whether machines possess intelligence, of whether they can think.

It might be said that Turing's test provides exactly what we have asked for, for it appeals to what people would 'ordinarily' say, though it does so in a more scientific, empirical fashion that contrasts, and does so favourably, with the more intuitive, apparently 'personal' way in which 'ordinary language' philosophers proceed. Turing was actually prepared to ask what ordinary language users would say when confronted with the task of discriminating between human and machine output. Turing's arguments certainly do confirm our point, which is that the question of whether a machine can think is one which *does* bear upon what is involved in our ordinary use of words like 'think', 'intelligent' and so forth, but Turing's proposal hardly offers an effective method of approaching these issues.

Turing's test is, in fact, an irrelevance to the very issue it is meant to address. Turing's design of his test *presupposes* the very things which the test is meant to demonstrate. The 'test', as described by Turing, is merely a colourful illustration of his reasoning. The crucial assumption is one which we have already identified and cast doubt upon. It is the assumption that if a machine can be designed to do what, in human beings, requires intelligence, then, in doing this, the machine must *also* be manifesting intelligence. It is, of course, only upon the basis of this that Turing can suppose that his question has any bearing on the issue of 'machine intelligence'. The machine which passes the Turing test is, of course, 'doing what intelligent humans do' in the sense that it is simulating human conversational performance, but the judgment that the machine's passing the test entails intelligence on its part is reasonable *only* if the simulation of such conversational performance is *assumed also* to involve intelligence. This, of course, is just the question that the Turing test begs. What the subjects in the (successful) Turing test say is that they cannot discriminate between the output of a machine and that of a person, that they cannot establish through interrogation of the two sources which is the machine and which the person. Nonetheless, if they were asked to say whether or not this showed that the machine was intelligent, couldn't they say that it *did*? And wouldn't such a judgment from a collection of ordinary language speakers be sufficient to dispose of our objections? If anyone should accept the verdict from ordinary speakers of a language, it should be us, it may be claimed.

Speaking a language, however, is not a matter of majority voting, and the fact that other speakers of the language might say one thing does not inhibit us, as fellow speakers, from saying another, quite different, thing. We may disagree with them. Ordinary language philosophy talks about the *meaning* of words and not about the substantive correctness of what people say. It is, of course, the case that, *in our ordinary language*, from the fact that someone could admit that they cannot tell that there is a difference between two things, *it does not follow* that there *is* no difference! Again, the string quartet is relevant. There is a situation in which a person cannot tell a difference, cannot tell the difference between a live performance and its recording. As speakers of the ordinary language, however, we *do* have to say that there *is* a difference between a live musical performance and a recording of it (at least in this kind of case). There is a difference between the Kronos Quartet themselves turning in a performance and our playing a CD of their concert. The fact that *every* individual subjected to our hearing test could not tell the difference does not establish that there is no difference. The test is set up so that they cannot, on the basis of *the musical sounds alone*, establish such a difference. The note-for-note identity of the playing and the superior sound quality of the recording, *ex hypothesi*, establish that no one could successfully discriminate *just by listening*. They might guess, and they might guess correctly. It might be that 100 per cent of our experimental subjects guess correctly when it is the quartet which is playing and when it is the CD player, but that does not establish, either, that there *is* a *detectable difference* between the two productions of musical sounds! *Guessing* does not count as 'successfully discriminating', and this is another respect in which the Turing test fails, for its subjects too might guess, and successfully. The simple fact is that the incapacity of subjects to *discern a difference* does not imply that *there is no difference*: only that there is no difference they can discern. This, we reiterate, is how we designed our musical test – there is no difference in *sound* that our subjects can use to discriminate between the two performances, but because there is no difference in sound quality we can hardly conclude that there are *no other real and discernible differences*. There are, indeed, many other differences: they just aren't ones which can be discriminated through the walls of a closed room. If someone were to look inside the room, they would be able to see quite clearly if it were occupied by the Kronos Quartet or by a hi-fi system. What someone's failure to tell the difference between two things establishes depends upon *the conditions of the failure*. That our experimental subjects cannot tell the difference between a string quartet performance and a recording of it only shows how the quality of recording has developed, to the extent where the copy is indistinguishable in sound quality from the original. It would be foolish indeed to suppose that because the group and the recording were identical in sound quality that it must therefore be that what ensured the quality of the sound in the live performance case also ensured the quality of the sound of the recording. The problems involved in getting records, tapes and CDs to match the quality of their sources are not, of course, remotely like those involved in producing a distinctive, outstanding quality sound on the part of a group of performers. The problems faced by the latter are those of playing skill, musical technique and creativity, etc., whilst the problems involved in the former, those of producing recorded sound comparable with the source of the sound, are engineering problems. It is, for example, the 'digital' character of the recording that contributes to its 'noise-free' reproduction, not its hold upon an instrument, the pressure of its bow, its fingering, etc.

Our musical test proceeds like the Turing test does with computing machines, which is that it conceals essential information from the subjects with respect to the discrimination they are being called upon to make, information which would ensure that they *would* be able to discriminate. The Turing test provides its subjects only with access to print-outs from the machine and the human being who are, respectively, to be interrogated as to their status as human or machine. It does not matter if the machine is fitted with an advanced voice synthesiser and that the voice is relayed through some device to ensure that, in sound quality, the two are indistinguishable. The test is, like our musical one, designed to eliminate the very things which would ensure a *detectable* difference, and is really only proof of a familiar and widely accepted point (much exploited by confidence tricksters) that if you go to sufficient lengths you *can* deceive people about the differences between two situations. The fact is, the machine and the human were both *concealed from the subject's sight*. The simple fact is that, were they not, experimental subjects in Turing's test could *immediately tell* that there was a difference between the two outputs; they could tell *from their source*, just as in the case of the string quartet. The logic of the Turing test is to ask this question: *overlooking the fact that this is a machine*, can a machine think?

Enthusiasts of the Turing test might maintain that something is indeed being begged, and that it is we who are doing the begging. We are, it could be said, manifesting a very parochial attitude towards things, responding as if it were *unthinkable* that anything other than a human being should have the power of thought. This kind of reactionary/progressive argument is, however, merely more of the bluster of which we have complained before. Our objection to the Turing test is simply this: that it is designed to make the difference between human and machine performance undetectable, by eliminating things which would normally contribute decisively to detecting those differences. The protest that we are *anthropocentric* (human-centred), seeking to confine intelligence and thought only to our own species, is one which, in fact, exposes a further assumption underlying the Turing test, which is that the differences between human beings and machines *are immaterial* to the question of intelligence. This is, we will shortly suggest, as absurd as the supposition that the difference of physical make-up is immaterial to the question of whether they are both *alive*. After all, if one cannot tell the difference between the machine and the human performer, one cannot tell the difference between something which is commonly thought to be alive and something which is commonly thought not to be. One could, therefore, conclude that there is no difference between the two, and that both are alive (or, perhaps, that neither are!). The latter argument is, of course, patently silly in a way that the argument pertaining to intelligence is. The latter *is* silly, but not so *obviously* so, it appears.

The supposedly 'reactionary' insistence upon the special nature of human beings may perhaps be attributed to our attachment to 'ordinary language philosophy' and to the work of the later Wittgenstein in particular. The latter has certainly been berated for reactionary breast-beating about the uniqueness of humanity. However, we might equally well be criticised for misrepresenting these views, for, certainly, Wittgenstein has been counted as a creator of the view of understanding-as-performance which the Turing test might be seen as instantiating.

Wittgenstein certainly argued against the idea that understanding was an inner state or process which accompanied activities. He certainly *did* insist that understanding was manifested in performance(s), that the demonstration that someone understands how to do the sums we are trying to teach him is given in what he can do, e.g., that he can do the sums for himself. Does the Turing test not express a very similar conception? What does it matter what, so to speak, goes on *in the machine* if the machine can achieve the performance, can match the standard? If 'inner states' or 'inner processes' do not matter, and if performance is the criterion of understanding, then surely the Chinese Room satisfied the criteria of understanding! Wittgenstein, on these terms, could be aligned with the functionalists, for he, like they, is saying that the question of how the performance is produced is *immaterial* to judging whether or not it shows understanding, for it does not matter what 'goes on inside' the machine (or creature) which shows the understanding.

Unfortunately, this can only pass on the basis of the most superficial reading of Wittgenstein. The idea that it does not matter *how* the performance is produced is, in this context, one which supposes that the idea of 'how the performance is produced' must be understood with respect to 'inner states'. Yet Wittgenstein's assiduous efforts *to remove* the 'inner/outer' dichotomy from the central place which it held within the philosophy of mind, together with his attempts – comparable to Ryle's – to eradicate the view that notions like 'understanding' were *'episodic'*, rather than 'achievement', verbs, only means that what goes on *in the head* is *irrelevant* to the determination *of whether someone is displaying understanding*, but this does *not* equate to a conviction that *the manner in which* a performance is produced is itself an *irrelevance* to the judgment as to whether it *displays understanding*. The fact is that someone's correctly answering questions about the sums which we give them to do *does* display that he/she understands the two times table. It certainly does not matter, does it, from the point of view of displaying understanding, how he or she came upon those answers? It does not matter whether he or she does the calculations in the head or with pencil and paper or whether he or she does them on an abacus. How he or she produces the performance is irrelevant. In *that* sense, it is true that how the performance was produced does not matter. If, however, someone is giving correct answers to our questions because these answers are being signalled to them by someone else, or because they are reading them out from a list of answers with which they have been supplied, then, although they might be giving the performance of someone who understands, and we might ourselves be *duped* into saying that they *did* understand, we would only be saying this because we were unaware of the way their results were being generated and we would, therefore, be wrong in saying it. Of course, the way in which the performance is produced *is* material to the determination that understanding is taking place, but the notion of what is involved in the performance's production has to do with *the way in which it is organised*, *not* with its generation through 'inner processes'.

One of Wittgenstein's main battles was against the inclination of philosophers to focus too narrowly upon things, against their inclination to isolate phenomena from the circumstances within which the phenomena acquired their very identity and only relative to which they could be properly understood. The idea that the conception of understanding-as-performance licenses the Turing test involves an inappropriately narrow focus upon some features of the performance itself, disassociating it from the background circumstances against which the question of whether one performance is comparable with, and shows the same as, another, must be posed. The narrowing of focus, especially given the strongly *naturalist* inclinations that are so widespread in modern philosophy, often takes the form of a focus upon immediate *physical* characteristics. If two patterns of behaviour – two performances – are indiscriminable in terms of their physical characteristics, then we should have to say that they are, in all respects, the same. However, when it comes to questions of understanding, the *bona fides* of the participants, and the legitimacy of the procedures by which they generate their performance, are involved in judging whether one performance is, indeed, the same as another, whether both are *authentic* performances. There need be no distinguishable *physical* differences between an authentic and an inauthentic performance. Consider the forged note.

We can conceive of forgers who, in their craft, acquire the skills for simulation that are comparable to those envisaged in advanced robotics. They can produce notes which are indistinguishable from the official currency, even down to their molecular constituents. They can produce a note which is physically indistinguishable from a government-issued note, identical in every respect, which means that it would possess the same serial number, etc. Such an identical character would not, however, establish that it was a *bona fide* item of the currency; the fact that two notes possessed the same serial number would not prove that they must *both* be legitimate, but that, in fact, they *could not be*, that only *one* of them could be legitimate. The fact that the two notes were identical in even their most refined physical characteristics would *not* ensure that they were *in all important respects* the same. Indeed, in respect of the considerations which matter to us, whether they are genuine items of currency, they could not be the same. The difference between a genuine and a forged item of currency does *not* reside in physical differences. By asserting that there *must be* physical differences between the two items, one seeks thereby to ensure that the *source* of the difference is unavailable. However, the determining source is, in principle, if not always in practice, existent and available, and it consists in *the authority with which* the notes are issued. The *legitimate currency* is issued *with the approval of a currency-issuing authority*, and is produced under such auspices, whilst the forgery is issued without that authority – and it is that *which makes it a forgery* (even though, for example, the contingent lack of a watermark may be, if noticed, the thing that *shows that it is* a forgery).

If we took this 'understanding-as-performance' view literally, and apart from the contexts within which it makes sense, we would have to rank the telephone's performance as being every bit as impressive as the most advanced digital computer imagined in debates about artificial intelligence. The telephone is an astonishing thing – it certainly simulates conversations to a degree which is indistinguishable from real conversations. One speaks into the mouthpiece of a telephone and responses emerge from the earpiece, ones which satisfy the standard of the Turing test. The telephone can do amazing things; it can not merely simulate conversation, it simulates individuals' conversations, giving the most astonishing impersonations of their voices, their attitudes and emotional conditions, and reproduces things which show that it is 'aware' of the most amazing range of details about these persons. Of course, the 'performance' of the telephone is not impressive in this way, nor is it, any longer, impressive technologically, for it has become such a familiar item in our world. The telephone does not understand anything, for the telephone's 'performance' is not a performance at all, since the telephone is simply a device for *relaying* the voices of persons: it functions only as a device whose vibrations simulate the air waves which the callers generate when speaking.

When Wittgenstein remarked that 'We only say of a human being and what is like one that it thinks' (as we quoted at the beginning of this chapter), his point was that part of the context against which we make judgments of performances is the character of the human physiognomy. What suffices to establish that a proper or correct performance is an authentic expression or manifestation of understanding is that *it issues from a human being.* Consider the following scenario. A school class is sitting out underneath a tree. The teacher asks a question and the pupil, immediately, without prompting or without access to an aid, answers it. The teacher can therefore conclude that the pupil understands. The teacher asks another question, and an answer is called out, but it does not come from any of the children. It seems, instead, to come from the tree. It is a correct answer. Does the teacher therefore conclude that the tree understands? Of course not. The teacher wonders if some person is hidden behind or within the tree. Suppose the teacher pursues the matter systematically, asking many questions and receiving many answers which 'show understanding'. The teacher then seeks to determine how this performance is produced, searches around and in the tree for someone hidden there, searches for hidden loudspeakers and so forth, and still finds nothing. Does the teacher then conclude that the tree *does* understand or, perhaps, that they do not know what is going on here, that *somehow* a trick is being played? What provides a test of understanding on the part of the pupils does not provide a test of *the tree's* understanding, for a tree does not count as the kind of thing that can understand, any more than do machines.

Hence, the fact that one of the parties to the Turing test is a machine is not immaterial to the conclusions that we should draw from the test. Indeed, we have seen that it is, in fact, *so* material to the conclusions that should be drawn from the test that the fact that one of the parties is a machine *must be concealed from the subjects*! The reason for rejecting the view that the performances of the human and those of the machine are the same performances and that both manifest understanding is precisely that *one of them is a machine* and that machines are *not* the sort of things that have understanding. The fact that the machine can 'pass' a test which tests for understanding in human beings does nothing to show that it understands, for the test does not test for understanding on the part of machines any more than the teacher's questions to her pupils test for understanding in trees. Computers cannot think because they are machines.

This conclusion will doubtless strike some as too simple, premature or even 'prejudicial'. How could the *mere fact* that they are machines rule out the prospect that their performances might exhibit understanding? Don't we need to scrutinise the 'evidence' here more carefully? There are, we know, those who would say that the judgment that these are machines would be too gross because, of course, the point about *computing* machines is that they are *very special kinds* of machines. Our objections only apply because we have focused upon the 'understanding-as-performance' idea, but this is by no means a necessary conception, and it can be argued that it is the *way* in which the machine operates that is the relevant consideration. This is the essence of the 'functionalist' conception which we have already encountered, and it is a conception which embodies a particular view of what 'thinking' is. It supposes a view that Ryle and Wittgenstein both disputed, namely, that thinking is a process that involves the manipulation of symbols. If thinking in human beings *is* the process of manipulating symbols, and if those processes could be simulated in a computer, then this would be more than mere simulation. If thinking is indeed nothing but the manipulation of symbols, then one need do nothing more, in respect of a machine, than to instantiate that process in it to have ensured that it thinks. If the operations of the machine are correctly describable as 'manipulating symbols', then they are also correctly describable as *comprising* thinking. The fact that computers are run by programs and that programs are comprised of symbols, is what might make it appear that this argument goes through. Once again, however, we are confronted with uses of descriptions such as 'manipulating symbols' which obscure very significant differences.

It is a perennial Wittgensteinian theme that an expression which describes activity does not thereby always describe the *same* activity. The simple question which needs to be counterposed to the functionalist argument, then, is whether, if it is true that people, when they are thinking, and computers, when they are running, are both manipulating symbols, we should therefore conclude that they are both instantiating the *same* kinds of operation. Someone who authors a page of text may be said to be 'manipulating symbols' in that he is laying these symbols (if we can agree to call words 'symbols') in ways which make up (in the sense of create or invent) a story. The printer who sets that page in type may also be described as 'manipulating symbols' (with the 'manipulating' playing a slightly more literal role here) and just as the author creates a page of type which tells the story, so the printer produces an identical product. Is not the printer, then, at least as much entitled to be considered as an author, as the creator, of the story that the printed words tell, as the person who initially typed the manuscript? To which the answer is, of course, that the printer is in no measure entitled to authorship of the manuscript. Even though the symbols being manipulated were exactly the same symbols, and though the objectives in each case were to lay the symbols out in the same sequences, the two operations are of quite different kinds. The author's operation is to come up with and write out a story, the printer's task simply to reproduce what the author wrote upon the printed page. 'Operating with symbols' is what the two parties are doing, but the fact that they are symbols is, in many ways, only incidental to the printer's work. It is not by virtue of the meaning they convey that the printer selects them, but merely by virtue of the fact that they conform to the pattern laid down in the author's text. The printer, like the inhabitant of the Chinese Room, could operate with these symbols entirely by virtue of their shapes and in complete disregard of their meanings, while the author is predominantly concerned with their meanings: a printer with no mathematical knowledge can set type for mathematical journals, and one with no French can set an article in that language, but an author with no mathematics cannot author a mathematical paper just as one with no French cannot write one in French. What the printer handles when he picks up lines of type are symbols, and in that sense he is operating with symbols, but in a completely different way from the author, for, of course, the author does not pick up lines of type, does not operate with symbols in the way in which the printer does.

The computer does 'manipulate symbols' but again in a sense which is even more attenuated than that which applies in the printer's case, one in which the fact that what is being manipulated is 'symbols' is *incidental* to the computer's operation. The computer operates on these entirely by virtue of their electronic character, by virtue of the kinds of electronic pulses which they are. The fact that these electronic pulses are (in complex, and more or less direct, ways) associated with symbols is one which is irrelevant to the computer's own operations. The symbolic character of that with which a computer operates is not relevant to it, but rather to *us, its users*. This is one respect in which the connectionist argument is useful to us, for it shows that the 'programming' of computers can proceed without the use, at each point, of symbolic programs. The value of symbolic programs is, of course, that they provide those who wish to run computers with convenient ways of accommodating to the computer's capacities, furnishing relatively accessible procedures for setting up the computer to do what they want it to do for them. Computers do what their programmers and users want them to do, and not what the computers themselves want to do.

There are, however, those who insist that computers can do other than what their programmers program them to do. We will concede the correctness of this claim. Computers malfunction, and programs have bugs. However, this is not what those who insist upon this point want us to concede. Their point must, rather, be taken to be this: computers can be *autonomous* from their programmers, they can exceed what they have been programmed to do, can initiate operations they were not explictly programmed to accomplish. The apparent relevance of such assertions presupposes an erroneous line of argument. Machines which have been programmed (either symbolically, or by transforming network connection strengths) to produce mathematical proofs may actually produce proofs which their programmers (or network trainers) had never thought of. This, however, does not demonstrate that the machines have deviated from or transcended their programming, but only that they are doing what they were programmed (or 'trained') to do. They were programmed/trained to generate proofs, not to generate proofs which had already, specifically, been thought of. There is no more *ingenuity* in the computer's producing a novel proof than there is in its producing a long-established one. Imagine arguing that a computer designed to produce poems had exceeded its programming because it had generated poems that the programmers had never thought of. Yet the whole point of the programming would be for it to produce poems that the programmers had never thought of, surely not to reproduce poems that had already been written! Our point concerns the expression 'programmed to do': a proof-generating program which generates a proof that its programmers had not foreseen was certainly not programmed to produce just that proof. It could not have been, on the grounds that the programmers had not envisaged that proof and hence could not have programmed for its particular production. A computer, though, is not programmed to produce, say, *this* proof, for it is not programmed to produce any *particular* proof, *neither this specific one nor any other specific one*. However, in actually producing *this* specific proof, the computer was, nonetheless, doing exactly what it has been programmed to do, and nothing more. It had been programmed to churn out all the proofs that would result from the mechanical application of its program's rules, and this proof is just one of those.

   The judgment, then, that a machine cannot think because it is a machine is no more hasty or premature than the judgment that the CD player's matching of the live performance does not manifest possession of musical skills. We know how the performance of the CD player is produced, and this does not involve the exercise or application of any musical skills. In the same way, we also know how the performance of the computer is produced and this does not involve, any more than the CD player's, any (mathematical, linguistic, etc.) *skills* at all on its own part. That the CD player can match the quality of a live performance is not the achievement of the player, but of its designers and manufacturers, and, by the same token, the computer's performance, however favourably it may compare with that of the most highly intelligent mathematician's or conversationalist's, is not the achievement of the machine, but, rather, of the designers, programmers and manufacturers of the machine.

   In the following two chapters we turn our attention to projects which are in important ways, offsprings of Turing's conception. We have mentioned that language mastery is taken to be one of the main and distinctive 'mental' powers of human beings – Chomksy himself treats language as unique to human beings amongst animals. Yet the programming of machines to emit linguistic output seems a very realistic possibility, and the installing of such a capacity in machines would seem to be an essential element in enabling them to pass Turing's test. We also said, however, that the simulations of human conduct which are alleged to show that machines can match people's competencies often involve only superficial resemblances to the performances that they simulate. We seek to give some documentation of this claim by examining attempts to computerise linguistic and conversational activities, arguing that these derive from very partial understandings of the activities in question.

6

Falling Short of the Programmatics: The Case of Computational Linguistics

In this and the next chapter we examine a number of developments within *computational linguistics* concerning computational natural language understanding and production which are germane to the themes we have been developing in previous chapters. In particular we will broaden our attack upon a computational theory of mind by explicitly turning our attention to the way in which natural language processing sustains a *computational theory of ordinary language*. Our intention is to show that such theories portray ordinary language use as subject to a *calculus of rules* and in so doing ignore Wittgenstein's powerful description of the role that language plays in social life and practical conduct. By fracturing language from social conduct, computational linguistics provides a theory of ordinary language use that construes rule-following as a mechanical exercise. Our purpose in the next two chapters is to disentangle this theory of ordinary language from the *engineering* ambitions within computational linguistics. Our argument is that whilst we can grant the acceptability of construing ordinary language use as mechanistic rule-following for the purposes of building computers, we cannot allow the way in which such a view is then pressed into the service of a theory of ordinary language use. In this chapter we show how across a range of important considerations in computational linguistics – syntactic and semantic processing and logic – a mechanistic theory of rule-following is compounded. We will then begin to develop our argument against such a theory which in the following chapter will be broadened and then brought to a conclusion by considering one development in depth: the idea of a conversing computer.

The advent of artificial intelligence propelled computational linguistics from the relative obscurity of its pioneering days in the 1950s and 1960s, when it primarily performed computational exercises on texts, into a prominent position within the two disciplines of computer science and linguistics. Its attempt formally to specify linguistic structure for computational purposes has not only promised new interface possibilities but has also reinforced the genetic and cognitive theories of language already abroad within linguistics.

Like artificial intelligence, computational linguistics is driven by the twin desires to build better technology and better to understand human processes. Thus there are two generally accepted motivations behind computational linguistics which are succinctly expressed by Allen: 'First, the technological motivation is to build intelligent computer systems, such as natural language interfaces to databases, automatic machine-translation systems, text analysis systems, speech understanding systems, or computer-aided instruction systems. Second, the linguistic, or cognitive science, motivation is to gain a better understanding of how humans communicate by using natural language' (Allen, 1987, p. 1). Allen concatenates these motivations into a general goal of computational linguistics which is 'to specify a theory of language comprehension and production to such a level of detail that a person could write a computer program that can understand and produce natural language' (Allen, 1987, p. 1).

Certainly, within its relatively short history, there has been no lack of programmatic claims within computational linguistics in this regard. For example, when Winograd built his SHRDLU (Winograd, 1972) program it was claimed that it would show the way towards the achievement of natural understanding for computers. Its abilities to 'interpret' questions and statements were described as primitive understanding and this, it was promised, heralded the development of more elaborate 'machine understanding'.

It has also been argued that 'Logic' programming languages such as PROLOG permit programmers to state what is to be processed, as opposed to how something is to be processed, thus permitting a programming problem to be described 'in logic' (Clocksin, 1984). Further, the representation of meaning has been tackled in procedural semantics through the idea of semantic and first order logic (Rumelhart and Norman, 1973; Winograd, 1972; Woods, 1968). Computational linguistics has, also, promised ways of representing knowledge utilising concepts drawn from artificial intelligence such as 'scripts' and 'plans', for developing natural language understanding for machines (Schank and Abelson, 1977; Schank and Riesbeck, 1981).

Readers of introductions to particular domains of computational linguistics such as natural language understanding would be forgiven for supposing that computational linguistics is the theoretical and practical instantiation of many of the ambitions within artificial intelligence to build intelligent systems. Thus the idea of the *articulate* computer (McTear, 1987) is founded on 'the specification of parsing algorithms and the study of their computational properties, the construction of knowledge representation formalisms that can support the semantic analysis of sentences, and the modeling of reasoning processes that account for the way that context affects the interpretation of sentences' (Allen, 1987, p. 1).

However, as we have observed before, Hubert Dreyfus (1993) has noticed the shortfall between the programmatic claims that are made on behalf of artificial intelligence and the actual systems that have been developed. In this respect readers of the introductions to computational linguistics would also soon detect that, set alongside the robustly stated motivations and the strongly expressed goals, are modest disclaimers when it comes to the descriptions of the *actual* technology that has been developed within computational linguistics. Thus, in their review of automatic natural language parsing, Spark Jones and Wilks (1985) emphasise the tentative status of the systems described in their collection which they introduce as demonstrating the possibility that working models *can*, rather than *have*, been built. Admittedly, their review is now ten years old and, within computer science in general this has proved to be a very long time within which massive hardware and software strides have been made. However, within the field of automatic natural language parsing we still find that the modest disclaimers continue.

Other domains of computational linguistics produce similar modest descriptions of the technology that has been developed. For example, in their review of computational linguistics, Gazdar and Mellish (1987) end their initial dismal review of the state of early machine translation on a high note: 'Thus, in 1970, the precursor of the present chapter reported that "so far, then, no large-scale commercial application of computers to translation exists". . . . By now things have changed radically in this respect, as we shall see in the final section' (Gazdar and Mellish, 1987, pp. 226–7). Accordingly, when we reach the final section of their article we are told that machine translation programs are now being used to do commercial translation, that their use saves time and money, and that commercial companies are investing heavily in their development. However, readers are then provided with a familiar disclaimer to the effect that machine translation programs are not indistinguishable from humans, for 'they all require either pre-editing of the input into some form they can accept, or post-editing to revise or replace the passages that they could not handle, or both' (Gazdar and Mellish, 1987, p. 244). In practice machine translation programs are *not* automatic translation machines but *tools* that translators can use to make *their* work of translation easier. In this respect, the direct comparison between machine translation programs is with other tools such as dictionaries, not with humans. This is not a general criticism of computer tools; indeed we are confident that such programs are very useful to translators, but when the technology produced is compared to the programmatic statements that precede them, the reason for the disclaimers becomes all too apparent.

Examinations of further systems that have been developed reinforce the impression that, to date, there is a gulf between the programmatics of computational linguistics and the actual systems based upon them. Thus the commercial databases that use natural language interfaces only use a highly restricted set of natural language inputs, and systems that are designed to develop grammars are totally dependent upon highly skilled operators and have not been automated. For example, text processing has not been made 'intelligent' and cannot accept commands and, further, expert systems are unable to articulate their reasoning for their consumers.

However, it is not only with respect to the development of technology for everyday use or work that we can find a disjuncture between the technology and the claims on which it is founded but, and perhaps more worryingly, also within the research developments in computational linguistics. Thus, for some of the issues within computational linguistics, the promises of early research seem to have stalled. For example, there is little evidence that the so-called primitive abilities of SHRDLU have 'evolved', as it was claimed they would, into an elaborate form of understanding. Also, the possibility of making declarative formalisms in languages such as PROLOG has still to be realised, and procedural semantics and networks have, it could be argued, fallen by the wayside. Further, the idea of representing natural language 'meanings' in logic has only resulted in very simple and very restricted programs that furnish natural language interfaces for interrogating databases. Whilst these may work for practical purposes, they fall short of the claim to be able to represent meaning.

It is important to stress that in this admittedly compressed comparison between the programmatics and the actualities of computational linguistics we are not marshalling an argument in the service of a wholesale attack upon computational linguistics. We are merely pointing to what is a legitimate observation to make about that field of inquiry, which is that there is a large gap between the programmatic statements that have been made on its behalf and the technology that has been developed. This gap could be taken as evidence of the difficulty in implementing natural-language-oriented programs, or it could be taken as evidence of the fact that the aspirations of computational linguistics have been laid on inappropriate theoretical foundations.

In our general attempt to clarify some of the problems of the contemporary philosophy of mind, we will, here and in the ensuing chapter, examine some of the ideas that are involved in a computational theory of language. The reason for this is not so much to criticise the computational systems that have been built, for we fully recognise the difficulties involved in developing even very simple natural language systems. Our main reason for examining the arguments of computational linguistics concerns their second goal, which is to gain a better understanding of human natural language. We maintain that the two goals create an ambiguity within computational linguistics which is forcibly seen in the way in which a mechanistic theory of rule-following (which may be acceptably developed for the purposes of building computer natural language processing systems) is inappropriately developed as a theory of ordinary language use amongst humans. Thus, to our way of seeing, a computational theory of ordinary language use is giving renewed vigour to an old confusion in the philosophy of language: that ordinary language use is constrained by a *calculus* of determining rules.

In the following arguments we are not taking issue with the formulation of language for the practical purposes of developing so-called natural language systems. We *are* taking issue with the idea that in formalising language using a computational model it is possible to gain a 'better understanding of how humans communicate by using natural language' (Allen, 1987, p. 1). Although we say that we are not criticising the systems that have been built, we have noted above that there is a shortfall between the programmatics and the development of natural language systems, and we will suggest that this may be the result of the very inappropriateness of a *computational model of language* itself.

Natural language understanding

We quoted from Allen that the objective of natural language processing is to be able 'to specify a theory of language comprehension and production to such a level of detail that a person could write a computer program that can understand and produce natural language' (Allen, 1987, p. 1). Within natural language processing the attempts to specify a theory of natural language have mainly revolved around what are considered to be two processing levels: syntax and semantics. Computational linguists are not in agreement about the relationships between these processing levels; for example, as Spark Jones and Wilks (1985) note, some argue that syntactic analysis has no place at all in theorising language understanding. Further, there are other levels at which sentences can be represented in computational linguistics such as at the lexical and morphological levels which tend to be assumed in syntactic processing. However, in general discussions of natural language understanding it is syntax and semantics that are emphasised.

In our discussion, we will use these emphases, not because they represent the boundaries of concern within natural language understanding, but because they can be used to highlight what, for us, are two problematics in the theories of language understanding provided by computational linguistics. The syntactic component of natural language processing can be used to highlight the way in which computational linguistics propounds the argument that the human use of language is determined by a calculus of rules, and the semantic component can be used to highlight the way in which semantic theories within computational linguistics nourish a cognitivist approach to language. In addition, we will consider the ways in which logic has been deployed to represent meaning, for in this we can see the two problems we are emphasising coming together.

Syntactic processing

The computation of a syntactic structure is based upon the formal specification of a grammar which provides for the structures which are 'legal' in a language, and the parsing technique employed which furnishes the method for analysing a sentence in order to resolve its structure as provided for by the grammar. Put simply, the goal of syntactic processing is to use the morphological and lexical analysis of a sentence in order to derive the syntactic structure, and the tools used to so derive that structure are a grammatical *formalism* and a *parser*.

Two simple grammatical formalisms can be used to begin to explore what is involved here. The first of these is a context-free grammar which consists only of rules that take the form: '⟨symbol⟩ ←

⟨symbol⟩₁ ... ⟨symbol⟩ₙ'.[1] The rules involved, *rewrite rules*, furnish the 'legal' structures of the language, how a sentence may be constructed through the 'legal' combining of its subparts, and how those subparts may be 'legally' produced. A simple representation of the output of a parser is a tree structure.

We can illustrate this with a simple sentence: 'Wes hates the gerbil'. In order syntactically to process this sentence, we need to furnish the rewrite rules that specify the 'legal' structures for English, such as the following: a sentence (S) may consist of a noun phrase (NP) followed by a verb phrase (VP); a VP may consist of a VERB followed by a noun phrase; a NOUN phrase may consist of a name or an ART (article) followed by a NOUN.[2] These rewrite rules can be expressed thus:

$$
\begin{array}{lcl}
\text{S} & \leftarrow & \text{NP VP} \\
\text{VP} & \leftarrow & \text{VERB NP} \\
\text{NP} & \leftarrow & \text{NAME} \\
\text{NP} & \leftarrow & \text{ART NOUN}
\end{array}
$$

Applying the rewrite rules to the sentence we are able to produce the following representation of the sentence 'Wes hates the gerbil':

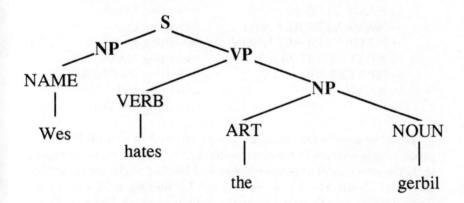

Two simple parsing techniques that may be applied to context-free grammars of this sort are top-down and bottom-up parsing. Top-down techniques involve decomposing the representation of a sentence into

1 n ≥ 1.
2 NOUN, ART and VERB are terminal symbols that cannot be decomposed any further, whilst NP, VP, and S are non-terminal symbols which can be further decomposed.

its subparts, then decomposing these subparts until particular word classes are arrived at which can then be checked against the input sentence. Thus in top-down parsing, the rewrite rules to find, for example, a NP, are used to look for the sequence ART ADJ NOUN. In contrast, bottom-up parsing uses the rules in a different way by taking a sequence that has been found (ART ADJ NOUN) and identifying it as a NP. Hence, for the sentence 'Wes hates the gerbil', a top-down parse would produce the following:

S → NP VP	
→ NAME VP	(rewriting NP)
→ Wes VP	(rewriting NAME)
→ Wes VERB NP	(rewriting VP)
→ Wes hates NP	(rewriting VERB)
→ Wes hates ART NOUN	(rewriting NP)
→ Wes hates the NOUN	(rewriting ART)
→ Wes hates the gerbil	(rewriting NOUN)

In contrast, a bottom-up parse would produce:

→ NAME hates the gerbil	(rewriting Wes)
→ NAME VERB the gerbil	(rewriting hates)
→ NAME VERB ART gerbil	(rewriting the)
→ NAME VERB ART NOUN	(rewriting gerbil)
→ NP VERB ART NOUN	(rewriting NAME)
→ NP VERB NP	(rewriting ART NOUN)
→ NP VP	(rewriting VERB NP)
→ S	(rewriting NP VP)

The other simple grammatical formalism used in natural language processing is a *recursive transition network*. A transition network represents the structure of a sentence in terms of labelled nodes connected by label arcs. Networks are to be crossed by finding routes or paths through them, and these paths are the sequences of labelled arcs. Thus, a sentence could be a network, and the labelled arcs could be a noun phrase and a verb phrase. This can be diagramatically represented as:

```
          enter     NP       VP      leave
S:   (a) ——→ (b) ——→ (c) ——→ (d) ——→ (e)
```

Another example of a network could be a noun phrase and the labelled arcs could be determiner and noun, thus:

$$
\begin{array}{ccccccc}
& \text{enter} & \text{determiner} & & \text{noun} & & \text{leave} \\
\text{NP:} \quad (a) & \longrightarrow (b) & \longrightarrow (c) & \longrightarrow (d) & \longrightarrow (e) \\
& & \text{pronoun} & & \text{adjective} \\
& & & & \text{leave} \\
& & & & (f) \longrightarrow (g)
\end{array}
$$

Both top-down and bottom-up parsing techniques can be used on transition networks, though using bottom-up techniques is recognised to be difficult.

Context-free grammars and transition networks are simple grammatical formalisms, and, within natural language processing it is recognised that they have inherent difficulties, for they are said to be unable to capture some syntactic phenomena such as 'agreement', a situation where the internal structure of one component of an analysis is dependent upon the internal structure of another. It has been necessary to augment the basic grammatical formalisms in one way or another, one of the most important augmentations being to transition networks, resulting in 'augmented transition networks' (ATN) (Kaplan, 1973; Woods, 1973). Further, many grammars for natural language processing have been developed, and these grammars can become quite complicated. Natural language computational processing has attempted to develop measures of 'good' grammars. However, the principles of syntactic processing remain for the augmented grammars as for the unaugmented ones, and it is the principles with which we are concerned in this chapter rather than with the details. The principles are that the grammar specifies allowable structure in terms of a set of rules for combining the parts of a sentence, and that the parser is a program that runs these rules on a sentence, the way in which the rules are run being either top-down, bottom-up, or a mixture, in order to arrive at an output that can be used to represent the sentence structure.

It should be plain from our considerations that the techniques of parsing we have described comprise a *search procedure*; the parsers *search* for the structure. Further, the types of syntactic processing we have considered are 'mechanical', they refer to the way in which a machine can perform set and programmed procedures on a text. They say nothing about the way in which human understanding is organised. New parsing developments based upon them, however, have explicitly proposed theories of human understanding. These developments have moved from a search-based conception of parsing to a *deterministic* conception where the parsing process is not so much engaged in searching alternative combinations to arrive at the correct one but uses current information to choose the correct interpretation.

The problem of ambiguity can be used to illustrate what this entails. Search-based parsers may find ambiguity problematic because the resolution of the ambiguity may reside further along a path that the parser is unable to develop because of the ambiguity. Deterministic parsers are able, however, to handle ambiguity using a *look-ahead* mechanism that encodes an ambiguity until further parts of the sentence are parsed. Quite simply, the look-ahead mechanism enables the parser to store ambiguous words until further input words have been inspected and then to return to the stored word with the parsed later words now as a resource for parsing the ambiguous word. Look-ahead mechanisms have been developed not only for words but also for whole constituents, such as noun phrases, of sentences. Interest in deterministic parsing was generated by Marcus' parser PARSIFAL (Marcus, 1980), which developed from the look-ahead mechanism. Crudely, the constituents of a sentence (noun phrases, verb phrases, etc.) are placed into a *stacker* and a *buffer* which are two temporary stores, and the parser is then the rule set that determines the action to be taken depending upon the contents of the stacker and buffer stores.

Syntactic processing is the heart of many of the natural language front ends that have been developed for the integration of databases.[3] These have proved to be effective in the retrieval and inputting of data and for its manipulation. In this respect, the formulation of language in terms of the construction of restricted grammars and their associated rules has proved to be productive of relatively effective tools through which the computational linguist has been able to develop workable, and often efficient, programs. At *this* level, the formulation of language is not problematic; it is merely a computational method to facilitate the development of computer systems.

However, some of the developments in syntactic processing do not rest their case there, but are used to address *human* understanding, and, consequently we can begin to discern the first seeds of confusion in the relationship between computer processing and human understanding. These seeds have been sown in the later development of deterministic parsing. One of the reasons why deterministic parsing has been developed is that for some within computational linguistics the search techniques of previous parsers do not model what they call the *human processing of language* as well as deterministic processing.

There are, however, two conflations at work here. The first is to slip into the use of concepts that are appropriate for human reasoning when

3 McTear, 1987, gives a useful summary of some of the major ones.

describing computer processing. We are being invited to view the computer as an *interpreting* machine. Consequently, parsing programs are offered as devices through which the machine, in processing sentences, is said to be interpreting them. The second conflation is then to view human understanding as mechanistic processing. Thus, machine processing, since it is claimed to be engaged in 'interpretation', is then offered as a model theory of human understanding.

This conflation is at work in Marcus' development of PARSIFAL. Marcus' basic contention is that *humans* parse sentences 'deterministically'. He also aligns this understanding of human parsing with Chomsky's *extended theory*, thus contributing to a psychological understanding of language. As Spark Jones and Wilks make clear, 'the interest aroused by Marcus' "deterministic hypothesis" has been focused more on the psychological claim being made than on the practical application of the model' (Spark Jones and Wilks, 1985). Marcus' conflation here has passed into the general consideration of syntactic parsing. For example, Allen (1987) discusses the preferences in 'human parsing' such as *minimal attachment* 'which involves a preference for the syntactic analysis that creates the least number of nodes in the parse tree' (p. 162); *right association* where 'all other things being equal, new constituents tend to be interpreted as being part of the current constituent under construction (rather than part of some constituent higher on the parse stack)' (p. 162); and *lexical preferences*, where 'each verb is classified by which prepositions indicate which PP [preposition phrase] must be attached to the VP and which ones are preferred to be attached to the VP (p. 164)'. These issues are, however, old familiar ones for they can be found in the 'Sausage Machine' (Frazier and Fodor, 1978) where overt claims were being made about 'human processing'. Deterministic parsing is then championed because it has a 'psychological validity', and syntactic parsing has moved from the simple mechanical processing of texts in order to represent their grammatical structure into the realms of a computational theory of language.

Our discussion here is not meant to imply that humans do not parse the syntactic structure of a sentence. Tedious English grammar lessons of our youth prove the contrary, where we whiled away many an hour applying the rules of English grammar we had been taught to sample sentences to deconstruct them into their constituent grammatical parts. We are, however, saying that this activity did not provide for our *understanding* of the sentences because we could perfectly well understand them without parsing them. Thus, our understanding did not comprise the application of a calculus of rules. We are also saying that our activity of parsing is not organised by applying some rules of grammar to information that we have stored in relevant parts of our brains. In saying this, we are trying to highlight two issues: a computational theory of language proposes that understanding, in part, consists of the application of a finite calculus of rules, to a sentence, which consists of information stored in the brain.

Both contentions contribute to the mystification of the use of rules in human conduct that has been criticised extensively by Baker and Hacker (1984b). The mystification derives from the way in which language is divorced from the practical circumstances of its use. Treating language as linguistic structures fails to recognise that meaning is tied to the activities that are accomplished in using language, and thus the meaning of a sentence is tied to the practical occasion of its use in the accomplishment of some practical activity, not to a deconstruction of its grammatical parts. However, it is not just within syntactic processing that we can come across the mists of these confusions but also within what to many in computational linguistics is the more important level, that of *semantic* processing.

Semantic processing

There is quite an intense debate within computational linguistics with respect to the relationship between syntactic processing and semantic processing (Spark Jones and Wilks, 1985). Whilst syntactic processing has been well established, it is argued that it is the semantic processing of natural language that is the real goal of natural language understanding on computers. The debate within computational linguistics revolves around whether syntactic processing is necessary: some see it as a step that can lead to semantic processing, others see no role for it at all in natural language understanding systems.

We have no interest in intervening in this debate, merely noting that those who would wish to entwine the semantic processing of language with the syntactic processing of language are explicitly arguing that understanding and meaning fall under the auspices of a set of rules. However, it is not just those who see syntactic processing as a step on the road to the full representation of a sentence who argue this, for when we turn to semantic processing we can plainly see that the idea that understanding and meaning may be brought under a system of rules has found explicit voice throughout computational models of language. Writing about the 'propositional content' of a sentence Ramsay proposes:

It is commonly believed that this propositional content may be extracted by combining the meanings of the individual words according to the semantic rules associated with each syntactic rule. This belief certainly underlies all non-trivial computer systems for natural language processing. . . . (Ramsay, 1986, p. 93)

and:

the analysis of meaning will proceed by associating semantic rules with each of the syntactic rules in our grammar. We will discover the meaning of a fragment of text by discovering the meanings of each of its component parts, and then applying the semantic rule associated with the overall structure of the fragment to these lower level meanings. (Ramsay, 1986, p. 95)

It is, therefore, argued that meaning is built up through the development of some rules for interpreting a noun phrase, the development of rules for combining the meaning of verbs and noun phrases so as to provide meanings for verb phrases, and then developing some rules for combining the meanings of noun phrases and verb phrases so as to give meaning to sentences.

One way in which this representation of the semantic structure of a sentence is developed in natural language processing is through *semantic grammars* (Burton, 1976), such as those to be found in the LADDER and SOPHIE systems. Semantic grammars combine syntactic and semantic knowledge into a single system of rules. However, the terms of the grammar are not syntactic categories but what are termed 'elements of meaning'. Instead of the grammar consisting of nouns, verbs, etc., it would consist of either words that occur frequently in, for example, the queries aimed at a database, or representations of items that may occur in queries. Semantic grammars, however, have a limited applicability for they are written for particular domains such as specialised databases. If they were to be applied to a different database, a different system of rules would have to be written.

Semantic grammars, like search-based parsers, are not intended to represent human activity but to provide for machine processing. That is, they are not intended to be part of a *theory* of natural language. However, one important way in which semantics is addressed within computational linguistics, *conceptual dependency theory*, is very much concerned to be a contribution to a theory of language inasmuch as it claims to represent *the way in which humans process language*.

Conceptual dependency theory utilises the Katz and Fodor (1963) idea of semantic primitives which posits that meaning can be represented in terms of the configuration of a standard set of semantic features. A simple set of features are binary, and are used to represent the meaning of so-called simple objects. Thus, to take two examples provided by Ritchie and Thompson (1984, p. 273); The meaning of dog is said to be:

(+ ANIMATE, − HUMAN, QUADRUPED, + CANINE)

and the meaning of bone is said to be:

(− ANIMATE, + PHYSICAL, + ANIMAL, + OSSEOUS).

Ritchie and Thompson note that these semantic primitives are not capable of representing the meaning of more complex structures such as 'The dog ate the bone' and remind us that Katz and Fodor's (1963) idea of 'semantic markers' was a partial formulation designed to address this problem.

Conceptual dependency theory may be viewed as an attempt to develop such a formulation. As expressed by Schank (1972) and Schank and Riesbeck (1981), it posits a limited number of semantic primitives: for example, primitive acts founded on an abstract understanding of transfer: ATRANS (abstract transfer) (e.g., the possession of an object); physical transfer (PTRANS); and mental transfer (MTRANS) (e.g., people talking together). ATRANS, for example, represents those activities involved in the transfer of the possession of an object and is intended to represent verbs such as 'give', 'take', 'buy', 'sell' and the like. Other primitive actions are those that pertain to bodily activity, for example, PROPEL, applying force to a bodily object, and MOVE, GRASP, INGEST and EXPEL. There are also 'mental actions' such as MBUILD, which refers to the performance of an inference, and CONC, which represents thinking.

'Slots' and 'slot fillers' are involved with these primitives. For example, PTRANS requires that its grammatical subject is physical, and the relationship between the slots and slot fillers is called a 'dependency' and consequently the relationship is understood as a 'conceptual dependency'. Thus through this theory, the meaning of a sentence can be represented as a conceptual dependency.

There are two points that need to be emphasised here. First, within conceptual dependency theory the representation of the sentence must include all of the information for its understanding. Thus, it is necessary to specify what information might be implicit. For example, if we take the sentence 'Wes tossed the gerbil to Jeff', it is necessary to specify that, in order to toss the gerbil, Wes had to pick it up. The second point is that it is necessary to specify the *inference* that may be drawn from the sentence. For example, in *tossing* the gerbil to Jeff (as opposed to passing it to Jeff), Wes was annoyed with the gerbil, or with Jeff, or with both of them. These are matters which have to be specified *for* the computer. However, the specification is based upon what humans can be said to infer from a sentence, and what, in terms of the information that is provided by the sentence, humans can expect. It is thus these *human activities* that are being formalised. In this respect, Schank is not just offering a way of representing the meaning of a sentence for the computer but is offering a theory of language for humans.

> Conceptual dependency theory makes the claim that language under-standing is knowledge-based and expectation-driven . . . that when we interpret sentences we are involved in a process, not of working out their structure but of working out what they say in relation to what we know, and that what we already know enables us to make predictions about what we hear. (McTear, 1987, p. 37)

Schank's theory places an emphasis on the role of what is called 'world knowledge' as well as on what he views as traditional 'linguistic' knowledge in understanding.

Schank, however, acknowledges that there are two major problems, as he sees it, with the theory. First, there is no mechanism to limit the inferences that can be drawn from a sentence, and secondly, the theory only deals with sentences. Attempts to address these two problems gave rise to the Yale language understanding programs, two of which we will mention here: SAM (Script Applier Mechanism) and PAM (Plan Applier Mechanism). These programs were variously founded upon the attempt to address the problems identified in conceptual dependency theory by representing the 'world knowledge' which Schank's theory posits as necessary for understanding.

The first of these involves the idea of 'scripts'. Scripts are used to account for the world knowledge that is necessary to represent the meaning of sequences of activities. Activities are thus 'scripted out' in advance and, upon encountering a situation that could fall under the auspices of a particular script, the script can be applied in order to understand the sequence of events. 'World knowledge' thus takes the form of sets of scripts. However, Schank and his colleagues argue that not only can scripts be programmed into a computer, but scripts are programmed into the human brain. Schank argues that humans store thousands of scripts in their brains, and that human understanding consists of the application of these stored scripts to everyday encounters.

'Scripts', however, are only seen to account for the way in which situations that have been previously encountered are understood, and it came to be argued by the Yale computational linguists that they cannot provide for the way in which people understand situations that are 'new' for them. PAM (Wilensky, 1981) is a program that is said to represent the way in which understanding is organised on those occasions utilising the concepts of 'plan' and 'goal'. Information is provided about the way in which people plan activities, what they need to know in order to achieve a goal, and what things count as goals that they want to achieve. PAM thus consists of the codification of what is called everyday knowledge about plans and goals and rules for applying this knowledge. However, as Schank argued for scripts, it is again argued for plans and goals that this is the way in which human understanding is organised. It is proposed that human understanding consists of divining the plans and the goals of some activity, that activities are to be accounted for in terms of their goals, and are to be understood in terms of accomplishing some plan.

Again, as with our consideration of syntactic processing, we are not attempting to cover all of the issues that are involved in the semantic dimensions of natural language understanding within the field. We have been selective, drawing out issues that are illustrative of important tendencies within computational linguistics. The tendencies that we are illustrating here are to use the procedures for programming computers to provide representations of the meaning of natural language inputs as theories of human understanding. In the attempts to develop semantic theories this has consisted of arguing that meaning and understanding: (1) are *processes*; (2) are rule-governed; (3) involve the application of stored scripts; and (4) require the attribution of a plan and a goal to an activity. We can find in some of the ideas in semantic processing a compounding of the issues which we highlighted in our consideration of syntactic processing issues pertaining to the objective of bringing language under a system of rules and assigning meaning and understanding to processes in the brain.

Logic and semantics

In our discussions of semantic processing we saw that, within conceptual dependency theory, it is necessary to specify the *inferences* that can be made with respect to a sentence. In order to be able to analyse the inferential possibilities of a sentence, some within computational natural language understanding have invoked logic. Logic has also been turned to in attempts to represent the meaning of sentences. Within natural language processing, first order predicate logic has been the mathematical formalism that has been most commonly employed in the representation of meaning.

First order predicate logic uses a set of symbols, rules for combining these symbols into terms and sentences, and rules of inference which specify the extension possibilities of sentences. A logical system starts off with an axiom (an initial set of sentences), and any sentence that can be derived from these using the inference rules is a theorem of the system. The symbols within the logical system are given meaning by associating the terms of the symbols with objects drawn from a given model and thus the sentences that the system is applied to become statements about the objects and how the objects are related. Consequently, symbols in the logical system are paired with objects in the model and rules of interpretation are used to determine how the meaning of a sentence is the product of the truth conditions that apply to its constituent components; are they true or false? A semantic structure can then be provided by, for example, connecting a 'logical sentence' with a given sentence in natural language. The meaning of a natural language sentence is then provided for in terms of a mathematical formalism. Examples of the symbols are 'logical connectives': *and* ($\wedge$), *or* ($\vee$), *not* ($\neg$), *implies* ($\rightarrow$); and 'quantifiers': *for all* ($\forall$), *there exists* ($\exists$). For example, we can represent the meaning of a sentence by associating a formulation with a sentence:

Graham enjoys Pedigree: E(G, P)
Graham is a southerner: G(s)
Pedigree is a beer: P(b)
All southerners enjoy Pedigree: $(\forall s)(\forall b)(CG(s) \wedge P(y)) \Rightarrow E(S, P)$

Ritchie and Thompson, however, raise questions about the use of predicate logic 'as a representational tool for natural language semantics' (Ritchie and Thompson, 1984, p. 371) because of the difficulty of relating models to the real world. This is not, however, a principled argument but a practical one, and they go on to argue that predicate logic could be used 'as a descriptive apparatus within a semantic theory', or by the introduction of 'more complex logics' (Ritchie and Thompson, 1984, p. 371).

Certainly, logic is an important feature of computing in many quarters. One of the reasons for this is that it provides a way of specifying the inferences that can be made with respect to natural language expressions and thus seems to offer the opportunity for the computer scientist to be able to equip a system with the necessary 'knowledge' it requires to process a sentence. Schank (1972) reminds us that the inferential possibilities of a sentence might seem obvious to humans but have to be explicitly spelled out in order to program computers appropriately. The rules of inference in a logical system enable the computational linguist to lay out, in a bounded fashion, and, further, to 'prove', the inferences that a sentence may give rise to.

Allen furnishes an illustration of a rule of inference in this sense. Taking the time-honoured proposition: 'All dogs loves bones and Fido is a dog. Thus Fido loves bones', Allen notes that in first order predicate logic this argument can be stated as the 'following rules, where D is a predicate true only for dogs, and LB is a predicate true only for objects that like bones:

$$\forall x.\ D(x) \supset LB(x)$$

$$\frac{D(\text{FIDO } 1)}{LB(\text{FIDO } 1)}$$

As Allen points out, this is read as 'If the formula $\forall x.\ D(x) \supset LB(x)$ and the formula D(FIDO 1) are true, then the formula LB(FIDO 1) must also be true' (Allen, 1987, p. 518). Allen then illustrates the use of such rules in computational terms in terms of a database 'if the first two formulas are asserted to be true in a database, you can add that LB(FIDO 1) is also true' (Allen, 1987, p. 518).

The fundamental place of logic within computational systems is also strenuously argued within *situation semantics* and its concern with logic and information. Situation semantics was first conceived by Barwise (1981), and developed by Barwise and Perry (1983) and, put simply, is an attempt to incorporate the idea that meaning is situatedly and contextually dependent in the formal scheme of a logical system. Situation theory develops the idea that the world of an 'agent' which can be animate (such as human) or inanimate (such as a machine) is made up of a collection of situations, such as 'situations which are referred to', and 'situations that an agent is given information about', and 'situations that an agent encounters' and the like. It contends that people vary their behaviour in the light of such situations and that behaviour is thus 'situation-dependent'. Within logic there is said to be a novelty to this approach because whilst an ontological scheme traditionally involves individuals, relations, and spatial and temporal locations, it does not involve *situations*. Within situation theory, situations are given the same ontological status as these other components.

This idea is thus understood to extend the purview of logic beyond the remit of the sentence. Barwise argues

> for a broader conception of what logic is all about than prevails among logicians. In particular [it is claimed] that ordinary usage of the words *logic, inference, information*, and *meaning* defines a natural subject matter that is broader than logic as presently studied. More specifically, I argue that logic should seek to understand meaning and inference within a general theory of information, one that takes us outside the realm of sentences and relations between sentences of any language, natural or formal. (Barwise, 1989, p. 37)

Devlin emphasises Barwise and Perry's idea of the *efficiency of language* – the idea that 'the same phrase or sentence can be used on different occasions, by different speakers, to mean different things' (Devlin, 1991, p. 217) – to highlight important features of language use that could be deployed within a formal framework. In order to gain a brief insight into the way in which situation semantics enters into logic we can briefly track through a number of the important points that Devlin makes with regard to speech acts and meaning.

First, he develops what he calls the 'utterance situation' u, which is the immediate context in which an utterance is delivered, with the connections between them designated as *connections*. Thus, to take Devlin's example, the meaning of the utterance 'A man is at the door' said by Jan to Naomi can be represented in the following way (where D is a door fixed by u):

$$u \models \ll\text{utters, Jan, A MAN IS AT THE DOOR, } L, t, 1\gg$$

$$\wedge \ll\text{refers to Jan, THE DOOR, } D, L, t, 1\gg$$

'Thus the speaker's connections link the utterance (as part of u) of the phrase THE DOOR to the object D' (Devlin, 1991, p. 218).

In addition to the utterance situation, Devlin suggests the 'discourse situation' d which attends to the fact that the utterance is part of an ongoing discourse. However, the discourse situation is part of an 'embedding situation' e by which he refers to any aspects of the world that are deemed directly relevant to the discourse such as its 'impact' – the change that is brought about in the embedding situation by an utterance. In addition, there is a 'resource situation' r, such as previously gleaned information. Finally, we have the 'described situation' *s*, which is 'that part of the world the utterance is about' (Devlin, 1991, p. 220).

Devlin consequently argues that these situations constitute a framework for analysing the meaning of (at least assertive) sentences. In short *any* (at least assertive) sentence can be understood in the following way:

> I consider an *utterance situation*, *u*, in which a *speaker*, a_u, utters a sentence, Φ, to a single *listener*, b_u, at a time t_u and a location l_u. The situation *u* may be part of a larger, *discourse situation*, *d*. (Otherwise we take $d = u$.) The situation *d* is part of some (possibly larger) *embedding situation*, *e*, that part of the world of direct relevance to the utterance. During the utterance, the speaker may refer to one of several *resource situations*. The utterance *u* will determine a *described situation*, $S_u = S_u (\Phi)$. (Devlin, 1991, pp. 232–3)

Devlin contrasts situation semantics with the set theoretic logic of Tarski, 1944, and by extension with Fregean logic, for it is Fregean logic that, in the main, computational linguistics has invoked in its consideration of logic. This logic, it could be argued, however, embodies the two problematic issues that have clouded thinking with respect to language which we have so far associated with the developments that we have been considering within computational linguistics. These are, first, that language can be brought under a systematic calculus of rules, and, secondly, that these rules stand *outside of* language. Whilst situation semantics may not encounter all of the problems this involves, it does not, however, as we shall shortly elaborate, escape them all.

Language and conduct

We have to stress, though it must be obvious, that in our considerations of natural language processing so far we have not been able to examine all of the many developments that have occurred within this prolific area of artificial intelligence; this has not been our aim. We have, rather, been concerned to highlight those aspects of natural language processing and understanding within computational linguistics which, either overtly or implicitly, contribute to the computational theory of mind and language that, we are arguing, is behind many of the contemporary confusions within the philosophy of mind. In this respect, we are at pains to emphasise that we are not attempting to undermine the attempts within computational linguistics to build computer systems that are intended to simulate aspects of the way in which humans use language. Formalising language in terms of, for example, a calculus of rules, or formally specifying the inferential potentials of a sentence, may be useful tools that can be appropriately deployed for the purposes of building such simulations. We take exception, however, when such formal models of language are then applied to language use by humans in the form of a theory of language.

From out of our short review emerge two, interconnected sets of issues that we want to emphasise as problematic within the theories of language developed in computational natural language processing. We stress that these problems are not *new* ones, indeed they are manifest across contemporary theories of language. The first set of issues is that language can be brought under the auspices of a set of constraining rules for its proper production and understanding. Baker and Hacker attribute the generation of a modern mythology about language to this argument: 'We shall find that the roots of the mythology which informs contemporary linguistics and philosophical theories of meaning lie in fundamental misconceptions about the nature of rules, rule-following and normative explanation' (Baker and Hacker, 1984b, p. 244).

However, although not a new misconception, it is one that is being revitalised by developments in artificial intelligence and computational linguistics and is being given a new lease of life to which, in our view, it is not entitled. The issue is manifest across a range of concerns within natural language processing. We have found it in (1) the way in which for some it is considered that syntactic parsing is a step in the determination of a semantic component; (2) the advent of deterministic parsing as a model of human understanding; (3) considerations of the applications of grammars; and (4) the models of thought and information presented in logical systems and specifications of rules of inference (we have implied this, but have yet to develop this point).

It is also perpetuated in the arguments concerning scripts, plans and goals. Although these are differentiated from rules they are nevertheless given the same role in theories of ordinary language use as that accorded to rules. The depiction of rule-following that is provided in computational theories of ordinary language use is that human conduct is *constrained* by a calculus of rules. Schank's arguments concerning scripts is that they *too* constrain human conduct, for human conduct is engaged in according to a pre-given script.

The second set of issues are also not new ones. They concern the way in which rules are said to be represented in the brain. The arguments that we have examined invoke the Chomskian idea that rules are formulated in neural systems. Again, this is not just the case for rules, it is also argued that scripts and goals are similarly represented in the brain. Within computational linguistics the approaches of semantic networks, and conceptual dependency theory with its origination of the idea of scripts and its emphasis on plans and goals, and its seeming success in implementing language systems on computers using these ideas, are breathing new life into old arguments.

These problems continue to arise because of the continuing insistence, reinforced by natural language processing, on divorcing language from the practical circumstances of its use, thus failing to appreciate the way in which Wittgenstein sought to emphasise language use as practical conduct. Wittgenstein took issue with the way in which language use was construed to be governed by a calculus of rules in Fregean logic. Within natural language understanding, language is seen to be constrained by a system of determining rules, and this can be most clearly appreciated by looking at the way in which logic has been used in artificial intelligence and computational linguistics which displays a Fregean heritage. We have yet, however, to demonstrate that, and thus we will initially pick up on Fregean logic in order to explore how the idea of a calculus of constraining rules poses a philosophical problem that is perpetuated in artificial intelligence and computational linguistics.

The major thrust of Fregean logic, one that we have found to be instantiated in various considerations of logic within computational natural language understanding, is that the rules of logic provide us with ways of reasoning *correctly*, and through which we can move from true premises to true conclusions. In this respect, the rules of logic are 'necessary rules'. Human reasoning does not *have* to follow them, but if *correct* reasoning is to occur then it will only do so under their auspices. The ability to make correct inferences is then *constrained* human reasoning; if reasoning is to be done correctly, it is circumscribed by these necessary rules. Further, it is decontextualised, organised outside of any particular occasions, and thus, for Frege, language has an *essence*.

We are not so much concerned to pick up and develop arguments about Fregean logic in particular.[4] However, extracting the core notions of 'constraint', 'decontextualisation' and 'essence' from out of his philosophy allows us to see how artificial intelligence and computational linguistics has, in its considerations of information processing, been nurturing a particular and problematic view of logic. As we have seen, the mathematical formulation of human thinking as constrained by rules for correct reasoning is used to specify the inferential possibilities – the *extension* possibilities as it is sometimes put – of a sentence *for the*

4 On this topic, see Baker and Hacker, 1984a.

computer. Further, we have also seen across a number of considerations of syntactic and semantic processing that the meaning of a sentence is understood to be constrained by the rules that account *solely for its structure*. In both cases, the issue of constraint involves the consideration of the sentence *removed* from its use within a social context. Thus, the inferential possibilities that a sentence may have, and the meaning that it may be given, are stipulated without reference to the role that the sentence might perform in some stretch of social conduct. If, however, language is reconciled with social conduct, the posited constraints become no more than arbitrary formulations, providing idealisations of use in context.

The reconciliation of language and conduct is provided in Wittgenstein's shift of the object of logical analysis from *language* to *language-games*. One of the mainsprings of Wittgenstein's thinking here is that language use and practical conduct are inextricably bound together. This has many implications for the way in which we might address logic, and for our purposes, the way in which we might understand the relationship between rules and language.

One important issue which Wittgenstein raises concerns the ideal of exactness of specification in logical systems. First, we have seen that the rules postulated within the logical systems currently used within computational natural language understanding are constraining inasmuch as they are claimed to circumscribe thinking exactly, and are wholly independent of context. However, is it possible *exhaustively* to formulate all the rules that might circumscribe a particular activity? As Wittgenstein writes:

> How should we have to imagine a complete list of rules for the employment of a word? – What do we mean by a complete list of rules for the employment of a piece in chess? Couldn't we always construct doubtful cases, in which the normal list of rules does not decide? Think, e.g., of such a question as: how to determine who moved last, if a doubt is raised about the reliability of the players' memories? (Wittgenstein, 1967, paragraph 440)

A further issue relevant to constraint is that judgments as to what could be complete, or encompassing, are tied to the practical circumstances of language use. In the continuation of the paragraph quoted above, Wittgenstein remarks:

> The regulations of traffic in the streets permits and forbids certain actions on the part of drivers and pedestrians; but it does not attempt to guide the totality of their movements by prescription. And it would be senseless to

talk of an 'ideal' ordering of traffic which should do that; in the first place
we should have no idea what to imagine as this ideal. If someone wants to
make traffic regulations stricter on some point or other, that does not
mean that he wants to approximate to such an ideal. (Wittgenstein, 1967,
paragraph 440)

The first point is crucial: that it is just not possible to constrain
language in terms of a calculus of rules because in actual conduct the
rules can proliferate for practical purposes which are not themselves
pre-specifiable in detail. Whilst having a finite set of rules might seem
to be a nice convenience for computational linguistics, the fact that in
practice the inferential possibilities of a sentence are partly dependent
upon its use in and as *human conduct* means that the specification of
inferential possibilities in terms of a calculus of rules can only serve as
an idealisation of those possibilities. There is a two-fold problem here.
The first part of this problem is that the exactness of specification
required for programming a computer is an illusion. As Wittgenstein's
second point above makes clear, criteria of exactness are purpose-
dependent, a point which goes unrecognised in artificial intelligence
arguments. The second part of the problem is that a myth is being
peddled within some quarters of computational linguistics that it *is*
possible exhaustively to specify these inferential possibilities. Language is not constrained in *that* way, and viewing it as such continues
to be a confusion to which computational linguistics, at least programmatically, is contributing. It might seem, however, that the 'situation
semantics' considered above is able to address this problem of constraint. Since situation semantic schemes for arriving at the meaning of
a sentence ground the analysis of the sentence within the various
situations that surround its use by factoring them into any representation of its meaning, situation semantics may be viewed as attempting to
include the practicalities of language use as a factor in its formal
schemes. In this respect, situation semantics may be viewed as breaking the Fregean mould of logic which insists that logical rules are
independent of context. As such, it is free from any charge of formulating inappropriate constraints on language use. Put simply, situation
semantics may be viewed as attempting to reconcile language and
conduct within logic.

But surely, all that situation semantics is doing is acknowledging
what has been obvious in many considerations of language, including
many parts of linguistics, that meaning is (in part) contextually dependent? The fact that this may be the case does not, then, mean that
this contextual aspect to meaning is subsumable under a set of

formalisms. Situation semantics is extending the range of factorable variables by incorporating 'the situation' in a logical system, but the way in which this is being done is exactly the same as the way in which other factors are built in, namely, in terms of their codification under a constraining formalism. The codification of the context in a mathematical formalism *must* be an idealisation of that context. In this respect, situation semantics has just as much a rigid constraint conception of language as set semantics, and whilst Devlin suggests that his logical system will look very different from that of Tarski, from our point of view it does not. Both systems view meaning as formalisable within a framework of codifable variables. Situation semantics is, on the one hand, making context a feature in a logical system, but, on the other hand, and this might sound strange, it is *decontextualising* 'context' in its formulation.

We would see that one of the points that Wittgenstein is making with respect to rules and language is that there are no *mechanisms* of grammar, no *calculus* of determining rules, *behind* reasoning, behind language. Rules can be a guide to action, but they do not constrain it in the way in which the viewpoint nourished by computational linguists proposes.

It is not just within the domain of the application of logical systems in natural language understanding that this rule-constraint myth is perpetuated. As we have seen, the idea that meaning can be determined by a set of constraining rules is endemic across all formal syntactic and semantic considerations. Thus, computational linguists seem to be bent on formulating rules that can be used to provide the meaning of a sentence. These formulations may be used to program computers; however, they are then also said to be representations of the ways in which humans determine meaning. There is a confusion here over the status of rules in human conduct which, although it runs deep in the philosophy of language, is being re-energised by computational linguistics. We can consider this by addressing Wittgenstein's distinction between an activity being *in accordance with a rule* and an activity that *follows a rule*.

One confusion that computational linguistics is contributing to within the philosophy of language concerns the extent to which it is necessary to have knowledge of the rules under whose auspices an action is said to fall. The argument that it is unnecessary to have explicit knowledge of the rules that are said to govern language is deeply rooted in Chomskian linguistics, where rules are placed outside the consciousness of individuals by being rooted in their physiology. Not only is it argued that persons need not know the rules that constrain their activities, it is also argued that, in principle, they could not know them because they are part of their central nervous system endowment. Some of the proposals that are made concerning language understanding within computational linguistics with respect to the rule-constrained nature of meaning and understanding seem unwittingly to accept the premiss that it is unnecessary for speakers to know the rules they are said to be following.

However, is this a sustainable argument? If we take somebody engaged in simple syntactic parsing we might describe what they are doing as applying some rules of grammar that they know to a given text, resulting in an analysis of its constituent grammatical parts. In such a case, we might confidently say that they know the rules and that they were following them, and consequently their actions were constrained by these rules. However, if we posited some *further* rules such as *how* they apply the grammatical rules by, for example, preserving 'minimal attachment', 'right association' and 'lexical preferences', then we might be less sure that such a person knows the rules. Could we still feel confident in saying that they followed the rules and that their activities were constrained by the rules? For champions of deterministic parsing, for instance, the rules they posit are rules that 'have psychological validity' even if people are unaware of the rules.

Waisman (1965), however, has something interesting to say that is relevant here. He furnishes an example of a person writing a sequence of numbers on the blackboard and asks if an observer can formulate the rule the person is using. Waisman proposes a number of rules any one of which would precisely cover the sequence. The point that Waisman makes from this example is that just because a rule can be formulated that would *cover* the action it describes, it does not follow that it can make sense to say that the person *followed* the rule in engaging in the activity. It would only make sense to say that the person followed the rule in producing the activity if they did so *knowingly*. Just because it is possible to formulate a rule that might provide for conduct does not mean that the conduct in question has indeed been constrained by that particular rule.

Waisman is working with the distinction that Wittgenstein makes 'between what one might call "a process being *in accordance with* a rule", and, "a process involving a rule"...'[5] As Bogen clearly put it, 'An activity *accords* with a rule if it exhibits regularities expressed by the rule. But it *involves* a rule only if agents actually use the rule to

5 Ludwig Wittgenstein, 1958, *Preliminary Studies for the 'Philosophical Investigations': The Blue and Brown Books*, p. 13. Oxford: Basil Blackwell.

guide and assess their action' (Bogen, 1972, p. 182). And, 'We cannot say a linguistic practice is governed by rules unless the speakers can apply the relevant rules to cases which fall under them, can determine which cases fall under them, and know what it is to apply the rules to the cases correctly' (Bogen, 1972, p. 182). Warnock provides a memorable example. On a journey from Oxford to Aberystwyth he notes that the route he takes may be the same one that we have marked on our map. Yet it hardly makes sense to say that he *followed* our marked route if he was unaware of it. His journey *accorded* with our map; it was not *guided* by it.

Formulating rules for implementing computer programs is one thing. However, the success (and we have argued that it is only a limited success) in programming computers which can produce simulacra of some aspects of human understanding by virtue of the formulation of some rules of language, is used as a basis for attributing the use of *these self-same rules* to actual human speakers and hearers. That is, rules of logical inference, semantic rules and parsing rules formulated within computational science are said to be *the* rules that govern natural language. The seeming success of programming some natural language systems is then giving succour to a problematic conception of the relationship between language and rules that resides in Fregean logic, Chomskian linguistics, and indeed in parts of the *Tractatus*. Wittgenstein's repudiation of some of his arguments of the *Tractatus*, however, exposes the fallacy of construing language in terms of rules *unknown* to speakers of that language.

We have focused our arguments upon rules. However, they are just as applicable to the application of scripts and plans in artificial intelligence accounts of human conduct. This is because, like rules, it is proposed that they constrain human conduct. Thus it is proposed that they govern human conduct and that like rules it is not necessary to *know* them. This is because again like rules, they are represented in the neural system of the brain. This brings us to the second set of confusions that surround the role assigned to rules, scripts and plans in computational theories of language use.

In his argument that scripts are stored in the brain, Schank perpetuates the Chomskian fallacy that rules are represented in a person's brain. Commenting on this, Baker and Hacker make the following points:

> We might start by questioning what it is for a rule to be 'represented' in somebody's brain or to have a 'neural realisation'. One can *formulate* a rule in English or French, *translate it* into German or Italian. One might call

such formulations 'representations of a rule', but then one certainly cannot formulate rules in neural synapses. For the medium of formulation must be symbolic, hence must be signs used by goal-directed creatures with certain purposes and in accord with certain conventions. One can represent a rule by a concrete symbol, like a signpost or a pattern to be followed or copied. But since neural synapses are not readily accessible nor observable, no one has ever represented a rule thus. For to represent a rule is to use an array of signs or symbols in a certain way and with a certain significance. We do so, and thereby render meaningful, noises, and inscriptions. But not neurons! (Baker and Hacker, 1984b, p. 296)

We have not argued that human beings cannot follow rules, or engage in some action that they have planned, or script out their activities in advance. Our argument has concerned *what it is* to follow a rule, and by extension, a plan and a script. Similarly, we are not arguing that human beings cannot represent a rule, but we take issue with the way in which within artificial intelligence *what it is* to represent a rule is presented. In artificial intelligence a rule, a plan and a script are represented in the *brain*. Baker and Hacker are making two points in this respect. First, that the medium of representation is symbolic. Thus a rule can be represented in a signpost and a plan may be represented in a drawing, and something may be scripted out on paper. But neurons are *not* a symbolic medium, nor are they observable and thus neurons are not the same order of medium that readily recognisable forms of representation take. Thus we can see that the signpost represents the rule; see that the plan represents the house; see that the map represents the terrain; see that the script represents the actions on the stage. We can see that somebody follows the signpost in taking a turn; see that somebody follows the plan in building the house; see that somebody follows the route on the map; see that the actors are following the script. But we just *cannot* see that the neuron represents the rule, or the plan or the script.

The second point that Baker and Hacker are making is that rules (and by extension) plans and scripts are used within courses of practical conduct for practical purposes. The medium of representation then is aligned to those practical purposes. Thus the rule is represented in the signpost and we follow the pointed end in order correctly to guide our journey; we use the plan in order to build the house correctly; we follow the map in order to find our way; we follow the script in order correctly to stage the play. The signpost, the plan, the map, the script are representations that are used for our purposes, they gain their intelligibility as representations within the course of action in which we use them. However, do we use neurons in the same way? Do we use neurons for our practical purposes? Does it even make sense to say that we *use* neurons? Do neurons gain their intelligibility within a course of action? Again, neurons are just a different order of phenomena from signposts, plans, maps and scripts, and thereby cannot be said to be media of representation.

We began this chapter by noticing that there is a shortfall between the programmatic claims and the systems developed within computational linguistics, which concerns one of the goals of computational natural language processing, which is to build better systems. We have latterly been examining the other goal we mentioned, which is better to understand how humans use language, and we have seen that the way in which this goal is approached is through a theory of natural language use that propounds that natural language use is constrained by a calculus of rules represented in the brain. We have argued that this is wrong. We believe that part of the reason why there is the shortfall between the programmatics and the systems is that the programmatics are based upon this theory. We turn now in the next chapter to a development in computational linguistics which we believe clearly demonstrates this: the conversing computer. In attempting to develop the conversing computer the ambiguity in artificial intelligence that we have referred to with respect to its engineering and its ambitions to develop theories of ordinary language use become stark, for here artificial intelligence is attempting to bring ordinary conversation under a calculus of constraining rules. We thus will continue our examination of the problematic character of construing language use as governed by a calculus of rules by turning to *the myth of the conversing computer*.

7

Can a Machine Talk?

In this chapter we will bring to conclusion our consideration of issues which have arisen earlier in the book. Once again, we will have to argue for a differentiation between the 'engineering' questions which are (legitimately) involved in the development of, in this instance, dialogical interfaces, and the construal of such ambitions, particularly with respect to the intimation that success in them will enable machines to do something that, hitherto, and significantly, it has been supposed that only human beings could do. The desire to make the latter kind of claim encourages the suggestion that if computers can be programmed to 'follow the rules of conversation' then this will show that machines are no less capable than are human beings of 'following rules'.

We have already made our case against the idea that programming machines to simulate 'mental' activities, rather than physical ones, somehow 'narrows the gap' between humans and machines, and will not repeat it here. We will, rather, focus upon a confusion which is encouraged by the ambition to design systems which 'talk like you and me', one which involves the conflation of very different kinds of 'rule-following'. The conflation is between the kinds of rules which are involved in writing computer programs, and those which are observed in the conduct of conversations, and there is, as a result, a developing misunderstanding about the extent to which the formulation of some rules for the organisation of conversation promises to facilitate the development of 'dialogical' interfaces.

In particular, it is claimed that because it is the case that there are *some* aspects of conversational organisation which are formulable as a set of rules and which can (relatively easily) be represented in a computer program, then the prospect of programming interfaces which *closely* simulate more than the superficial features of conversational transactions is at hand. However, this expectation is based upon a misinterpretation of the part that such rules play in the organisation of conversational activity. With respect to the development of 'computers that talk like you and me', we would expect, once again, to see the now-familiar pattern of high aspirations and subsequent disappointment, with a few small successes being incautiously taken to signify the imminent prospect of immense progress. There is, in fact, a tension between the understanding of how 'conversation' works which is embedded in the attempts to design interfaces and some of the sources from which those attempts purport to derive their understanding of conversation.

Dialogical interfaces

So far, our consideration of computational theories of language use has focused upon natural language *understanding*. This is, however, only one side of the processing coin, the other being natural language *generation*. Turning to natural language generation we find, however, that further promises are made that make the shortfalls between the programmatics and the systems even more noticeable. These promises concern what to many in computational linguistics is the ultimate goal of all natural language processing, which is the development of a *dialogical or conversing machine*.

Though natural language processing encompasses a broad range of linguistic phenomena, a central goal which is often cited in both the technical and the popular literature is the production of a human-like dialogue interface: for example, 'In some ways, the notion of a computer with which one could carry on an ordinary conversation represents the ultimate aim of all research in natural language processing' (Lehnert and Ringle, 1982, p. 199); and: 'This book is about one particular task that we'd like a computer to do. Wouldn't it be nice to just sit down at some computer terminal and tell the computer, in whatever language you speak, some task that you want done and have the computer do it?' (Reichman, 1985, p. xi). More circumspectly, yet in a generally supportive vein, McTear writes: '[The articulate computer: fact or fiction?] This is the question with which we began this book. I hope I have been able to show that the notion of an articulate computer is not pure fantasy and indeed that considerable progress has been made in this important area of AI [artificial intelligence]' (McTear, 1987, p. 225).

Though we consider the development of a conversing computer to be another overweening ambition within computational linguistics that compounds a theoretical confusion over what it is to engage in dialogue or conversations, we cannot simply set it aside on the basis of the arguments we have already given against other theories of natural language processing. The reason for this is that some of the proponents of a conversational machine view themselves as going beyond the traditional boundaries of their discipline and have, themselves, been critical of the more orthodox research in natural language processing. They argue that *their* discipline's traditional concerns with the linguistic structure of the sentence cannot provide an understanding of how complex and protracted sequences of sentences can comprise a coherent dialogue and thus, in order to build a conversing machine it is necessary to move the boundaries of natural language processing beyond conventional linguistic structures by studying actual *conversation or dialogue*.

The fact that the emphasis moves from the grammatical structure of the sentence to 'the course of a conversation' may suggest that there has been a recognition that language use is about action-in-interaction which might enable a distancing from the problems that we have identified as afflicting prior work in natural language processing. This awareness might be encouraged by a further recognition of the extent to which the sequencing of turns in a conversation does not conform to a 'mechanical' conception; its succeeding turns are not generated by the automatic operation of a procedure. However, rather than the examination of conversation being used to call into question the underlying concept of mechanically generated sequences, the attempt has been made to absorb the understanding of conversation into that underlying conception, and it is this particular point that is the main focus of subsequent discussion. We thus turn in this chapter explicitly to examine the idea of a *converging computer*. We intend to show that, in the same way in which the concept of 'intelligence' is used with such careless abandon within the general field of artificial intelligence, so too within the subdiscipline of computational linguistics, the term 'conversing machines' is profligately used.

To begin with, we should note that, although the developments which we will consider here are relatively new, the very idea of a conversing machine is not a new one nor is it just associated with those in computational linguistics who are showing interest in the structure of ordinary dialogue and conversations. The question/answer systems that can be traced from Weizenbaum's (Weizenbaum, 1966) ELIZA program through Winograd's (Winograd, 1972) SHRDLU to the numerous natural language front ends that have been developed for particular databases employ a dialogical or conversational model.

However, the more recent developments within computational linguistics (and some of the developments which are taking place outside of the discipline and which are being offered as relevant to it) are part of a reaction to the characterisation of question/answer systems *as* dialogical or conversational systems. It is argued that these systems do not facilitate 'genuine' conversation and dialogue. Whilst critics of question/answer systems do not query the foundational concepts upon which they are based, such as those of 'knowledge structures' and 'rules of inference' that we have examined in the previous chapter, they do, nevertheless, contend that question/answer systems fail to realise the possibility of developing dialogical or conversational machines because they are not based upon a proper understanding of dialogue and conversation as linguistic phenomena.

For example, Lehnert and Ringle argue that language parsers are not capable of approximating conversation: 'Systems that process only the surface linguistic features of a dialogue will never be able to achieve even a rudimentary approximation of genuine dialogue behavior' (Lehnert and Ringle, 1982, p. 200). Reichman (1985) echoes this when she argues that most programs that can parse and seemingly generate language do so at the level of the sentence but that conversation or dialogue takes place *across* sentences. This means, she suggests, that it is possible to find different sorts of phenomena or greater frequencies of some phenomena in conversation when compared to sentences. For example, she describes how conversation involves what she calls 'elliptical utterances' and how in conversation there is a greater use of anaphoric and deictic references. For Reichman, the fact that conversation embodies such features means that reference has to be made to some preceding part of the conversation in order to make sense of some current utterance or reference, and, consequently, grammar parsers which only operate at the level of the sentence are not capable of capturing this feature of conversation, and cannot, therefore, hope to achieve effective simulations. In order to develop a system that is capable of *conversing* with humans it would be necessary, on Reichman's arguments, to replicate features of human conversation.

Reichman further argues that there is more to dialogue and conversation than what is said, 'in so many words' (by which she means that dialogue and conversation are dependent on tacit knowledge), and that grammar parsers are not robust enough to handle this feature of talk. Ringle and Bruce (1982) suggest that this is because, whilst the imputed underlying structures are the object of searching analysis, they are context-dependent, and do not provide a method for generating systems that are independent of a particular database:

> Depth in a particular micro-world is achieved through careful restrictions in the domain of discourse and extensive analysis of human belief/goal structures within that domain. The weakness of such a system is not so much that it would fail if its repertoire of expected structures were exceeded . . . but rather that it gives no insight into general methods for establishing user sensitivity that would be domain independent. . . . What we should be looking for instead are methods of establishing user sensitivity that depend on generalizable dialogue components and that would, therefore, be portable from one domain to another. (Ringle and Bruce, 1982, p. 216)

Consequently, for some in artificial intelligence and computational linguistics who see that the goal of natural language processing is to develop a conversing computer, the traditional linguistic concerns with syntax and semantics as instantiated in the grammar parsers involved in question and answering systems do not provide them with descriptions of linguistic phenomena that would enable them to develop a 'truly' conversing machine. Rather, it is argued, what is required is an analysis of conversation and dialogue: 'To study the underlying structures and mechanisms involved in human dialogue, one must engage in empirical analysis of actual human conversations' (Lehnert and Ringle, 1982, p. 200).

Accordingly, there have been attempts to develop ways of applying studies of conversation and discourse to the design of conversing machines. One of these has been to take a broadly discourse-analytic tack and to examine what knowledge of discourse structures consists of and how that knowledge is used to structure discourse. The formalisation of that knowledge and its use in a model can, then, it is assumed, be used to implement discursive computer systems. The other initiative with which we will be concerned is the application of the descriptions of various conversational mechanisms developed within the sociologically grounded field of *conversation analysis* (Sacks, 1993a; 1993b) in order to provide foundations for the development of conversational machines.

Studies of conversation and discourse

Discourse structures

Those who are pursuing a discourse-analytic approach within computational linguistics are attempting to impose linguistic analysis upon conversational phenomena in order to construct a formal model of discourse structure and knowledge that can be subsequently used in the development of a computer system. Although numerous initiatives are being taken in this direction we will concentrate upon just one of them which we believe to be not only relatively sophisticated but also representative of principles that can be found in the others. The model is the one that is described in Reichman's (1985) book *Getting Computers to Talk Like You and Me* and the principle is one of *formalising* conversation.

Reichman's model is based upon two main components: a *context space* and a *conversational move*. A context space is used to describe a number of utterances on a single issue. For example, an *issue context space* involves the assertion that something is true or false, good or bad, possible or impossible. Context spaces are made up of conversational moves which are discourse interactional units such as presenting a claim, explaining a claim, supporting a claim or challenging a claim. Discourse or conversation is, according to Reichman, built up through numerous context spaces, which are, in their turn, built up from out of various conversational moves. Any context space is usually functionally related to preceding context spaces and this allows speakers and hearers to understand the coherence of conversation.

Consequently, the structure of conversation or discourse can be hierarchically portrayed in the same way in which linguistic structure can be, for, it is claimed, in the same way in which a verb in syntax can be supported by an adverb, so too can a claim be supported by an explanation. Reichman argues that it is knowledge of this hierarchical structure that enables participants to follow what she describes as the 'flow' of conversation and which relates to the production of discourse markers and the use of anaphoric reference.

Reichman formalises the idea of context spaces by arguing that they all have the same structure because they all consist of the same slots to be filled, and she represents this in the following terms:

TYPE　　　　　　　　　　the name of the context space

DERIVATION　　　　　　　whether the claims in the context

	space were explicitly stated by the speaker or inferred by the system
GOAL	the function of the conversational move, e.g., support, challenge
CONTEXTUAL FUNCTION	(1) Method: the method used to perform the conversational move, e.g., analogy (2) Co-relator: specific reference to context space to which the current move is related
SPEAKERS	a list of speakers who have produced utterances within the context space
STATUS	the role of the context space in the discourse, e.g., whether foreground or background
FOCUS	the status of individual elements within the context space

(Reichman, 1985, p. 52)

When the context space is an 'issue context space', Reichman adds three extra slots: one each for claim, topic and support. 'Issue context spaces' are also divided into debatative, which have yet further slots for counter-claims and counter-supports to be made by antagonists and protagonists, and non-debatative, which have no such slots. Reichman adduces the following example:

A: I think if you're going to marry someone in the Hindu tradition, you have to – Well, you – they say you give money to the family, to the girl, but in essence, you actually buy her

B: it's the same in the Western tradition. You know, you see these greasy fat millionaires going around with film stars, right. They've essentially bought them by their status.

(Reichman, 1985, pp. 55–6)

Reichman describes the structure of B's utterance (context space 2, A's turn being context space 1) in terms of context space structure thus:

TYPE	Issue
DERIVATION	Explicit
GOAL	Generalisation

CONTEXTUAL	Method: Analogy
FUNCTION	Co-relator: C1
SPEAKERS	B
STATUS	Active
FOCUS	It (buying and selling women) – high focus Western tradition – medium focus

(Reichman, 1985, pp. 55–6)

The second major component in Reichman's conversational model is a 'conversational move', which she illustrates in an examination of the following extract of conversation:

```
1   D:  you and I are very close in this room right
2       now but we don't have the same
3       environment because I'm looking at you,
4       I'm seeing the window behind you. You're
5       not seeing the window behind you
```
(Reichman, 1985)

Reichman is interested in accounting for how the statement (in lines 2–5) can be heard as a supporting statement to the claim that D and his co-conversationalist do not share the same environment. She proposes that there are three elements at work here: a claim, a support and a principle (in the above example, that if two people share the same environment they will see the same things). The general principle is then applied by mapping it onto instances of the class (the argument here) of which it is a generalisation. Thus, one element in providing for the hearing is what Reichman calls a process of *instantiation*.

The second element is a rule of logic, in this case, *modus tollens*, which Reichman formulates as: 'Given two facts A and B, and the assertion that A implies B, then if you know that B is not true, you can conclude that A is not true.' With respect to the case at hand, Reichman is then able to say of the example: 'If two people share the same environment, then they will see the same things (if A then B). We (D and R) are two people and "things" is "the window behind you". (Instantiation). I can see the window but you cannot (B is not true). Therefore: We do not share the same environment (A is not true).' For Reichman, this model not only constitutes a framework for the interpretation of utterances within conversation, but also constitutes a framework for the generation of conversation.

Reichman's model is one of the more developed attempts to investigate the structure of dialogue or conversation with the explicit intention of using the results to implement a system for the development of a conversing machine. As we mentioned, however, she is not alone. For example, Lehnert and Ringle (1982), Grosz (1978 and 1981), and Brady and Berwick (1983) have also attempted to develop an understanding of the structures of conversation or dialogue for machine implementation, and they share in common with Reichman the ambition to render the generation of conversation accountable to a formalisation of standard processes and rules. We have used Reichman merely to stress these features of computational linguistic treatments of conversation and discourse because of the relative sophistication of her model.

We want to highlight two aspects of Reichman's model, for they are indicative of the prematurely or inappropriately formalising thrust within computational linguistics. First, Reichman is proposing that discourse is the product of the completion of obligatory elements, and, consequently, she is proposing a process model which is comprised of standardised slots. Thus, the model proposes that every conversation consists in the same processes and has the same slots. Second, the slots are the product of a set of rules, rules of inference.

We will critically return to these formalisms at a later stage in this chapter, but now move on to examining another form of investigation into the organisation of conversation that is being offered to computational linguistics: conversation analysis.

Conversation analysis

Work within conversation analysis has involved the development of a number of conversational and dialogical systems. For example, Frohlich and Luff (1990) discuss the 'advice system', which was a demonstration computer system built to show how members of the general public who required welfare rights advice could be served by computer. Frohlich and Luff argue that a conversation-analytic approach may be taken towards processing problems and describe how the advice system draws on various studies and what they call 'findings' in conversation analysis. Thus, Sacks, Schegloff and Jefferson's (1974) description of the simplest systematics for the organisation of turn-taking for conversation is said to provide a resource for the control of turn-taking for the system. Also, Schegloff, Jefferson and Sacks' (1977) description of error and repair initiation is invoked in their description of a repair control for the program. Further, the control of the opening sequence is said to be based upon Schegloff's extensive work on the opening section of conversation (Schegloff, 1968; 1979; and 1986), and the control of the closing sequence, it is claimed, is founded on Schegloff and Sacks' (1973) description of the closing section of conversation.

In order to give some flavour of how conversation analysis is being used in the advice system, we can provide as an example a description of the way in which the system is designed to *preclude* certain activities from following other activities. For instance, the system prevents users from making a *statement* following a system *question*. This preclusion has been designed into the system in order to simulate a feature of the organisation of *adjacency pairs* (Schegloff and Sacks, 1973). This feature is that some utterances in conversation project a 'conditionally relevant next turn' (Schegloff, 1968) to be occupied with particular activities. For example, conventionally, a question projects that specifically designed answers should occupy the next turn. The advice system has been designed to mimic this sequential organisation and thus precludes other activities from occupying the 'answer slot'.

In another use of conversation analysis, Gilbert, Wooffitt and Fraser (1990) describe the 'sundial project', which was intended 'to develop a computer system which is capable of "conversing" with members of the public over the telephone to answer simple queries such as the time of arrival of particular air line flights or the times of trains' (p. 237). They describe how the system operates with respect to 'turn-taking', 'opening sequences', 'closing sequences' and 'question–answer sequences', and argue that the system is based upon the description of these sequences within conversation analysis.[1]

Both the discourse-analytic approach and the so-called conversation-analytic approach argue that conversing machines will only be possible if the systems are built in such a way as to enable them to engage in conversation or dialogue in the manner in which humans talk to one another. In order to so equip the machines, it is argued, computational linguists must develop a thorough understanding of the principles through which human discourse is ordered and organised.

---

1 The collection of studies that the two examples of the advice system and the sundial project are taken from – Luff, Gilbert and Frohlich (1990) – offers, in the main, the relevance of conversation analysis for the development of so-called conversing machines, a relevance that has been further explored in the American Association for Artificial Intelligence meetings of 1990 which mounted a workshop: *Workshop on Complex Systems, Ethnomethodology and Interaction Analysis* (Gilbert, 1990).

We do not want to take issue, here, with the attempts to use empirical studies of discourse and conversation to derive the specifications for the development of computers to simulate human conversation. However, the suggestions which are being put forward by those who favour discourse-analytic and conversation-analytic approaches have also promulgated understandings of human conversation and the relationship between computer processing and human conversation which we consider problematic in a number of ways. First, conversation and dialogue are mechanically portrayed in the argument that conversation consists of predetermined or 'given' processes and slots. This is explicitly argued in the discourse-analytic stance and implicitly nourished in the so-called conversation-analytic stance. Second, both positions fail to recognise that computers only simulate human conversation, arguing that processing rules and rules of conduct have the same ontological status with respect to the processes and actions that fall under their auspices. Third, and to us this is the nub of the matter and the prime problem which gives rise to the first two: both positions argue that human conversation can be assimilated under sets of constraining rules. Ironically for those who are offering up conversation analysis to computational linguistics, *it is exactly the contrary case that conversation analysis sustains*. In order to develop our argument, we will first consider the way in which conversation has been construed as rule-constrained.

Rules, conversation and computers

Within the diverse literature on conversation it *is* possible to find many studies that use 'rules' as part of their descriptive apparatus. For example, within the broad framework of 'discourse analysis', the idea that there are rules of, for example, sequencing is well established. Levinson provides a summary of some fundamental properties of discourse and conversation models to which, he says, most discourse analysts would subscribe. One of these is that 'conversational sequences are primarily regulated by a set of sequencing rules stated over speech act (or move) types' (Levinson, 1983, p. 289).

Conversation analysts have also formulated a number of rules that relate to sequencing. Probably the best-known work in conversation analysis to those who are outside the area is Sacks *et al.* (1974), 'A Simplest Systematics for the Organization of Turn-Taking for Conversation'. This paper provides a partial formulation of turn-taking in conversation in terms of a model which consists of two components and a *set of rules*. One component, a *turn construction component*, represents the grammatical building blocks with which talk in a turn may be constructed. A crucial feature of turn construction *units* is their use in co-ordinating the transfer of speakership, for it is at their *possible completion* that the transfer of speakership is co-ordinated. Sacks *et al.* describe these places as *turn transition relevance places*. They are important loci in the organisation of turn-taking for conversation which have often been overlooked in subsequent discussions of turn-taking, yet, as we will see, within Sacks *et al.*'s model their occurrence is *not* formally represented. We mark this point now, but take it up in more depth in our subsequent examination of building computer programs using this model of turn-taking.

The other component in the turn-taking model is the *turn allocation component*, which refers to techniques which allocate a next turn to a next speaker. The set of rules are those that govern turn construction and provide for the allocation of a next turn to one conversationalist with the minimisation of gap and overlap. They are:

(1) For any turn, at the initial transition-relevance place of an initial turn-constructional unit:

   (a) If the turn-so-far is so constructed as to involve the use of a 'current speaker selects next' technique, then the party so selected has the right and is obliged to take next turn to speak; no others have such rights or obligations, and transfer occurs at that place.

   (b) If the turn-so-far is so constructed as not to involve the use of a 'current speaker selects next' technique, then self-selection for next speakership may, but need not, be instituted; first starter acquires rights to a turn, transfer occurs at that place.

   (c) If the turn-so-far is so constructed as not to involve the use of a 'current speaker selects next' technique, then current speaker may, but need not, continue, unless another self-selects.

(2) If, at the initial transition-relevance place of an initial turn-construction unit, neither 1a nor 1b has operated, and, following the provision of 1c, current speaker has continued, then the rule set a–c reapplies at the next transition-relevance place, and recursively at each next transition-relevance place, until transfer is effected. (Sacks, Schegloff and Jefferson, 1974, p. 704)

On the face of it, it might be appealing to view this model as furnishing the rules of conversational organisation required by computational linguists in their attempts to develop conversing machines, for the components and the rules would seem to be the type of grammatical building blocks and causal rules they require. Undoubtedly Searle

(1986) for example, has taken Sacks *et al.* to be formulating a set of *causally* operative recursive rules for replicating turn-taking in conversation. An important feature of the 'Simplest Systematics' paper by Sacks *et al.* is being overlooked here by those who focus upon the 'rule-governed' component of the model, which is that it not only provides a rule system with a recursive structure, but it also describes the turn-taking arrangement as one which is *'participant-managed'*. The distorting effect of such neglect upon the understanding of the way in which the 'rule-governed' component features in the model cannot be underestimated, for it is clearly the intent of Sacks *et al.* to argue that the 'turn-taking arrangements' and their normative structure, that is, the rules, are such as to require *local* management in their actual implementation.

The elucidation of the way in which 'current speaker selects next' techniques work involves reference to another form of conversational organisation, *adjacency pairs*, which, as we have seen above, has been picked up by those who would wish to offer conversation-analytic ideas as a resource for the development of seemingly dialogical machines. Their interest in this regard is accounted for by the fact that Schegloff and Sacks' description of the relationship that exists between the adjacent parts of an adjacency pair is cast in some respects in a *formal* way which would allow them to recast the description in rule formulations. Schegloff and Sacks note the following features of adjacency pair sequences:

> Briefly, then, adjacency pairs consist of sequences which properly have the following features: (1) two utterance length, (2) adjacent positioning of component utterances, (3) different speakers producing each utterance . . . , (4) relative ordering of parts (i.e. first pair parts precede second pair parts), and (5) discriminative relations (i.e. the pair type of which a first pair part is a member is relevant to the selection among second pair parts). (Schegloff and Sacks, 1973, p. 238)

Gilbert, Wooffitt and Fraser (1990) recast the adjacency pair organisation as a grammatical formalism and express the relationship that holds between pair parts as a grammar rule:

adjacency pair ---> first part, second part

Here, the rule consists of a 'head' and a 'tail' joined by the connector ---> which means 'can consist of'. Gilbert *et al.* build up a whole range of rules that formalise the description of the adjacency pair relationship between utterances as described by Schegloff and Sacks. Thus:

adjacency pair ---> question, answer
adjacency pair ---> question, insertions, answer
adjacency pair ---> summons, response
adjacency pair ---> offer, acceptance
adjacency pair ---> offer, insertions, acceptance
insertions ---> insertion, insertions
insertions ---> insertion
insertions ---> question, insertions, answer
insertion ---> question, answer
                    (Gilbert, Wooffitt and Fraser, 1990, p. 248)

Conversation is not, however, only organised by mechanisms such as the adjacency pair which operate at an 'utterance-by-utterance' level of organisation. It can also be seen to be organised in terms of the unit 'a single conversation'. The course of a conversation is not one which proceeds on a purely utterance-by-utterance basis, for it involves also a projected structure, turns currently being taken being designed to prepare the way for subsequent activities. One way in which this can be seen is that 'sections' of conversation which are oriented to the overall management of the unit 'a single conversation' are produced, such as an 'opening section' – in which parties may propose the kind of conversation they anticipate participating in – and a 'closing section' – wherein, for example, utterances play the part of indicating the possibility that the conversation can now be brought to a close. Whilst both of these sections of talk display an utterance-by-utterance organisation, they *also* display an orientation to the management of the conversation 'as a whole'. For example, Schegloff's (1986) work on conversational openings richly details the component parts that can be used to make up a conversational opening. He describes how there are core opening sequences which are organised in terms of pairs of utterances: (1) The summons/answer sequence which organises the opening, and confirms the openness of a channel of communication; (2) the identification (and/or recognition) sequence which organises a sensitivity to the interlocutors who are involved in the conversation; (3) the greeting sequence which provides, amongst other things, for mutual participation; (4) the 'howareyou' sequence which provides for the early introduction of matters that have a joint priority over other matters. Schegloff writes: 'Each of these sequences is ordinarily composed of conventional parts with determinate and differential sequential consequences. It is by the deployment of these in the unfolding series of turns organised by these sequences that "normal" openings get constituted' (Schegloff, 1986, p. 118).

The opening section has, as Schegloff observes, a 'routine' character. Two other sections of talk that also display this 'routine' character are the 'closing sections' of conversation and the sections of talk involved in 'topic closure'. Descriptions of routines of conversation might then seemingly be available to formalisation and Schegloff even notes the interest of the seemingly formulaic character of a section of talk as a routine, 'in "artificial intelligence" studies on the production and processing of natural language use' (Schegloff, 1986, p. 113).

In order to take issue with the way in which it is theorised by those who take a discourse-analytic approach, as well as by those who favour a conversation-analytic stance, that conversation can be formalised in terms of a set of rules that constrain its production, we will examine the various domains of conversational organisation that conversation analysts have examined and which would have to be formalised in terms of a set of constraining rules *if the idea of a conversing computer could be made intelligible*. We focus upon conversation analysis not only because it has been directly misconstrued by some whose theorising we wish to attack, but also because, as a discipline, it has developed a depth of analysis that surpasses other attempts to grapple with the organisation of conversation.

The unformalisability of conversation

The first domain is that of turn-taking. Although the turn-taking model is indeed a *formalisation* of turn-taking, it is, importantly, only a *partial formalisation*. This represents the extent to which turn-taking can be formalised. We noted in our description above that turn-taking is co-ordinated around possible turn transition places, and how conversationalists are able to project in advance of arriving at them, a turn's possible completion, candidate transitional relevance places. However, whilst the 'Simplest Systematics' paper includes a formal description of both turn allocation and turn construction components and of a rule set that constrains the ordering of speakers, it *does not* include a formal or formalised description of *transition relevance places*.

Sacks *et al.* present a rich array of empirical instances that clearly display that persons do, in their turn-taking activities, orient to the co-ordination of turn-taking around transition relevance places yet they do not provide a formal specification of the projection of possible completion places a formal specification of the organisation of transition relevance places. No doubt some may see this as a failure of the model and may argue that it would, in principle, be possible to formalise this feature of turn-taking around, for example, the syntactic structure of the turn construction units. Yet, the very material that Sacks *et al.* use to display conversationalists' orientation to turn transition relevance places also shows that syntactic structure is not the sole determiner of a turn's possible completion for they clearly demonstrate that turn transition relevance places are the *interactional achievement* of the parties to the conversation for each and every turn that is taken. Thus, although it may be possible to project from its onset what the end of a turn could possibly look like, using, for example, its syntactic structure (e.g., the turn is initiated with a 'wh-' word and upon the completion of the 'wh-' construction a next speaker may be ready to begin to speak), nevertheless the unfolding course of the turn may change that construction, rendering any projection of a transition relevance place only the projection of a *possible* transition relevance place. Thus, it is clear from Sacks *et al.*'s description that, whilst the projection of possible completion is a feature of turn-taking, it does not, itself, fall under the auspices of a set of formal criteria: 'possible completion is something projected continuously (and potentially shifting) by the developing course and structure of the talk' (Schegloff, 1991).

The point that we are emphasising is not just that the model that figures in the 'Simplest Systematics' paper does not, as it might seem to some, offer a formal model that could be implemented on a computer, but that Sacks *et al.*'s description of the way in which turn-taking for conversation is organised illustrates the (in principle) *unformalisable* character of *all* features of conversation turn-taking.

We can illustrate this point by emphasising one aspect of Reichman's model (Reichman, 1985: see above) which is that it is intended to be a process model. Conversation analysis has shown how the movement from one speaker to another, from one turn to another, is not a simple matter of mechanically moving from one pre-given slot to another pre-given slot within a conversation, but is, rather, a matter of locally managing and achieving that movement through a whole range of unformalised activities. That is, conversation is not so much a matter of turn succession but of *utterance design*, and the range of features involved in utterance design are not captured in a formal process model of which Reichman's is an example. The specification of 'adjacency pairs', for example, simply indicates the relationship between 'utterance types' – if an invitation is given, then an acceptance or rejection of it is an *appropriate* next action. However, knowing that an acceptance or rejection of an invitation is an appropriate next action is a very considerable distance from knowing just what to say to effect that appropriate next action, from being in possession of the *specific form of words* which will perform the recognisable action of (say) rejection. The conversationalist must formulate, must *design* the specific form of words which will perform that action, and the character that they will have will depend upon, *inter alia*, the specific form of words in which the invitation was issued, the nature of the invitation, the relationship between the giver and recipient of the invitation, etc., etc. (Note that we cannot, of course, exhaustively list all the assorted considerations which potentially might enter into the formulation of an offer.) The person accepting the invitation has, then, to form an utterance which, for example, 'ties' it to the invitation, shows appreciation of the nature of the invitation, for example, that an invitation to this event is something special and shows appreciation of (for example) the largesse involved in offering the invitation.

There are many aspects of utterance design which, although they do not feature explicitly in the Sacks *et al.*'s model, are, nevertheless, recognised by them as important for the co-ordination of speaker transfer. Thus, there has been extensive examination of the way in which a turn is constructed so as to be sensitive to the identity of co-conversationalists (Schegloff, 1992). Given that identities can be variously formulated and that upon one occasion it may be that one identity is procedurally relevant whereas on another, another identity may be procedurally relevant (even though it is the 'same person'), then formulations of the identity of 'questioner' may not be relevant for the way in which conversation is actually designed, nor even for some particular question.

There are many other aspects of utterance design that have been emphasised by conversation analysts as bearing upon speaker transfer. For example: where a turn is placed within a protracted sequence of utterances bears upon the organisation of turn-taking (Sacks, 1975). Also of note are: the sound patterns that have antedated them (Schegloff, 1986a); the purposes of interlocutors and the availability of shared knowledge (Sacks, 1986); the specifics of the relationship being carried out by the talk (Sacks, 1986); the business being done (Drew, 1992); and the delicacy of the matters to be handled (Schegloff, 1980); and so on. The relevant point about the extensive collection of such studies is, here, however, that they are *unformalised*. We cannot show for each of these areas of analysis *how* they display the unformalisable character of conversation since that would take much more space than part of a single chapter; however, what we claim is that these studies describe the *localised and particularised nature of the 'determinants' of utterance design and turn articulation and exhibit the ways in which these are evasive of efforts at representation in formal abstractions.*

Sacks *et al.* unequivocally stress this point by characterising their model of turn-taking as 'context free but context sensitive'. A significant part of their purpose in so doing is to recognise the endless variety of social transactions which can be conducted through alternating turns at talk.

Elsewhere, it has been argued (Button, 1990) that the rules involved in speaker transfer that form a part of the Sacks *et al.* model do not represent rules that can be implemented on a computer to generate conversation. Hirst, however, has objected: 'this is hardly an in-principle argument against computer use of CA [conversation analysis] rules. Case-based reasoning, while far from being a completed science, is, nevertheless a well-established subfield of artificial intelligence, and seems to hold considerable promise for being able to do what Button says can't be done' (Hirst, 1991, p. 222). Hirst's argument here is a demonstration of what happens when the 'Simplest Systematics' is wrenched from out of the context of the rest of the work on utterance design within conversation to which we have alluded. As we have noted, within the 'Simplest Systematics' the point is made that turn-taking is co-ordinated with respect to a whole host of other activities which are contingently deployed in the unfolding course of the turn. In this respect, it is not a matter of providing computer science the means for moving from a case-based example to a generalised situation, be-cause the whole point is that it is not possible to formalise conversation in such a way as to furnish *any* such generality. Thus no computer can be given such putative generalisations.

In order to be scrupulous, however, we do recognise that some aspects of the 'Simplest Systematics' would seem to suggest that certain dimensions of turn-taking are formalisable. This is because the rule set that is provided would seem to be a formalisation that covers and standardises all of the phenomena of turn allocation. However, even the formalisms that *do* appear in the model are not the order of formalisms that would be required to program a computer. That is, unlike the rules that are involved in the programming of computers which have a causal relationship to the processing they bring about, the rules involved in the organisation of turn-taking are *not* causally deter-minative. This is an issue which is forcefully displayed in a recent debate between Searle and Schegloff.

Searle (1986) has described the rules that figure in the 'Simplest Systematics' as causal mechanisms which operate to distribute turns amongst speakers in a mechanical, algorithmic fashion. For Searle, this means that the rules involved in speaker transfer determine that the person who starts talking *gets* to keep on talking. Schegloff (1991), however, makes the point that the rules which were formulated in the 'Simplest Systematics' are not causally determining in this way, since starting to talk does not entail that the initiator gets to keep on talking, but rather, as he argues, they *end up* keeping on talking. Searle mistakenly supposes that it is *the rules* which organise the taking of turns within the conversation, but, Schegloff argues, this is precisely *not* what those who formulated those 'rules' intended by them, to the extent that Schegloff is now brought to regret calling them 'rules' in the first place. It is *the parties to the conversation* who determine the distribution of turns at talk amongst themselves. They treat the 'rules' of turn-taking as incumbent upon them, so that should they, for example, end up in a situation where more than one person is talking at once – one of the fundamental features of conversation enumerated by Sacks *et al.* is that *at least and not more than one person speaks at a time* – they will react in ways which ensure that such 'overlap' is immediately terminated. It is the fact that *the parties* to the conversation treat the 'rules' as incumbent upon them, as specifying requirements on the order of their conversational activities, which leads us to talk of them as being *'oriented'* to the rules, but those rules do not apply themselves: they must be applied by those who 'orient' to them.

We have already spoken of the necessity for *the parties* to the conversation to 'manage' the implementation of these 'rules'. To explain a little further and perhaps, thereby, to clarify our meaning, let us consider the distribution of turns at talk. If one thinks of programming a computer interface in such a way that the computer and a user are related dialogically, then one may well be thinking in terms of a two-party exchange, and this might enhance the illusion that it is *the rules* which distribute the turns. After all, if two persons are engaged in conversation, then the turn-taking has an automatic aspect in the sense that if one is currently speaking then the other is, *must be*, the next speaker. However, conversations are not invariably two-party exchanges, and in a multi-party interchange there is nothing in the rules which selects any next speaker. It is a feature of the 'rule' structure that a current speaker *can* select a next speaker – can, for example, direct a question at a named party in the conversation, e.g., 'Do you agree, John?' – but there is nothing that *requires* that a current speaker should in any way nominate a next speaker. The 'rules' specify that selection by a current speaker has *priority* over self-selection, that if the current speaker selects a next speaker then that one is entitled to the next turn, but it is, of course, *the speaker, not the rules*, who makes such a selection. If the current speaker does not select next, then the next speaker is chosen by 'self-selection', but this precisely means that – in a multi-party conversation – the turn is not allocated to anyone, that the parties to the conversation must select the next speaker from amongst themselves. The 'rules' allowing self-selection allow the possibility of *competition for turns* – a current speaker arrives at a possible turn transition place but does not select a next speaker, in which case, the next speaker may self-select and, of course, several participants might seek to select themselves as potential next speaker. If the current speaker asks a question of the parties to a conversation then several of those might possess the answer to that question and undertake to answer that and find, thereby, that they are involved in violation of the rule that one person should speak at a time, in which case they will now have to organise their talk so that the order required by the rule is restored, that one of them is the answerer of the question. The *parties to the conversation* must determine which of them is to be 'next speaker' – thus, in addition to specifying turn-taking rules, conversation analysis provides (unformalised) descriptions of 'floor-seeking' techniques which conversationalists may use to determine who does speak next from amongst those that the rules would entitle to speak next.

It is worth adducing another basic but important point about conversation analysis which is significant for those who aspire to program computers to 'talk like you and me', or, at least, are thinking of using conversation analysis as a basis for programming dialogic interfaces. The point is that the 'rules' of conversation also generate many of the 'troubles' of conversation. The 'rules' of turn-taking are superficially those for *orderly* conversation – they effectively *stipulate* what orderly conversation is to be – namely, that there should be no 'gap' between the turns of speakers, that one and only one person should talk at a time, etc. The rules then ostensibly provide for orderly conversation and it might, therefore, be thought that to program an interface on the basis of these 'rules' would be such as to ensure an orderly alternation of turns between machine and user, but nothing of the sort is ensured. The example we have just given of 'next speaker' selection indicates that it is the self-same turn-taking rules which can give rise to their own violation – the fact that the 'turn transition places' are only *possible* turn transition places can result in overlapping talk, in one speaker seeking to talk before another has completed a turn; the *possible* turn transition place proved, in retrospect, not to be an *actual* transition place.

Similarly, the possibility that next speakers can self- select also means that there can be competition for next speaker place, that more than one party can attempt to be next speaker and that several can start talking at once – the attempt to comply with the turn distribution and speaker selection 'rules' can result in violation of the requirement that only one person should speak at a time. In the same way there are arguments in conversation analysis that misunderstandings and confusions can be *generated* by the 'rules' and procedures for the production of ordinary talk, and so interface programmers should not imagine that implementing conversation analysis will provide them with dialogic exchanges which are any less disorderly than those in which conversationalists ordinarily engage.

We are, therefore, arguing that the 'rules' which order conversation do not provide a set of algorithms which allocate the turns in a conversation nor otherwise causally determine the sequence of any actual conversation. The 'rules' are normative, and if they allocate anything it is *entitlements* not turns. The rules specify what is *legitimate* in conversation and the parties to conversation do (prevailingly) *respect* those requirements, demonstrably seek to preserve or restore the situation that these *norms* require. However, it is through *the ways in which they organise their talk, the ways in which they structure their utterances* that the parties to conversation ensure that the conversation complies with those rules, make it happen or bring it about that their turns at talk alternate without gap or overlap or that a situation of all-talking-at-once is terminated. It is the extent to which parties to conversation must contrive – most typically *ad hoc* – their ways of bringing about the orderly alternation of turns at talking that we have sought to capture by talking about 'orientation' to the 'rules', and we have sought to contrast this with the kind of algorithmic formulations which are necessarily those of computer programming. Thereby we hope to have shown that implementing the 'rules' of conversation on computers involves the *transformation* of their character, that those 'rules' simply cannot function in the program in the way in which they do in conversation. We have, further, been suggesting that the difficulty of implementing such 'rules' on a computer in ways that can engender anything but the most superficial simulations of conversation has probably been underestimated because the position of the 'Simplest Systematics' for turn-taking within conversation analysis has been misunderstood.

Despite our prior claims to the above effect, authors like Fraser and Wooffitt (1990) persist in arguing that computers orient to rules. They are not, we think, aware of the full panoply of our arguments nor do they necessarily comprehend their meaning. They set out to show that far from being determined by rules, computers, in executing some processing instructions, are orienting to rules in the same way that it may be possible to describe some action conducted by humans to display an orientation to a rule. Thus Fraser and Wooffitt argue that in being able to provide an answer to a typed-in question, the front end of a database is *orienting* to a rule in the same way in which humans may be said to orient to a rule when they answer a question which they have been asked. However, in the light of the argument we have been making, the claim that computers orient to rules is clearly an example of the sort of confusion we have been addressing throughout this book and which arises because of the failure to distinguish between engineering developments, in this case computer processing, and what they mean for what we can say about human conduct.

Hirst makes a similar argument, for he believes that computers *use* rules as resources. Hirst invokes a previous argument against the conflation of programming rules and rules of human conduct (Button, 1990) and attempts to rebut it by listing the ways in which conversation analysis has described rule use in the production of conversation. He fails to see that there is any distinction to be made between the use of rules by humans as described by conversation analysts and computer processing according to programmed rules:

> I am at a loss to see the contradiction. Any backward-chaining Horn clause theorem prover or planner with appropriate meta-rules can be viewed as using its rules as resources in exactly the ways I described. [His description is of human uses of rules provided by the conversation analytic literature.] Indeed, the ability of a second utterance to transform a prior utterance surely *requires* having rules such as 'that upon the production of a question, the next utterance should be an answer'! Button seems to be saying nothing more than that CA [conversation analysis] rules must be represented declaratively, not procedurally, so that they can be deliberately and explicitly invoked with a view to their effect. But far from precluding their use by a computer, this argument suggests that they fit very nicely into present-day AI [artificial intelligence] reasoning systems! (Hirst, 1991, p. 222)

We need to clear up some misconceptions here. First of all, it is not the case that answers *transform* prior utterances into questions. The intelligibility of an utterance as an answer is, in part, bound to the preceding utterance being hearable as a question. Thus Hirst is saying that something that, in part, gains its sense by its sequential placement next to a question transforms that prior utterance into the something that gives it sense. This argument is itself plainly nonsensical. Hirst seems to assume that the argument turns upon whether there are certain features of conversation which could not be produced by a computer, that is, simulated on a machine, and that, therefore, the 'backward-chaining Horn clause theorem prover or planner with appropriate meta-rules' would directly rebut the kind of arguments we are putting here. He misses the point, which actually pertains to the difference between the part that 'rules' play in programs and the part that they play in the conduct of conversationalists, and that, therefore, the production of 'useful similarities' between the output of computers and the performance of conversationalists cannot just consist in the straightforward programming in of the turn-taking rules, or other rules formulated by conversation analysts. The issues pertain not to whether some specific feature of conversation can be simulated but, as always, what will have been achieved by such simulations. The difference which cannot be bridged is, of course, that between achieving conformity with social norms and being driven by an algorithmically designed program. The computer is not sensitive or responsive to the *normative* character of those rules, it does not produce output which accords with them because it recognises the legitimacy of the demands which the turn-taking 'rules' impose upon it, or the legitimacy of the entitlements to talk which those 'rules' distribute. The fact that a computer is connected to a database which enables it to generate the answer to a user's query does not mean that it knows the answer to that query – any more than the calculating machine understands, subscribes to or applies the mathematical norms on the basis of which it has been programmed. As Stuart Shanker has argued, discussions of artificial intelligence are bedevilled by the failure to recognise that computers provide mechanical analogues of normative activities, but do not themselves instantiate compliance with norms (Shanker, 1987a; 1987b).

In part, the origin of Hirst's confusion over the way in which a computer 'uses rules' originates in misunderstandings of the way in which 'rule' is used in the conversation analytic literature that they cite and which we have been trying to clarify. However, they also originate in a failure to understand what a computer is, for, in Fraser and Wooffitt's case, arguing that a computer can orient to rules and, in Hirst's case, that a computer uses rules, they are propounding very worn artificial intelligence ideas with which we have been contending throughout this book. Hirst, at least, sees where the thrust of the argument that he wishes to undermine comes from:

> Underneath, this discussion [about the difference between rules of human conduct and programming rules] seems to be little more than a bad version of the old, familiar anti-AI [artificial intelligence] arguments about Turing tests and Chinese rooms, about the limitation of physical symbol systems, about whether one needs to distinguish between a system that is explicitly following a certain rule from one that merely acts as if it is. It seems to me that for HCI [human–computer interaction] the question is whether we can build a computer system whose conversations are use-

fully similar to those of humans, and it doesn't matter whether or not Button wants to call them merely simulacra. (Hirst, 1991, pp. 222–3)

Hirst is quite correct to separate the question of whether one can build computer systems whose interfaces feature 'conversational' organisation which are 'usefully similar to those of humans' from questions as to whether these would then provide something more than 'mere simulacra' of people's conversational activity, but his way of doing so reflects the point at which there is often considerable *ambiguity* in artificial intelligence work.

Those involved in practical 'artificial intelligence' projects – including the building of 'dialogical' interfaces – can, with our full assent, proclaim themselves to be engaged in a strictly technical pursuit and its practical problems, to be concerned to use ideas of conversational organisation taken from the social studies literature, for example, to solve those problems and to be designing pieces of technology in ways which will enhance and facilitate their use. However, if they do claim this, then their work will be of interest to the extent that clever pieces of new technology are, but it will not be of any other significance than that, and will carry no more *philosophical* import than the invention of the 'speak your weight' machine.

For Hirst's *engineering* purposes, the point he is making in the above quotation is impeccable. However, he should be aware that this point can only be conceded to him at the cost of divesting the artificial intelligence/human–computer interaction venture of any sense that it is a special or exceptional kind of engineering venture because it is engaged in mechanising 'mental' phenomena, and therefore, one which has far-reaching intellectual significance, and which encroaches upon the distinction between the human and the mechanical. Hirst ought, then, to be quite happy with Button's argument – that the 'conversational' outputs of computers are simulacra – for these do not bear upon and would not diminish the value of his engineering work on dialogic interfaces, but he does not meet these arguments with such equanimity, seeking, rather, to *reject* them, and indicating, thereby, the ambiguity which we have mentioned between the presentation of artificial intelligence as a straightforward engineering exercise in mechanisation and as something which has particular significance because of its infringement upon the idea of the distinctiveness of 'the human'. It does, not, then, matter if dialogue interfaces are 'mere simulacra' of conversations and involve systems that 'merely act as if' they were following rules, for this is irrelevant to the practicalities of engineering such interfaces, but this does *not* mean that the point that these *are* simulacra, and that they involve systems which 'merely act as if' they follow rules, becomes redundant: if those who undertake such constructions wish to imply – as it seems to us they often do – that their very modest achievements in that direction provide grounds for the rest of us to engage in fundamental rethinking about the structure of our deepest conceptual distinctions, then we shall need to reinforce the point at every turn. It is, in our view, important to make unequivocally clear that the 'conversing computer' – and certainly the faltering steps towards the construction of such a device – provides no basis whatsoever for such rethinking.

Though we have said so before, we should reinforce the point that the above remarks are not offered in *defence* of a hierarchical distinction between 'human' and 'machine' nor out of a conviction that any sense of our human self-worth should derive from or depend upon the supposition that it is the possession of 'mental' faculties that sets us apart, and which could be threatened by the 'mechanisation' of 'mental processes'. Our objection is, rather, and pervasively through the book, to the philosophical 'talking up' of the modest, if not flimsy, achievements of *bona fide*, interesting, creative, but otherwise unremarkable, technical and scientific ventures and to the creation, thereby, of illusions about what has been (or more likely will be) proved by progress in such ventures. The programming of dialogic interfaces according to the 'rules of conversation' establishes *nothing* with respect to the question of whether machines 'follow rules'.

One further, final, point. An important source of misunderstanding of 'conversation analysis' is to look upon it as a species of linguistics, with its 'turn-taking rules' viewed as a grammatical formalism. We have in mind the way in which adjacency pair organisation has been represented within such formalisms. The developments of these formalisms, however, overlooks the extent to which the relationship between adjacency pair components such as questions or answers is a relationship between *actions* and not between linguistic structures. The dislocation of language from action that we addressed in the previous chapter is again manifest in the way in which the adjacency pair's organisational properties described by Schegloff and Sacks have been misrepresented as rules of grammar. The study of conversation by conversation analysts is not concerned with 'utterances' as linguistic forms but with the *actions which utterances do*. Understanding that conversationalists accomplish action-in-interaction when they talk to one another has a number of consequences for the proposals to develop conversational machines.

In order to begin to address these we can first note that the analysis of turn-taking which we have been commenting upon was itself subordinate to the fact that turns are turns within a conversation and are designed to build 'the unit: a single conversation'. There are two consequences of this. First, turns at talk do not, as they would seem to within Reichman's description, merely 'occupy' slots which are pre-allocated for them. Rather, they are constitutive of the organisation of the conversation of which they are a part. This means that the formulaic characterisation of utterances as, for example, occupying question slots, providing, by rules of grammar, for answer slots, may not comprehend that a question may be produced that orients to the management of the conversation as 'a whole'.

Thus, for example, a question asked in the opening section of a conversation such as 'Are you busy?' may, in providing for possible affirmative or negative answers, also be part of managing the conversation as a unit, for it may provide for some protracted or curtailed conversation, even making 'conversing' itself a non-starter for that occasion (Schegloff, 1986). The mere formalisation of a grammatical rule that connects an answer to a question is not, here, taking account of what may be done *in* asking a question, and what may be done *in* answering a question. The design of turns at talk as, for example, questions and answers, is, consequently, a matter of managing social interaction, not instantiating some rules of grammar.

The second consequence of recognising that conversation is not a matter of filling pre-allocated slots is that the formalisms of a grammatical rule connecting, for example, questions and answers overlooks the fact that questions do not project answers, but project answers to *this* question. The fact that an utterance is *'the* answer' to a question, or *any* kind of admissible answer, is not something which is determinable from its formal features. The candidacy of an utterance for the characterisation of answer might be derived from its sequential placement next to a question but whether it is *the* answer depends upon (1) what the question asks about and (2) what would answer the question. Thus the question 'Are you busy?' asked in the opening section of a conversation may ask 'Have you got time to talk?', in which case, 'I'm waiting for John to phone me' might be the answer. However, if the question 'Are you busy?' asks an actor if he/she is working, then the reply 'I'm resting' could be recognisably the answer. 'I'm waiting for John to phone me' and 'I'm resting' do not gain their status as candidate answers from their intrinsic grammatical features but from their placement as a response to the question, and importantly, they gain their intelligibility as candidate answers to *that* (situated) question. In other words, questions and answers are not just slots in a conversation which contain utterances joined together by grammatical rules; they are amongst the very vehicles through which the conduct of social life is done.

In this respect, merely seeing sections of talk as rote routines gone through slot by slot, as in Reichman's model, or as staged routines that are gone through in order to get into and out of conversation, as in Frohlich and Luff's, and Gilbert, Fraser and Wooffitt's models, misses the contingent nature of the interactional and moral work that is done through openings and closings. The thrust of work on sections of talk such as openings and closings that has taken place in conversation analysis is to display how, through a variety of conversational actions, participants are able to negotiate with one another the contingent constraints under which they may, for example, proceed with their conversation, constraints that then become a resource they use to manage the overall development of their talk. This is not to say that they might not have negotiated such constraints on other occasions and that they are not familiar with them or cannot recognise them. But it is to say that such negotiations are contingently done, and done again for each and every time conversations are initiated, and that only by ignoring the contingent interactional work that is done through such a section of talk as an opening could they be conceived of as slots or steps in a pre-given routine. Routines they may be, but rote they are not, for 'the routine is an achievement' *of* the contingent circumstances of its production (see Schegloff's 1986 paper, 'The Routine as Achievement').

This is not, however, just a criticism of those who have proposed that, for example, adjacency pairs can be formalised in terms of rules of grammar but also an illustration of the fact that to disassociate turns at talk from the social activities that are accomplished within them will result in abstractions that cannot account for the design of turns at talk as they figure within human conversation. We have seen how, within computational linguistics, the move to develop a conversational machine involves a turning to the organisation of conversation itself in order to divine the rules that govern its production. Understanding those rules, it is argued, would allow computational linguists to write programs based upon those rules. We have, in this last section, been attempting to show, however, that conversation is not formalisable in this way and thus the actual study of conversation, far from being a resource for the developing of a conversing machine, is a resource for displaying the fallacy that is at the heart of the idea that a computer can converse.

Elsewhere (Button and Sharrock, forthcoming), we have examined in more depth one element of the argument which we have considered here which is, specifically, the way in which conversation analysis has been abused by some in their claims that they have built conversational interfaces. We stressed there that conversation analysis may have a utility in guiding designers in the development of *simulacra* of conversation. Nothing we have argued in this book undermines that. More fundamentally, however, we have been – once again – confronting and challenging the conception of the nature of language which pervades that work, a conception which regards language as the merely mechanical generation of utterances, and which regards the production of such utterances as disengaged from the life and activities within which they are produced. The result is an underestimation of the extent to which the capacity to talk and to carry on a conversation involves the possession of something other than purely 'linguistic' skills, and, indeed, of other things than skills. Whilst we are insistent that talking and carrying on conversations is, in important respects, a matter of 'rule-following', we have been concerned to argue that it is not *only* a matter of 'rule-following'. We have, furthermore, been seeking to insinuate the point that *insofar* as it is a matter of 'rule-following' what is important is how that 'rule-following' is conceived, and it must not be supposed to involve the application of a calculus. The idea of 'rule-following' as a matter of employing a calculus was, of course, the supposition of Wittgenstein's *Tractatus* and the critical butt of his *Philosophical Investigations*. This accounts for our emphasis upon the understanding of rule-following in 'conversation analysis', and our insistence that the operation of the 'turn-taking arrangements – though rule-governed – is not there conceived as the application of a calculus, though it is perhaps mistaken for such by those who are concerned to adapt 'conversation analysis' to the needs of programming interfaces. The superficial resemblance to a calculus may, however, give a misleading impression as to the ease with which conversational turn-taking can be programmed.

Science fiction can successfully trade in such impressions but, as McTear observes, computational science finds it more difficult to live up to the impression it wishes to give. In the conclusion to his book *The Articulate Computer*, McTear invokes the fictional computer HAL from Arthur C. Clark's *2001* in order to show just how far we have yet to go within computational linguistics: 'When we compare the limited powers of conversation of the systems described in this book with HAL's sophisticated performance, we can see how much has yet to be accomplished in the computational modelling of conversational competence' (McTear, 1987, p. 226). However, although pointing to the gap between the claims and the actualities, McTear compounds the very confusion that we have addressed throughout this book, which is that it is possible through future developments to close the gap. McTear sees that 'there is still much to be accomplished'; this sentiment assumes that objections such as ours are momentary and that future advances in computer technology will prove us wrong. We hope, however, that the arguments that we have been making, throughout, will go some way to undermining this misplaced confidence, for the issues which we have been addressing here are *conceptual*, not *empirical*, ones, and accordingly will not be settled by whatever spectacular advances in computer technology may lie ahead of us, even a HAL.

Conclusion: 'None of the Above'

We cannot emphasise strongly enough the extent to which our arguments have been designed, not to advance *any* (alternative) 'theory of mind' nor any (alternative) 'philosophical psychology' in opposition to those positions which prevail in contemporary discussions, but rather to undermine the very idea that there are genuinely scientific problems in this domain for which theoretical solutions could legitimately be sought. We certainly have not tried to resuscitate the 'logical behaviourism' which is sometimes – and, we have claimed, inappropriately – ascribed to Gilbert Ryle. The need to advance a theory or theories only arises if there are problems to be solved by their construction, and it is to casting doubt upon *the authenticity of the supposed problems* of 'philosophical psychology' that our lines of argument in this work have been exclusively devoted. It is for this reason that we have sought to return to examine the sources of recently influential kinds of philosophical psychology rather than to discuss extensively their most up-to-date and fashionable forms, seeking to show that it is far from necessary to set up these putative 'problems' in the ways in which they have been set up. We have, *inter alia*, tried to show that in order to pose these 'problems' it is necessary *already* to have accepted a great many *tendentious* philosophical presuppositions. Effectively, one is confronted in many current discussions of the issues with philosophical positions which *create* the very problems to which they purport to offer solutions.

Consider, for example, one of the main inspirations for the contemporary recrudescence of mentalism, Noam Chomsky's arguments about language acquisition. Chomsky is strongly inclined to sensationalism, and his claim that language 'grows' and is not learned is, of course, meant to sound like an argument which directly – and sensationally – confronts what anyone would otherwise suppose. We would normally speak of what the growing infant does as 'learning its first language' and would take it entirely for granted that the child learns that first language from other people in its environment, as is evidenced by the fact that the child comes to speak the same language as its kin and peers do. Hence, to *deny* that children learn language *sounds like* a challenge to the above commonplace suppositions. In fact, though, it is nothing of the sort, for, of course, the inclination of children progressively to master their native tongue in accordance with their progressive exposure to its use is both patent and uncontroversial. There are two other, similarly uncontroversial, aspects to language learning which deserve mention here, both of which bear upon its *biological* character: (1) it is, of course, the case that full-blown language is almost, if not entirely, distinctive to human beings, that it is *natural* to these creatures in a way it is not to other species and (2) that language learning is a function of maturation.

The uncontroversial character of these latter two contentions is not to be considered a *theoretical* matter, but is something which is entirely and pervasively manifest in human practice. We do not find individuals striving to teach cows, dragonflies or woodpeckers to talk, nor even encouraging budgerigars to emulate more than a few simple phrases. No one *in practice supposes* that other biologically distinct species can learn language with the facility that humans do (not even Bonobo apes!). Secondly, and again in practice, parents of infants only develop anxiety about their child's incapacity to manifest developing mastery of the language at a certain age because, of course, they recognise full well that the capacity to utter becomes available only beyond a certain point in the maturation process.

Despite appearances, then, Chomsky does not actually cast doubt upon the contention that children *do* learn language. He *appears* to do so, though, and the suggestion that language grows *rather than* being learned aids the impression that he is saying something revolutionary and controversial. Chomsky's arguments do not, in fact comprise a *straightforward* challenge to talk of children as learning language, for it is a challenge *only to a certain philosophical construal* of what 'learning language' is. *If* one supposes that learning a language is like figuring out a theory, *then* Chomsky's argument is: it is not possible to *learn* such a theory from others. Note, however, that the argument already incorporates one of Chomsky's own philosophical premisses, that knowledge of a language is akin to knowledge of a theory. Note also that the idea of learning as a matter of *hypothesising* is part of this (philosophical) apparatus. *If* hypothesising is something which is done *in a language*, then, of course, two alternative possible conclusions are engendered: (1) The infant *cannot* learn language because it has no language in which to formulate the hypotheses which allegedly constitute knowledge of language. However, children patently *do* learn language, so, as far as Chomsky is concerned, (2) it must therefore be the case that they are in possession of language before they can speak, or give any other manifestation of possessing a language. They must have some language *other than* their 'native tongue' in which to formulate the hypotheses which will facilitate mastery of that native tongue, and hence must have a language which *they did not learn*.

The assumption that knowledge of a language is akin to knowledge of a theory is further productive of Chomsky's case that language *cannot* be learned. The adoption of that assumption involves the supposition that the relation between the child's 'knowledge of language' and the speech of those who socialise the child is a relation between *hypothesis* and *evidence*, and Chomsky can now import further philosophical argument about 'the underdetermination of theory by evidence'. This holds that for any corpus of data there is an infinite array of possible theories which could encompass it, and there is no reason, therefore, why different parties seeking to induce a theory for a corpus of data should select the *same* theory: there is nothing to prevent different children from hypothesising different theories for the same language *unless* there is something innate in them which ensures that different children will settle on the same hypotheses. In other words, the children do not *hypothesise* at all. Hence, Chomsky's argument now *retracts* a premiss he had introduced in the first place – that language learning is necessarily a species of *hypothesis formation*. But if he had not introduced that conception, there would have been no need to pursue the sequence of dilemmas which he went on to derive from it.

Chomsky's treatment of language learning as theory construction spawns the notorious 'new sentence' problem. The language learner is seeking to project a set of generalisations which will encompass the whole range of sentences which can be generated in the language – this is roughly what 'grammar' is in Chomsky's conception. The 'underdetermination of theory by evidence' argument means, then, that although the child must seek to project universal generalisations from a limited corpus of data, how could the child make any such inferential projection from the limited set of utterances which have been heard so far? There is, Chomsky wants to argue, an unbridgeable gap between 'the data' and 'the theory', between the particular and the general. The child has been exposed to *these* sentences so far, but, if it is to be able to generate new sentences of its own (and not just repeat those already heard), it is compelled to extrapolate from these select few sentences the principles which shape the form of *all* sentences in the language. Let us suggest a comparison in order to illuminate what is being supposed in all this, and to show to what extent such suppositions are unnecessary.

A person learns to drive by practising driving around the route on which he will be subjected to his driving test. He drives round and round the same few streets, being instructed in how to brake, turn, signal, etc. at appropriate points on those streets. He has learned to drive this route. When he is licensed to drive, he will be entitled to make a potentially infinite number of road journeys (subject, of course, to mortality). He will be entitled to make innumerable 'new journeys'. But he has only been taught to drive these few neighbourhood streets, so how will it be possible for him to make any journeys he has not made before, how will he be able to drive effectively and safely in *all kinds* of conditions when he has been taught how to drive in only a very few conditions?

The answer is (of course) that the seeming problem here is a product of the way in which the learning situation *is described* in the first place. The driver is not being taught to drive these few streets, but is being taught, *on that route*, how to drive a car, how *generally* to operate a vehicle, make allowance for traffic conditions, attend to signals, and to find and negotiate a way around pretty well *any route*. In being taught to look down the next road before turning into it the learner is being taught not just to negotiate *this* junction, but is being shown how, in general, to look out for hazards and what to take notice of – this corner, that oncoming car, are treated, in the context of the driving lesson, as *instances* of the general patterns and hazards of driving. Though the learning might be confined to this route, the learner driver is not being taught how to drive this route alone, but is being taught, by means of experience on this route, how to drive *anywhere*. Much the same applies with respect to 'the problem' of the way in which 'finite linguistic resources' allow the possibility of 'infinite linguistic productivity' which Chomsky seeks to engender but there is no 'problem' here which is not disposed of by the simple recognition that the provision of techniques for open-ended combination provide for such 'infinite' productivity. Someone who has mastered the techniques of sentence formation and a modest vocabulary has the (theoretical) capacity to produce sentences without number, just as a competence with the eighty-eight keys on a piano (theoretically) gives one the capacity to produce endless amounts of music.

Chomsky's characterisation of the learning situation makes it sound like there is an inferential or inductive gap between the particular and the general, but, as should be plain, learning such as that involved in the driving lesson does not, *cannot*, involve such a gap. When a learner is shown for the first time how to turn on the ignition he is not expected to ask, in each subsequent lesson: 'How do I start the car?' The learner is being shown, the first time the ignition is demonstrated, not how to start the car *this time*, but how to start the car *any time*. The learner is presented with *the standard way* to start a car, is presented with it *as* the standard way.

Wittgenstein's fundamental argument about the 'private language' is that in being taught words we are provided with 'rules for their use'. This is not some arcane doctrine which need involve intellectual convolutions about the idea of rules, but draws our attention to the most patent and uncontroversial facts about teaching the meaning of words. It is not as if in teaching a child to use the word 'Daddy' we are teaching it how to use the word on *this occasion* such as to present the child with a 'projection problem' as to how to use the word on the next occasion. We are teaching the child how to use the word on *this and uncountably many other occasions*, as a term of address and designation for this person. Learning to use the word *is*, in this sense, learning a rule for its use, learning how to position the word not just now, but at any time. Unless the learner comprehends that he is being provided with instruction in or demonstration of policies for the *consistent* deployment of words then he is not learning *anything*.

One final formulation to try to make our point as clear as possible: teaching an infant the meaning of a word and its grammatical role is a matter of teaching *a generality*, of showing the infant a *way of going on*, in which the particular words and the sentences they make up function as instantiations. The alleged logical 'gap' between the 'old sentence' on which one has, so to speak, learned and the 'new ones' one has yet to utter or hear is spurious. The roads on which one has learned to drive are not in any logically relevant sense disconnected from those on which one has not yet driven. The specific and the general are not discontinuous here, to be linked only by the leaping of an inferential chasm. The way in which a norm is taught, displayed or demonstrated through instantiation is more akin to what is often called an 'internal' relation than it is to the external relation between an event and the empirical generality which covers it. The 'new sentence' problem is *entirely* the creation of Chomsky's mode of argumentation: learning through being given instantiations of language is no more problematic or mysterious than is the way in which being taught to handle and employ one's first spoon provides a basis for one's subsequent adept handling of cutlery.

To complain that we give no *alternative* to Chomsky's account of how language is learned would be entirely misplaced, just as it would be to attribute to us any behaviourist account. We (need) have no account *whatsoever* of how language is learned beyond the utterly un-controversial observations that it takes place in the course of biological maturation and in relation to other speakers. The reiteration of these platitudes does not imply any *alternative* conception to Chomsky's, for, as we have already mentioned, Chomsky's own work presupposes these same bland points. Do we not, then, leave Chomsky's problem unsolved? Are we not compelled, as Fodor so often insists, to accept something like Chomsky's account for want of a better one? But our argument has been against accepting Chomsky's *problem*, not his sol-ution. The problem, we have just argued, is *entirely* the creation of Chomsky's supposition that learning a language is akin to constructing a theory. Chomsky's problem, in this connection, is not an empirical one about the way in which people actually do learn language, but is, instead, a *philosophical* one about whether it is *possible* for people to learn language. Since, patently, they *do* learn language, then that ques-tion has to be construed in a peculiar sense: (1) *Given* that people do learn languages and (2) *given* that learning language is a form of theory construction (with further assumptions about the underdetermination of theory by evidence, etc.), *then* (3) learning a language is impossible. If one disputes the second 'given', then the problem evaporates in its entirety. This 'given' itself derives from contestable, mentalistic assumptions, e.g., that *achievements* such as 'learning' must be (mis)conceived as 'mental activities' (in this case, as comprising the putative 'mental operations' of thinking, abstracting, inducing, inferring, etc.), necessitating the conclusion that in order to learn a language the infant must already be capable of thinking prior to being able to speak. Without Chomsky's assumptions (and a highly tendentious bunch they are!), there is no need at all to suppose that language learning is *impossible* and hence *no need to explain how it actually is possible*. Chomsky's entire venture rests upon the *unjustified* supposition that mastering a technique involves constructing a theory, and nothing more substantial than that. Take that away, and. . . . If, then, we *cannot* acknowledge any necessity for an 'explanation' of language acquisition of the sort that Chomsky demands, then we can scarcely be accused of putting forward the *wrong sort* of explanation, be it behaviourist, logical behaviourist or otherwise.

At the beginning of this argument, we said that the fundamental disagreement with most of those we have criticised is not in respect of the nature of 'mind' or of 'psychology' but is, instead, over the part which language is understood to play in human life, and about its consequent role in philosophy. Indeed, the issue is whether the understanding of language is itself a *psychological* question at all. The starkest opposition is between someone who supposes that language is a vehicle for the operation of an internal process of thought and someone who maintains that language is part of the organisation of practical affairs. Note, though, that we do not say that it is the *purpose* of language to facilitate practical goals. The argument (derived, of course, from Wittgenstein) is, rather, that language is created in the course of and as *part of* practical affairs.

Chomsky is an exemplary protagonist of the former view, that language is the medium in which the inner process of thought takes place, and associatedly, therefore, of the view that the study of language is a contribution to the study of mind. It should not be forgotten that one of Chomsky's accomplishments has been to parlay linguistics into psychology, to argue that the study of the structure of language, that is, of its grammatical rules, *is* the study of 'mental phenomena'. The effect of this position is, however, the *dissociation* of speaking a language from the *other* activities in which people engage, as if the *system* of language could be described and understood in complete abstraction from the patterns of life in which the speakers of the language otherwise engage.

Consider the case of the so-called 'folk psychological' concepts. Those who claim that these comprise *a system for explaining and predicting behavioural regularities* are, in effect, assuming what we could call a 'spectatorist' view of the role of language. According to such a (mis)conception, we use words like 'belief', 'intention', 'thoughts', 'desire', 'expectation' and others exclusively to talk about people's behaviour in order to account for the regularities it exhibits and to predict its course, as if our linguistic engagements with others, within which such words are routinely used, consisted solely of efforts extrinsically to figure out and predict such regularities. Winch attacked a related misconception of Popper's. Popper had argued that 'social institutions' are just explanatory 'models' introduced by the social scientist for his own explanatory purposes, but Winch replied that the very identification of much of human conduct by anyone presupposes social institutions: saluting presupposes armies and their rules of comportment, buying and selling presupposes markets, writing a cheque presupposes a banking system, and voting for someone presupposes representative political institutions, and so on. These 'institutions' are not 'simply invented by people who wanted to *explain* what happens' (Winch, 1958, p. 127), but enter into their lives in a *variety* of ways. The spectatorist view of our 'psychological' concepts commits a similar error. It is as if we first observed other people engaged in a host of activities, and *then* required some terms with which to describe and explain the regularities in what they do. Against this (impoverished) view, we would note that we use (such) language not just to talk *about* other people, but to talk to them as they talk to, and with, us, to enter into *variegated* lines of conduct with them. To neglect the richness and diversity of our myriad involvements with people in which (*inter alia*) 'psychological' concepts are put to work, and to portray a purely detached and instrumental characterisation of their usage, is to present a caricature of them.

Indeed, those who promote such a characterisation dub such concepts 'folk psychological' precisely because they presume that they have a function directly parallel to that envisaged for the theoretical terms of a scientific psychology. Indeed, these terms may prove, according to some, to *be* the theoretical terms of such a psychology. The role of these concepts is construed along 'spectatorist' lines, is construed as that of explaining and predicting the behavioural regularities of other creatures – predominantly, but not exclusively, of human beings.

Consider, however, what such an account does *not* explain (any more than do *any* of the 'mentalistic' accounts): namely, *why anyone speaks* at all. This is not something which the 'mentalist' theorists give any sign of recognising as a problem, for they simply take it for granted that people do *speak to each other*. Given, however, that language is the medium for processing thought, there is a question as to why it should also serve as the medium of speech. One can argue that the purpose of language is to *express* thought, and that speaking is thus the vehicle for the public expression of thought. But why should individuals *need* to express their thought aloud? It cannot be that when they hear what they say they then know what they are thinking! If one genuinely accepted the point about the purpose of speech being the expression out loud of thought, then one would need to add the suppressed presupposition, which is that they need to speak to express their thought *to other people*.

We certainly do not wish to assert that the speakers of language may never be described as speaking (or writing) in order to express their thoughts, and we certainly do not want to deny that they ever speak out loud in expressing their thoughts to themselves. Even if we were to accept – and we do not – that language had any *specific purpose* (or some few purposes), we would not be much impressed with the idea that the purpose was to permit individuals to express their own thoughts to themselves. They *can* do this, of course, but their doing it is a comparatively rare occurrence, and does not even begin to encompass the vast diversity of other things which people do when they speak.

Wittgenstein's emphasis upon language as part of the 'natural history' of humanity is directed not towards identifying a different, this time *correct*, purpose for language. It is, rather, designed to break with the idea that language develops for any kind of *purpose*, not least because of the idea that language must have some purpose, for that requires that the purpose and the means of satisfying it be conceivable *before* the possession of the language which is to satisfy the purpose. Here we have a measure of agreement with Chomsky, Fodor and those like them who hold that one could not think to the extent of being able to think out a language *without the aid of such a language*. Wittgenstein, however, sees this not as reason to insist that, therefore, human beings must possess some 'inner' language which enables them to engender (not just acquire) a language. He draws, rather, upon the alternative possibility, that language can arise, so to speak, *from nothing*, that language *can arise out of that which is entirely pre-linguistic*. This, certainly, is his point about the maturation of the child, the way in which pre-linguistic relations develop *and facilitate* the learning of language, the communication with the child being *founded* in 'primitive' and 'natural' reactions, the acquisition of language itself being an *elaboration* of and around these reactions. In the same way, it can be imagined, language itself can have arisen out of pre-linguistic patterns of human reaction and has been *continuingly* and *increasingly* elaborated around those reactions. There is absolutely no need to be held in thrall to the classic metaphysical postulate that so strongly underwrites the Chomsky/Fodor account, that language can only develop out of language. The subsequent idea that *the brain* must evolve in such a way that somehow (aspects of) language must be built into it, fully independently of having expression or utility in the lives of those possessing such brains, is surely no more plausible – is, indeed, surely a good deal *less* plausible to *anyone* not in the thrall of the notion that language must come from language – than the claim that language arose in the course of and out of the evolution of collective human life and the many, varied and often progressively elaborated patterns of reaction and activity which make up the evolution of that life.

Rather than looking for a 'purpose' which would explain why

human beings should speak to each other we can take it as part of the 'natural history' of human beings, and that it is *just as much* a natural aspect of people's language that it is a medium of their relations. We do *not* say here 'a medium of communication', for 'communication' is only one thing people do in and with their speech. We do not wish to be sociologically imperialistic, any more than we want to give ground to imperialism in the name of psychology, so we will not say that language is a social *rather than* a psychological phenomenon. We will just say that it is *just as much* a social as it is an individual one. Those of more or less mentalistic persuasion will perhaps admit that language is a social matter, but such acknowledgement will be at best perfunctory, and the role of language as a part of social life will be treated as a secondary, derivative feature which can be treated as incidental to the understanding of language.

Insofar as those we are criticising aspire to create a psychology, it might seem that our criticism is unfair, for they can surely attend to the individual aspect of language to the exclusion of its 'social' dimension? However, to counter us in this way is to overlook the fact that the drive to create a psychology of the kind one finds in Chomsky, Fodor and their cognitivist colleagues does not involve an effort to bring language within the remit of an established psychology, but is an attempt to create a psychology on the model of the study of language, out of the conviction that language is a *primarily*, if not *essentially*, 'mental', and therefore psychological, phenomenon. It is, further, the case that the proposed isolation of 'psychological' aspects of language is not *accomplished* on the basis of any careful discrimination and disentangling of the supposedly psychological and social aspects of language, but is, rather, *claimed* on the basis of *stipulating* that they can indeed be separated and isolated from one another in this way. That is to beg the question of whether they *can* be so separated.

The allocation of language primarily to the 'mental sphere' gives rise to what we would see as a 'parallel track' treatment of language and other aspects of human activity, as though the role of language were simply to provide a commentary upon human activities which would, in any case, exist and continue were there no such language. To explain this, let us revert to the case of the 'folk psychological' concepts, and engage in some reduction *ad absurdum*. It is as though people went about booking railway tickets and holidays, pleading guilty in court, disciplining their children and driving home from work, but were witnessing each other doing these things without properly understanding them. They observed 'behaviours', but could not explain or predict these. In order to explain and predict them, then, they must engage in *theorising*, must speculate as to how these behaviours are to be explained. It is hard to know from the 'folk psychology' story whether some genius is supposed to have coined the 'folk psychological' concepts or whether there was some massive convergence by all individuals upon just these concepts. However, this is incidental to our argument.

We imagine, then, in a 'spectatorist' world, that someone is puzzled by someone else's booking a seat on a train. Our observer of this puzzling behaviour has the wonderful theoretical idea that this person is booking a seat on a train *on purpose*. This now explains what he is doing and, given that our imaginary 'any person' theorist is of the mentalistic persuasion, the explanation involves the postulation of an inner state, the 'purpose', which brings about this behaviour, the booking of the seat. At the most primitive level, the question is posed: how could the notion of someone's booking a seat on a train *on purpose* add to or explain his activity of 'booking a seat on a train'? The very activity of 'booking a seat on a train' *is* the activity of arranging a rail journey, purchasing a ticket, establishing the reservation of a particular place on the train *in advance* of *preparing* subsequently to board and travel upon that train, so that to say that someone who 'books a seat on a train' *has a purpose* is not necessarily to add *anything* to what has already been said in describing his activity as 'booking a seat on a train'.

The more serious point, here, is the idea that one can have human activities taking place in orderly and standardised ways *without language*, with language then being contrived to explain and predict that behaviour. The idea of persons booking train rides, arranging holidays and so forth, without language, is, of course, an utter absurdity. Our language develops *along with* (but not merely as a 'parallel track development' to) the formation of activities. One does not develop the game of tennis, for example, and then having brought it to the state of organisation it now has, contrive a vocabulary for it. As part of developing the game of tennis that we have, one introduces into it the practice of keeping and calling scores, and one contrives terms in which those scores can be kept and called, and the formation of that vocabulary is not to be understood in terms of the psychology of human individuals but on the basis of the exigencies and history of the game of tennis.

The concepts of so-called 'folk psychology' do not connect with the facts of a specific activity in the ways in which 'Love', 'Deuce' and so on do to the activity of playing tennis, but our point has been that they are, nonetheless, best understood by being considered in terms of the part that they play in activities, albeit that they play a role (often a *varying* role) in a wide *range* of activities. Thus, as we have argued, the role of 'belief' is not effectively examined on the basis of its treatment as a theoretical notion designed to predict behaviour, but is more usefully considered in relation to (*inter alia*) the practice of grading relayed information, that its most vital *up-front* role in such comments is to indicate how much the information being relayed is worth. Understanding where beliefs are attributed to people, and what beliefs they are, originates not from a theory of inner states but from the examination of how people stand with respect to the acquisition of information. Someone who believes that the ice will not support his own weight is someone who has not yet gone out on the ice: one way to ascertain whether or not the ice will support him is to venture out on it, but if one is in doubt about its ability to give support, then one will not venture out and is denied the means of establishing for certain, of getting to *know*, that it won't. So one's information on the weight-bearing capacities of the ice is less than conclusive: one believes (as opposed to being absolutely confident) that it won't support one's weight.

Thus, such supposedly 'folk psychological' terms as 'believe' derive their capacity to explain and predict people's actions – *when they are usable to do these things*, which is not by any means their only or main role – from their involvement in the gradation of information and its employment in action. Thus, in this respect, the notion of 'belief' plays a role (and again, *inter alia*) in *co-ordinating* or *aligning* people, allowing them to show where they respectively stand relative to some matter of fact or the trustworthiness of an individual.

The inspection of the place of such words within (to use a loose expression loosely) 'language games' simply gives a very different picture of the character and meaning of those words from that which one gets by simply, and really quite arbitrarily, assigning them to a 'folk psychology'. The aim of such an inspection is certainly not to prepare the way for any theory of 'the phenomena' to which such words might be (mis)taken to refer. The argument that many of the key problems in philosophical psychology are spurious and that, therefore, the theories which are offered in resolution of those 'problems' are otiose, has been made before and has been frequently dismissed. The dismissals of it are, however, characteristically out of hand: they are, alas, *not* based upon attempts to undertake rival or competing conceptual investigations of the requisite detail on the part of those intent upon the preservation of the goals of theorising. We would also point out that repeated criticism of a line of inquiry which pursues the 'quiet weighing of linguistic facts', as though this were *itself* a venture in speculative psychological theorising, does not ensure the cogency of the criticism. For example, the approach we have outlined here cannot be condemned on the grounds that it denies that 'mental states' are *causes* of actions when, in fact, they are such causes. The argument we have advanced has been that philosophers who construe mental states as 'causes' often treat the word 'because' as though it were a term with an invariably causal use, when it is not. Our arguments, then, stand or fall upon issues concerning how words-in-the-language actually function, and those who espouse speculative psychology have not troubled themselves to develop any *method* to ensure that their characterisations of words-in-the-language are accurate.

Insisting that the word 'because' invariably signals a causal relationship does not establish that it does, and it leaves the question: how would one *establish* that it does? In this work, we have been much concerned with defending and attempting to reinvigorate a *methodology*, drawn from Wittgenstein and Ryle, for handling such questions, as with matters of analytical detail.

The recurrent attempts to understand and explain the speech and related conduct of individuals which isolates them from, extracts them out of, their networks of activities and relationships will commonly render those activities mysterious indeed. We frequently cite Harold Garfinkel's complaint (Garfinkel and Sacks, 1990) that his social science colleagues often suppose that taking away the walls is the best way of revealing what keeps the roof up. Garfinkel's complaint seems like a felicitous reformulation of Wittgenstein's worries about a good deal of philosophy. Despite our disclaimers, however, we will no doubt be read as having been participating in philosophy, as having sought to advance, perhaps surreptitiously, an alternative 'theory of mind and behaviour'. If we have offered anything that may remotely be construed as a theory, it would be a 'theory of language', but only if the word 'theory' is used in the most attenuated sense. We cannot pursue the objectives sought after by the contemporary 'philosophy of mind' because we do not accept that it has formulated genuinely coherent problems to begin with. Demonstrating that its *apparent* problems are not genuine ones has, thus, been the central preoccupation of this collaborative work. To state our position as starkly as possible: we refuse to become embroiled in the spurious antinomies which permeate so much of philosophy, psychology and sociology, which polarise realism/constructivism, idealism/materialism, dualism/monism, realism/instrumentalism, behaviourism/mentalism. We favour *none* of the above.

Bibliography

Allen, J. (1987). *Natural Language Understanding*. Menlo Park, California: Benjamin/Cummings Publishing Company.

Baker, G. P. and Hacker, P. M. S. (1984a). *Frege: Logical Excavations*. New York: Basil Blackwell and Oxford University Press.

Baker, G. P. and Hacker, P. M. S. (1984b). *Language Sense and Nonsense*. Oxford: Basil Blackwell.

Barwise, J. (1981). Some Computational Aspects of Situation Semantics. In *19th Annual Meeting of the ACL*. Association for Computational Linguistics.

Barwise, J. (1989). *The Situation in Logic*. Stanford: Center for the Study of Language and Information.

Barwise, J. and Perry, J. (1983). *Situations and Attitudes*. Cambridge, Mass.: Bradford Books/MIT Press.

Blank, D. S., Meeden, L. A. and Marshall, J. B. (1992). Exploring the Symbolic/Subsymbolic Continuum: A Case Study of RAAM. In J. Dinsmore (ed.), *The Symbolic and Connectionist Paradigms: Closing the Gap*. Hillsdale, NJ: Lawrence Erlbaum.

Bogen, J. (1972). *Wittgenstein's Philosophy of Language*. London: Routledge & Kegan Paul.

Brady, M. and Berwick, R. C. (eds). (1983). *Computational Models of Discourse*. Cambridge, Mass.: MIT Press.

Brentano, F. (1924). The Distinction between Mental and Physical Phenomena. In O. Kraus and L. McAlister (eds), *Psychology from an Empirical Standpoint*. London: Routledge & Kegan Paul, 1973.

Broad, C. D. (1951). *The Mind and Its Place in Nature*. New York: Humanities Press.

Burge, T. (1979). Individualism and the Mental. *Midwest Studies in Philosophy*, IV, 73–121.

Burge, T. (1986). Individualism and Psychology. *The Philosophical Review*, XCV(1), 3–46.

Burton, R. R. (1976). *Semantic Grammar: An Engineering Technique for Constructing Natural Language Understanding Systems*. Bolt, Beranek & Newman. Report No. 3453.

Button, G. (1990). Going Up A Blind Alley: Conflating Conversation Analysis and Computational Modelling. In P. Luff, N. Gilbert and D. Frohlich (eds), *Computers and Conversation* (pp. 67–90). San Diego, Cal.: Academic Press.

Button, G. and Sharrock, W. W. (forthcoming). On Simulacrums of Conversation. In P. Thomas (ed.), *Social Aspects of HCI Design*. Cambridge: Cambridge University Press.

y Cajal, S. R. (1972). *Histologie du Système Nerveux*. Reprinted by Consejo Superior Investigaciones Cientificas: Madrid.

Carnap, R. (1932–3). Psychology in Physical Language. *Erkenntnis*, 111.

Churchland, P. (1979). *Scientific Realism and the Plasticity of Mind*. New York: Cambridge University Press.

Churchland, P. (1984). *Matter and Consciousness*. Cambridge, Mass.: MIT Press.

Churchland, P. S. (1980). A Perspective on Mind-Brain Research. *Journal of Philosophy*, 77(4).

Churchland, P. S. (1986). *Neurophilosophy: Toward a Unified Theory of Mind/Brain*. Cambridge, Mass.: MIT Press.

Clarke, A. (1991). In Defense of Explicit Rules. In W. Ramsey, S. P. Stich and D. E. Rumelhart (eds), *Philosophy and Connectionist Theory*. Hillsdale, NJ: Lawrence Erlbaum.

Clocksin, W. F. (1984). An Introduction to PROLOG. In T. O'Shea and M. Eisenstadt (eds), *Artificial Intelligence: Tools, Techniques and Applications* (pp. 1–21). New York: Harper & Row.

Cook, J. (1969). Human Beings. In P. Winch (ed.), *Studies in the Philosophy of Wittgenstein* (pp. 117–51). London: Routledge & Kegan Paul.

Cook, J. (1980). The Fate of Ordinary Language Philosophy. *Philosophical Investigations*, 3(2), 1–72.

Coulter, J. (1979). The Brain as Agent. *Human Studies*, 2(4).

Coulter, J. (1991a). Is the 'New Sentence Problem' a Genuine Problem? *Theory and Psychology*, 1(3).

Coulter, J. (1991b). The Informed Neuron: Issues in the Use of Information Theory in the Behavioral Sciences. In W. Rapaport (ed.), *Cognitive Science Technical Reports No. 7*. SUNY: Buffalo.

Coulter, J. (1993a). Consciousness: The Cartesian Enigma and Its Contemporary Resolution. In J. V. Canfield and S. G. Shanker (eds), *Wittgenstein's Intentions* (pp. 173–94). New York: Garland Publishing.

Coulter, J. (1993b). Materialist Conceptions of Mind: A Reappraisal. *Social Research*, 60(1).

Coulter, J. (1993c). Neural Cartesianism: Comments on the Epistemology of the Cognitive Sciences. Conference on Reassessing the Cognitive Revolution. York University, Ontario.

Coulter, J. and Parsons, E. D. (1991). The Praxiology of Perception: Visual Orientations and Practical Action. *Inquiry*, 33(3).

Cowan, J. D. and Sharp, D. H. (1988). Neural Nets and Artificial Intelligence. *Daedalus*, 117(1).

Davies, M. (1991). Concepts, Connectionism and the Language of Thought. In W. Ramsey, S. P. Stich and D. E. Rumelhart (eds), *Philosophy and Connectionist Theory*. Hillsdale, NJ: Lawrence Erlbaum.

Dennett, D. (1978). *Brainstorms: Philosophical Essays on Mind and Psychology*. Cambridge, Mass.: Bradford Books.

Dennett, D. C. (1987). *The Intentional Stance*. Cambridge, Mass.: Bradford Books, MIT.

Descartes (1985 translation). *The Philosophical Writings of Descartes. Vol. 1* (J. Cottingham, D. Murdoch, trans.). Cambridge: Cambridge University Press.

Devlin, K. (1991). *Logic and Information*. Cambridge: Cambridge University Press.

Dinsmore, J. (1992). Thunder in the Gap. In J. Dinsmore (ed.), *The Symbolic and Connectionist Paradigms: Closing the Gap*. Hillsdale, NJ: Lawrence Erlbaum.

Drew, P. and Heritage, J. (eds). (1992). *Talk At Work: Interaction In Institutional Settings*. Cambridge: Cambridge University Press.

Dreyfus, H. L. (1993). *What Computers Still Can't Do*. Cambridge, Mass.: MIT Press.

Fodor, J. A. (1968). *Psychological Explanation: An Introduction to the Philosophy of Psychology*. New York: Random House.

Fodor, J. A. (1975). *The Language of Thought*. New York: Thomas Crowell Co.

Fodor, J. A. (1980). Methodological Solipsism Considered as a Research Strategy in Cognitive Psychology. *The Behavioral and Brain Sciences*, 3, 63–110.

Fodor, J. A. (1981a). On The Impossibility of Acquiring 'More Powerful' Structures: Fixation of Belief and Concept Acquisition. In M. Piattelli-Palmarini (ed.), *Language and Learning: The Debate Between Jean Piaget and Noam Chomsky*. Cambridge, Mass.: Harvard University Press.

Fodor, J. A. (1981b). Methodological Solipsism Considered as a Research Strategy in Cognitive Psychology. In J. Haugeland (ed.), *Mind Design*. Cambridge, Mass.: MIT Press.

Fodor, J. A. (1983). *The Modularity of Mind: An Essay on Faculty Psychology*. Cambridge, Mass.: Bradford Books, MIT Press.

Fodor, J. A. (1987). *Psychosemantics*. Cambridge, Mass.: Bradford Books, MIT Press.

Fodor, J. A. (1990). *A Theory of Content and Other Essays*. Cambridge, Mass.: MIT Press.

Fodor, J. A. (1994). *The Elm and the Expert: Mentalese and Its Semantics*. Cambridge, Mass.: MIT Press.

Fodor, J. A. and Pylyshyn, Z. (1988). Connectionism and Cognitive Architecture: A Critical Analysis. In S. Pinker and J. Mehler (eds), *Connections and Symbols*. Cambridge, Mass.: Bradford Books, MIT Press.

Fraser, N. and Wooffitt, R. C. (1990). Orienting To Rules. In N. Gilbert (ed.), *Proceedings of the Workshop on Complex Systems, Ethnomethodology and Interaction Analysis*, American Association for Artificial Intelligence (pp. 69–80). Boston.

Frazier, L. and Fodor, J. A. (1978). The Sausage Machine: A New Two-Stage Parsing Model. *Cognition*, 6, 291–325.

Frohlich, D. and Luff, P. (1990). Applying the Technology of Conversation to the Technology for Conversation. In P. Luff, N. Gilbert and D. Frohlich (eds), *Computers and Conversation* (pp. 187–220). San Diego, Cal.: Academic Press.

Garfinkel, H. and Sacks, H. (1990). On Formal Structures of Practical Action. In J. Coulter (ed.), *Ethnomethodological Sociology*. London: Edward Elgar.

Gazdar, G. and Mellish, C. (1987). Computational Linguistics. In J. Lyons, R. Coates, M. Deuchar and G. Gazdar (eds), *New Horizons in Linguistics 2*. Harmondsworth: Penguin Books.

Gilbert, G. N., Wooffitt, R. C. and Fraser, N. (1990). Organising Computer Talk. In P. Luff, N. Gilbert and D. Frohlich (eds), *Computers and Conversation*. London: Academic Press.

Gilbert, N. (1990). (ed.). *Proceedings of the Workshop on Complex Systems, Ethnomethodology and Interaction Analysis*. American Association for Artificial Intelligence. Boston.

Grossberg, S. (1987). Competitive Learning: From Interactive Activation to Adaptive Resonance. *Cognitive Science*, 11, 23–63.

Grosz, B. (1978). Discourse. In D. Walker (ed.), *Understanding Spoken Language*. New York: Elsevier North Holland.

Grosz, B. (1981). Focusing and Description in Natural Language Dialogue. In A. Joshi, B. Webber and I. Sag (eds), *Elements of Discourse Understanding*. Cambridge: Cambridge University Press.

Hacker, P. M. S. (1987). *Appearance and Reality: A Philosophical Investigation into Perception and Perceptual Qualities*. Oxford: Basil Blackwell.

Hacker, P. M. S. (forthcoming). Seeing, Representing and Describing: An Examination of David Marr's Computational Theory of Vision.

Hebb, D. (1949). *The Organisation of Behavior*. New York: John Wiley.

Heil, J. (1992). *The Nature of True Minds*. Cambridge: Cambridge University Press.

Hempel, C. G. (1949). The Logical Analysis of Psychology. In H. F. Feigl and W. Sellars (eds), *Readings in Philosophical Analysis*. New York: Appleton-Century-Crofts.

Hinton, G. E. (1989). Connectionist Learning Procedures. *Artificial Intelligence*, 40, 185–234.

Hinton, G. E. (1992). How Neural Networks Learn From Experience. *Scientific American*, 267(3).

Hinton, G. and Sejnowski, T. (1986). Learning and Relearning in Boltzmann Machines. In D. E. Rumelhart and J. L. McClelland (eds), *Parallel Distributed Processing: Explorations in the Microstructure of Cognition, Vol. 1: Foundations* (pp. 282–317). Cambridge, Mass.: MIT Press.

Hirst, G. (1991). Does Conversation Analysis Have a Role in Computational Linguistics? *Computational Linguistics*, 17(2), 211–27.

Hodges, A. (1983). *Alan Turing: The Enigma*. New York: Simon & Schuster.

Hunter, J. F. M. (1977). Wittgenstein and Materialism. *Mind*, LXXXVI (344), 518–19.

Johnson-Laird P. (1983). *Mental Models.* Cambridge, Mass.: Harvard University Press.

Kaplan, R. M. (1973). A General Syntactic Processor. In R. Rustin (ed.), *Natural Language Processing.* New York: Algorithmics Press.

Katz, J. J. and Fodor, J. A. (1963). The Structure of a Semantic Theory. *Language,* 39(2), 170–210.

Kenny, J. P. (1985). *The Legacy of Wittgenstein.* Oxford: Basil Blackwell.

Lehnert, W. G. and Ringle, M. H. (1982). Conversation and Discourse. In W. G. Lehnert and M. H. Ringle (eds), *Strategies for Natural Language Processing.* Hillsdale, NJ: Lawrence Erlbaum.

Levinson, S. (1983). *Pragmatics.* Cambridge: Cambridge University Press.

Luff, P., Gilbert, N. and Frohlich, D. (eds). (1990). *Computers and Conversation.* London: Academic Press.

Lycan, W. G. (1991). Homuncular Functionalism Meets Parallel Distributed Processing. In W. Ramsey, S. P. Stich and D. E. Rumelhart (eds), *Philosophy and Connectionist Theory.* Hillsdale, NJ: Lawrence Erlbaum.

MacKay, D. (1954). On Comparing the Brain with Machines. *American Scientist,* 42.

McCulloch, W. S. and Pitts, W. H. (1943). A Logical Calculus of the Ideas Immanent in Nervous Activity. *Bulletin of Mathematical Biophysics,* 5, 115–33.

McTear, M. (1987). *The Articulate Computer.* Oxford: Basil Blackwell.

Malcolm, N. (1984). Conciousness and Causality. In D. M. Armstrong and N. Malcolm (eds), *Consciousness and Causality: A Debate on the Nature of Mind* (pp. 3–66). Oxford: Basil Blackwell.

Malcolm, N. (1986). *Nothing Is Hidden.* Oxford: Basil Blackwell.

Marcus, M. P. (1980). *A Theory of Syntactic Recognition for Natural Language.* Cambridge, Mass.: MIT Press.

Marr, D. (1980). *Vision: A Computational Investigation into the Human Representation and Processing of Visual Information.* San Francisco, Cal.: W. H. Freeman.

Millman, J. and Taub, H. (1965). *Pulse, Digital and Switching Waveforms.* New York: McGraw-Hill.

Mills, C. (1993). Wittgenstein and Connectionism: A Significant Complementarity? In C. Hookway and D. Peterson (eds), *Philosophy and Cognitive Science* (pp. 137–57). Cambridge: Cambridge University Press.

Minsky, M. and Papert, S. (1969). *Perceptrons: An Introduction to Computational Geometry.* Cambridge, Mass.: MIT Press.

Morelli, R. and Brown, M. (1992). Computational Models of Cognition. In R. Morelli (ed.), *Minds, Brains and Computers: Perspectives in Cognitive Science and Artificial Intelligence* (pp. 18–28). NJ: Ablex.

Pinker, S. and Mehler, J. (eds). (1988). *Connections and Symbols.* Cambridge, Mass.: MIT Press.

Pinker, S. and Prince, A. (1988). On Language and Connectionism: Analysis of a Parallel Distributed Model of Language Acquisition. *Cognition,* 28, 73–193.

Place, U. T. (1988). Thirty Years On – Is Consciousness Still a Brain Process? *Australasian Journal of Philosophy,* 66(2).

Place, U. T. (1992). Eliminative Connectionism: Its Implications for a Return to an Empiricist/Behaviorist Linguistics. *Behavior and Philosophy*, 20(1), 21–35.

Putnam, H. (1960). Minds and Machines. In S. Hook (ed.), *Dimensions of Mind*. London: Collier-Macmillan.

Putnam, H. (1965). Brains and Behavior. In R. J. Butler (ed.), *Analytical Philosophy, Vol. 2*. Oxford: Basil Blackwell.

Putnam, H. (1981). Reductionism and the Nature of Psychology. In J. Haugeland (ed.), *Mind Design*. Cambridge, Mass.: Bradford Books.

Putnam, H. (1988). Much Ado About Not Very Much. *Daedalus: Journal of the American Academy of Arts and Sciences*. Winter 1988: issued as Vol. 117, No. 1, of the Proceedings of the American Academy of Arts and Sciences, special issue on artificial intelligence.

Quine, W. V. (1960). *Word and Object*. Cambridge, Mass.: MIT Press.

Quine, W. V. (1961). *From A Logical Point of View*. New York: Harper and Row.

Quine, W. V. (1981). *Theories and Things*. Cambridge, Mass.: Harvard University Press.

Quine, W. V. (1987). *Quiddities: An Intermittently Philosophical Dictionary*. Cambridge, Mass.: Harvard University/Belknap Press.

Quinlan, P. T. (1991). *Connectionism and Psychology: A Psychological Perspective on New Connectionist Research*. Chicago: University of Chicago Press.

Ramsay, A. (1986). Computer Processing of Natural Language. In M. Yazdani (ed.), *Artificial Intelligence: Principles and Applications* (pp. 65–105). London: Chapman & Hall.

Reeke (Jr.), G. (1989). Synthetic Neural Modelling. In R. Pfeifer, Z. Schreterz and F. Foyelman-Savlie (eds), *Connectionism in Perspective*. Oxford: Elsevier Science Publishers.

Reichman, R. (1985). *Getting Computers to Talk Like You and Me: Discourse Context, Focus and Semantics*. Cambridge, Mass.: MIT Press.

Ringle, M. and Bruce, B. (1982). Conversation Failure. In W. G. Lehnert and M. Ringle (eds), *Strategies for Natural Language Processing*. Hillsdale, NJ: Lawrence Erlbaum.

Ritchie, G. and Thompson, H. (1984). Natural Language Processing. In T. O'Shea and M. Eisenstadt (eds), *Artificial Intelligence: Tools, Techniques, and Applications* (pp. 358–88). New York: Harper & Row.

Rumelhart, D. (1991). Foreward. In W. Ramsey, S. P. Stich and D. E. Rumelhart (eds), *Philosophy and Connectionist Theory*. Hillsdale, NJ: Lawrence Erlbaum.

Rumelhart, D. E. and McClelland, J. L. (1986). *Parallel Distributed Processing: Explorations in the Microstrucutre of Cognition, Vol. 1: Foundations*. Cambridge, Mass.: MIT Press.

Rumelhart, D. E. and Norman, D. A. (1973). Active Semantic Networks as a Model of Human Memory. *IJCAI*, 3, 450–7.

Rumelhart, D. E., Hinton, G. E. and Williams, R. J. (1986). Learning Representations by Back-Propagating Errors. *Nature*, 323, No. 6188, 533–6.

Ryle, G. (1971a). *Collected Papers, Vol. 1: Critical Essays*. London: Hutchinson.

Ryle, G. (1971b). *Collected Papers, Vol. 2*. London: Hutchinson.

Ryle, G. (1973). *The Concept of Mind.* London: Penguin Books.

Ryle, G. (1987). *Dilemmas: The Tarner Lectures (1953).* New York: Cambridge University Press.

Sacks, H. (1975). Everyone Has to Lie. In M. Sanches and B. G. Blount (eds), *Sociocultural Dimensions of Language Use* (pp. 57–9). New York: Academic Press.

Sacks, H. (1986). Some Considerations of a Story Told in Ordinary Conversations. *Poetics,* 15.

Sacks, H. (1993a). *Lectures on Conversation: Vol. I.* Oxford: Basil Blackwell.

Sacks, H. (1993b). *Lectures on Conversation: Vol. II.* Oxford: Basil Blackwell.

Sacks, H., Schegloff, E. A. and Jefferson, G. (1974). A Simplest Systematics for the Organization of Turn-taking for Conversation. *Language,* 50, 696–735.

Schank, R. C. (1972). Conceptual Dependency: A Theory of Natural Language Understanding. *Cognitive Psychology,* 3(4), 552–630.

Schank, R. C. and Abelson, R. F. (1977). *Scripts, Plans, Goals and Understanding.* Hillsdale, NJ: Lawrence Erlbaum.

Schank, R. C. and Riesbeck, C. K. (eds). (1981). *Inside Computer Understanding.* Hillsdale, NJ: Lawrence Erlbaum.

Schegloff, E. A. (1968). Sequencing in Conversational Openings. *American Anthropologist,* 70.

Schegloff, E. A. (1979). Identification and Recognition in Telephone Conversation Openings. In G. Psathas (ed.), *Everyday Language: Studies in Ethnomethodology.* New York: Irvington.

Schegloff, E. A. (1980). Preliminaries to Preliminaries: 'Can I Ask You a Question?' *Sociological Inquiry,* 50.

Schegloff, E. A. (1986). 'The Routine as Achievement'. *Human Studies,* 9(2/3), pp. 111–51.

Schegloff, E. A. (1991). To Searle on Conversation: A Note in Return. In J. Verscheuren (ed.), *On Conversation.* Amsterdam: John Benjamin's.

Schegloff, E. A. (1992). Reflections on Talk and Social Structure. In D. Boden and D. Zimmerman (eds), *Talk and Social Structure.* Cambridge: Polity Press.

Schegloff, E. A., Jefferson, G. and Sacks, H. (1977). The Preference for Self-correction in the Organization of Repair in Conversation. *Language,* 53.

Schegloff, E. A. and Sacks, H. (1973). Opening Up Closings. *Semiotica,* 7.

Schwartz, J. T. (1988). The New Connectionism: Developing Relationships Between Neuroscience and Artificial Intelligence. *Daedalus,* 117(1).

Searle, J. (1980). Minds, Brains, and Programs. *The Behavioral and Brain Sciences,* 3(3).

Searle, J. (1983). *Intentionality.* Cambridge: Cambridge University Press.

Searle, J. (1986). Introductory Essay: Notes on Conversation. In D. G. Ellis and W. A. Donohue (eds), *Contemporary Issues In Language and Discourse Processes* (pp. 7–19). Hillsdale, NJ: Lawrence Erlbaum.

Searle, J. (1992). *The Rediscovery of the Mind.* Cambridge, Mass.: Bradford Books, MIT Press.

Shanker, S. (1987a). AI at the Crossroads. In Brian Bloomfield (ed.), *The Question of Artificial Intelligence* (pp. 1–58). London: Croom Helm.

Shanker, S. (1987b). Wittgenstein versus Turing on the Nature of Church's Thesis. *Notre Dame Journal of Formal Logic,* 23(4).

Smith, P. and Jones, O. R. (1986). *The Philosophy of Mind: An Introduction.* Cambridge: Cambridge University Press.

Smolensky, P. (1987). The Constituent Structure of Connectionist Mental States: A Reply to Fodor and Pylyshyn. *Southern Journal of Philosophy,* XXVI (Supplement), 137–63.

Smolensky, P. (1988a). On the Proper Treatment of Connectionism. *The Behavioral and Brain Sciences,* 11, 1–23.

Smolensky, P. (1988b). Putting Together Connectionism – Again. *The Behavioral and Brain Sciences,* 11, 59–74.

Spark Jones, K. and Wilks, Y. (eds). (1985). *Automatic Natural Language Parsing.* Chichester: Ellis Horwood.

Stich, S. (1982). On the Ascription of Content. In A. Woodfield (ed.), *Thought and Content.* Oxford: Oxford University Press.

Stich, S. (1983). *From Folk Psychology to Cognitive Science: The Case Against Belief.* Cambridge, Mass.: Bradford Books, MIT Press.

Tarski, A. (1944). The Semantic Conception of Truth and the Foundations of Semantics. *Philosophy and Phenomenological Research,* 4, 341–75.

Turing, A. M. (1950). Computing Machinery and Intelligence. *Mind,* 59, 433–60.

von Helmholtz, H. (1977). Physiological Optics. In R. Cohen and Y. Elkanda (eds), *Helmholtz's Epistemological Writings.* Dordrecht: Reidal.

Waisman, F. (1965). *The Principles of Linguistic Philosophy.* London: Macmillan/St. Martin's Press.

Weizenbaum, J. (1966). ELIZA – A Computer Program for the Study of Natural Language Communication Between Man and Machine. *CACM,* 9, 36–45.

Wilensky, R. (1981). PAM. In R. C. Schank and C. K. Riesbeck (eds), *Inside Computer Understanding.* Hillsdale, NJ: Lawrence Erlbaum.

Winch, P. (1958). *The Idea of a Social Science and Its Relation to Philosophy.* London: Routledge & Kegan Paul.

Winograd, T. (1972). *Understanding Natural Language.* New York: Academic Press.

Wittgenstein, L. (1958). *Philosophical Investigations.* Second edition. Oxford: Basil Blackwell.

Wittgenstein, L. (1967). *Zettel* (G. E. M. Anscombe, ed., G. H. von Wright and G. E. M. Anscombe, trans.). Oxford: Basil Blackwell.

Woods, W. A. (1968). Procedural Semantics for a Question-answering Machine. In *Fall Joint Computer Conference* (pp. 457–71). New York.

Woods, W. A. (1973). An Experimental Parsing System for Transition Network Grammars. In R. Rustin (ed.), *Natural Language Processing.* New York: Algorithmics Press.

Index